THE FASHION AND FUTURE OF HISTORY

THE FASHION AND FUTURE
OF HISTORY

Historical Studies and Addresses

by

Bernadotte E. Schmitt

THE PRESS OF WESTERN RESERVE UNIVERSITY

Cleveland   1960   Ohio

PREFACE

The studies and addresses here presented are part of the fruit of fifty years of diligent and perceptive exploration in the field of history. Dr. Schmitt's distinguished career, crowned this year with the presidency of the American Historical Association, has been one of extraordinary variety. A Rhodes Scholar in his youth, his academic career began at the University of Wisconsin; he attained professorship at Western Reserve University; taught then at the University of Chicago, where he is Andrew MacLeish Distinguished Service Professor Emeritus of Modern History. Dr. Schmitt was for seventeen years editor of the *Journal of Modern History*, and for seven more a special assistant in the Department of State. His book, *The Coming of the War 1914*, won the Pulitzer Prize for History in 1931, and his other books and writings are too numerous to list here.

Of these writings, certain ones have been selected for publication in this form because it is felt that their permanent value deserves a wider audience than that to which they were originally offered. One, at least, was privately circulated under seal of secrecy because of references to living persons. These are now dead, and the reasons for secrecy no longer obtain. Hence a record of permanent value is, for practical purposes, made available for the first time.

The Press of Western Reserve University presents here some of the mature reflections and representative studies of one of America's most distinguished historians.

Fifty Years of Exploring History

This paper was first delivered to the Graduate History Club of the University of Chicago as a "Valedictory" when I retired from my professorship in 1946. Since then I have added to it, and the present title refers to the time elapsed since I received my Ph.D.

*　　*　　*

I became a historian by accident. My father was a professor of mathematics in the University of Tennessee, and he made me take all his courses, including calculus and differential equations. I memorised the necessary formulae and worked the problems, but I was bored by them. What I really liked was chemistry, but in quantitative analysis and mineralogy I found that I lacked manual dexterity, and often I had to juggle the figures to obtain the results which the professor demanded. Obviously, I was not cut out to be a professional chemist. Then, in April 1905, I was elected a Rhodes Scholar from Tennessee, and I had to decide upon a course of study in the University of Oxford. I had had my fill of Latin and Greek, for which Oxford was famous; I did not wish to be a lawyer. As I had not studied history in college, I decided to give it a try in Oxford.

So, in October 1905, I entered upon what was then called the Preliminary Examination in Jurisprudence, a one-term course consisting of English history, two books of Gaius' *Institutes* of Roman law, and a dash of logic. At the end of two months' very hard work, I passed the examination, and in January 1906 I registered in the Honour School of Modern History, which meant that in June 1908 I would be taking an examination in 11 papers—English history, political, constitutional, religious, economic; a period of European history (1414-1598 was my choice), a special subject studied from original sources (mine was the Italian wars from 1494 to 1516), political science (chiefly Aristotle and Hobbes), and political economy (largely John Stuart Mill). These examinations were more formidable than those which I took later in obtaining a Ph.D.

Although I went to a good many lectures, my instruction depended chiefly on a weekly meeting with my tutor, in my case the Rev. Arthur Henry Johnson, of All Souls College, the author of several standard texts on European history. Each week I read an essay, about half an hour in length, on an assigned subject. "The Jonner" then discussed my effort, usually taking the opposite side in the argument, and criticized my style. The subject of my first essay was "Was Magna Charta a Feudal Document?" In all, I wrote about fifty essays. Among the subjects were "Was the Foreign Policy of Queen Elizabeth Vacillating?", "Did the Stamp Act Cause the Loss of America?", "Explain Aristotle's Theory of Slavery". If I have any gift of historical exposition, it results from the extraordinary training I received at Oxford. I was lucky enough to gain a First Class, for which my college —Merton—awarded me a prize of £10, with which you could buy a lot of books in 1908.

From Oxford I went to the University of Wisconsin, where I had obtained a fellowship, for two years' graduate work. The department of history at Wisconsin was one of the best in the United States, including such men as Frederick Jackson Turner, Dana Carleton Munro, Alfred L. P. Dennis, Carl Russell Fish, and Victor Coffin. In Madison I was introduced to loose-leaf notebooks, a vast improvement over the bound books used at Oxford, and to the ubiquitous 3 x 5 card. These cards are no doubt useful for bibliographical purposes, but I am convinced that they are the bane of good historical writing, for in writing term papers and theses, students are apt to copy one card after another, without regard to literary style. The best writing I have ever done was, I think, a little book, *Triple Alliance and Triple Entente,* which I produced entirely from memory. To be sure, after the first draft was finished, I verified some facts, quotations and dates, but it was much more fun writing without being dependent on the little white cards, and I always warned my graduate students against them.

Turner was the principal star in the firmament. He would come to class with a great stack of notes on half-size sheets. Knowing his subject from A to Z, he spoke spontaneously, but from time to time he would read a quotation from the sources, picking up the proper sheet of paper without hesitation. Munro, whose learning was prodigious, had a conversational style of lecturing; often he seemed to be making an after-dinner speech. Dennis was the scholar *par excellence.* He was fully equipped with 3 x 5 cards, gave you a full bibliography, and delivered carefully worked out lectures, in which he repeated all important points three times in three different ways. Coffin and my father had taught in a preparatory school in Virginia when I was three years old. When I arrived at the University of Wisconsin twenty years later, he took a personal interest in me and was very helpful. He came to class without books or notes, sometimes in a golf suit or tennis clothes, and offered the most finished lectures in elegant English. This made a profound impression on me, and I hoped that some day I might achieve the same mastery. Ultimately, at Chicago, I was able to dispense with notes.

I should also mention George Clark Sellery, who once asked me to lecture for him; he became dean of the graduate school and is still going strong at 88, the sole survivor of the department of my day.

In course of time I wrote my thesis, doing this without any direction. Dennis, who sponsored it, went abroad for a year, and no one else in the department was interested in the subject. As I finished chapters, I took them to Coffin, but he never criticized them. The night before the final examination, he invited me to come out to his house. He asked me a number of questions—and more or less repeated them the next day at the examination. Nevertheless I nearly failed that examination. My minor was political science under Paul S. Reinsch, later United States minister to China. One day in the spring of 1910 two squirrels playing in the treetops of a Madison street evidently had a fight, for one came tumbling down. It landed on the head of a horse, which dashed away and ran into a buggy in which Reinsch was about to take a drive. Reinsch was severely injured and was ill for months. So I was examined in political science by a summer visitor whom I did not know, and I did very badly; I always suspected that I failed that part of the examination but was passed by the grace of the department. Some years later, I was teaching one summer in Madison, and I was called upon to examine some one whom I had never seen before. I recalled my experience to my colleagues, some of whom had been present at my examination; needless to say, the young man passed. While I was very happy to receive my Ph.D., I was aware that my thesis needed some revision before publication; in my early years of teaching, there was no time to revise it, and in the end, I was content when the University of Wisconsin published an abstract of it.

From Wisconsin I went, in 1910, to Cleveland as an instructor in history at Adelbert College, the men's college of Western Reserve University. I was sorry to go, for I felt "demoted" from a great university to a small college, where I taught freshman history from the fall of the Roman Empire to the end of the nineteenth century. Actually, this was the best thing that could have happened to me, for I was treated as an equal by my seniors (Henry E. Bourne and Elbert J. Benton) in the department and given a free hand to conduct my courses as I saw fit. My advanced course began with the Congress of Vienna and came down to date. In 1910 only one text book covered the ground, C. D. Hazen's *Europe Since 1815*, and even it was pretty sketchy after 1905. So it was necessary to read European newspapers and magazines to keep the course up to date. This was an important step in my career.

Equally important was the fact that I had spent the summer of 1906 in Germany, where I enjoyed myself and where living was more comfortable than in Britain or France. But I was disagreeably impressed by the omnipresence of the army and the glorification of the navy, and by the atmosphere of militarism, especially after I was pushed off the sidewalk in Berlin by a strutting officer. In May 1911 I wrote a letter to the *Nation* saying that Germany was the greatest obstacle to the maintenance of peace, and in January 1914 I delivered a lecture at Western Reserve on "Germany in the Reign of William II", in which I expressed the fear that Germany was preparing to precipitate a European war. I was widely denounced at the time (there was a large German population in Cleveland), but six months later I was hailed as a prophet!

After this I went on to write my first book, *England and Germany*, a study of the relations between the two countries from 1740 to 1914, published in 1916. It was kindly reviewed by Sidney Fay in the *American Historical Review*, and this led to a lasting friendship which has in no way been disturbed by the circumstance that we put forth conflicting views of the responsibility for the war of 1914. Fay's *Origins of the World War*, published in 1928, took a lenient view of Germany's responsibility, whereas my book *The Coming of the War 1914* (1930) laid the chief burden on Germany. This has always troubled me. We had both taken advanced degrees at eminent universities, and I suppose that the technical instruction given at Harvard and Wisconsin was much the same. We used the same documents and read the same biographies and memoirs in preparing our respective books—and came up with quite different interpretations. It is sometimes asserted that we are both prejudiced because Fay studied in Germany and I in England, but surely there is more involved than that. Is there something wrong with our methods of historical study and training when two scholars draw such conflicting conclusions from the same evidence?

The reviews of *The Coming of the War*, were, on the whole, unfavorable, chiefly because the book was highly critical of Germany. By 1930 Germany had in no small degree recovered (in the United States, at least) from the obloquy generated during the war years, and Fay's book had met with wide acceptance. Because mine did not follow Fay, it was not taken seriously; when it was awarded the Pulitzer Prize for History in 1931, there was a loud outcry in some circles. Certainly the criticism of my book was based partly on emotion. After the outbreak of the Second World War in 1939, many persons told me that originally they had thought that I was wrong, but that after Germany had a second time unleashed war, they realized that I had been right!

During the second German war there was published in Italy a book on *The Origins of the War of 1914* by Luigi Albertini, one-time owner and editor of the *Corriere della Sera*, who had been dispossessed by Mussolini. Albertini was able to use evidence not yet published when I worte; while not accepting my views *in toto,* he definitely put the chief responsibility for the war of 1914 on Germany. When the English translation of his book appeared in the 1950's, its findings were generally accepted by the reviewers. In other words, book reviewers are affected by the "climate of opinion." In 1930 that climate was favorable to Germany; after 1945 it was not. While attending the Eleventh International Congress of Historical Studies at Stockholm in August 1960, I was told by two German scholars, youngish men in their late twenties or early thirties, that they agreed with my views, although it was unpopular to say so in Germany.

Since 1914 I have devoted most of my time and energy to reading books and lesser writings on foreign politics and diplomatic history. In 1914, as was to have been expected, the writers of every country (with occasional exceptions) exonerated their own country of responsibility for the war and blamed the other side. But since then thousands of documents from many archives have been released and hundreds of personal memoirs have been published, and this new evidence has furnished material for a large number of books written by Austrians, Englishmen, Frenchmen, Germans, and Italians about the responsibility for the war and its *Vorgeschichte.* Yet in 1939 the views expressed were not very different from those put forward in 1914. Thus the question that troubles me about Sidney Fay and myself is not confined to ourselves but embraces the historians of all western Europe.

Nor is this divergence of opinion exclusively a matter of national prejudice. I have read some books on diplomatic history written by Communists, and the story they tell is so different from that offered by the bourgeois historians of capitalist Europe and America as to be scarcely recognizable by the latter. I note that a German Communist is as rabid as a Russian one. In view of all this, I have no doubt that it will be impossible in any foreseeable time for any historians to prepare a diplomatic history from 1871 onwards which will be acceptable to the peoples of western Europe and of the United States, let alone to those of the Soviet Union.

The "war guilt" controversy of the First World War was over the question of responsibility for the catastrophe. There was no question of responsibility for the second war: Hitler's guilt was conceded everywhere outside of the Axis countries. But there has been some debate as to President Roosevelt's part in the involvement of the United States. Several writers, two of them professional historians, have charged that Roosevelt deliberately contrived to have the Japanese attack us because he knew that Congress would not of its own volition declare war on either Japan or Germany. I am not a specialist on this problem (although I have read a good deal of the evidence), but I note that this thesis has been generally rejected by the historians who reviewed the challenging books. As there has been no revival of the charge in recent years, we have probably heard the last of it, at least for some time.

During the past decade, the bitterest controversy developed over the Suez Canal crisis of 1956.[1] John Foster Dulles, the late secretary of state, had long been under attack, and lately Sir Anthony Eden, the British prime minister of the time, has published his side of the

---

[1] Written in April 1960, before the Summit crisis of May.

story. Historians will certainly do well to be wary. Not only is the evidence not all in, but we are too close to the event to see it in perspective. Sir Edward Grey, the British foreign secretary in the years before 1914, once remarked that he would be very interested to read what history said about his policies. According to him, the foreign office was not guided by clear-cut aims and ideas, but lived from day to day and dealt with questions as they arose. So I hope that I shall live long enough to see what the historians of, say, 1975, conclude about the Dulles-Eden row.

But, although my own activity has been devoted principally to diplomatic history, it has not been exclusively so. During the years I spent at the University of Chicago (1924-1943) I taught subjects other than diplomatic history and I edited the *Journal of Modern History* (1929-1946) —experiences which led me to other pastures. Looking back over the fifty-five years which have elapsed since I began to study history, my deepest impression is that of the changing character of historical study. At Oxford, the approach was overwhelmingly political, that is, the emphasis was on government and politics, diplomacy and war. John Richard Green's protest against "drum-and-trumpet" history expressed in his famous *Short History of the English People* found little echo. It was much the same at Wisconsin, although more effort was made to study economic and social history.

In my memory two books stand out as marking a significant change in American ideas. The first was James Harvey Robinson's *The New History*, published in 1911, the other Charles A. Beard's *Economic Interpretation of the Constitution*, published in 1913. The old-fashioned political history has been going out of favor ever since. There was not much left of it at Chicago in my day. About thirty years ago the intellectual approach to history began to be popular, and books on the history of ideas are being published in increasing numbers. And now a former president of the American Historical Association tells us that our "next assignment" is to investigate the role of psychology and psychiatry in the historical process. If all of this is elementary, it serves to warn us that with the coming of the age of space, many of our historical values may be called in question. This does not worry me. Changing conceptions help to keep history vital. Heaven forbid that history should ever become what Voltaire once called it, *un faible convenu,* a tale agreed upon.

Several specialized aspects of history have always appealed to me, such as the role of chance. The best illustration I know of is the murder at Sarajevo in June 1914, which set off the First World War. After the first attempt to kill the Archduke Francis Ferdinand had failed, the plans for the royal party were somewhat changed, but the chauffeur of his car was not told of the new route and at a certain corner he began to turn, as originally prescribed. He was forced to stop and back up—and at that moment the assassin Princip, standing there, seized his chance to shoot. But for this mishap, it is unlikely that the Archduke would have been killed and therefore most improbable that war would have broken out in the summer of 1914. At Gallipoli, in 1915, the Turks had exhausted their ammunition after the great attack of March 18 and were preparing to flee as soon as the Allies renewed their attack the next day—which they did not do. In our day, we remember that the Japanese were not detected approaching Pearl Harbor because the officer responsible for searching the skies had gone off duty and had not been replaced. In an earlier time, neither Lee nor Meade had planned to fight at Gettysburg, but met there by accident. The role of chance, *fortuna* the Romans called it, must not be exaggerated, but is sometimes just as important as great forces and the actions of great men.

Then there is the part played by people's health. Of recent years numerous books have appeared dealing with the medical history of famous persons. It seems clear that Napoleon was quite unwell on the day before Waterloo and on the day of the battle, which he was slow in beginning—accounted by the military critics his great blunder —because he was physically exhausted in the early morning. Was William II *geisteskrank* (as the Germans say) —which would explain many of his foolish and dangerous actions? To what extent was Woodrow Wilson's attitude towards the Senate in 1919 brought about by physical and mental weariness? Again, this is something not to be overworked, but also not to be forgotten.

Still a third specialized approach is represented by Hans Zinnser's *Rats, Lice and History*, which I found fascinating.

In fifty years one learns that each generation writes, or rewrites, history according to its own taste. In the 1920's, books about Theodore Roosevelt and Woodrow Wilson were heavily partisan because they had been strongly controversial presidents, but recent biographies of

both men have been unprejudiced and scholarly. In my own experience, Bismarck furnishes the best example. The first account of him
that I read—in 1909—was that in C. A. Fyffe's *History of Modern
Europe* published in 1889, which was distinctly critical. Then during
the reign of William II, its outward glitter seemed to prove the
soundness of Bismarck's work, and the treatment of the Iron Chancellor was generally laudatory. But when Germany crashed in 1918,
inevitably the question was raised whether the political system set
up by Bismarck was not more to blame for losing the war than
the poor judgment of the general staff. In the days of the Weimar
regime, criticism of Bismarck was widespread among historians. Then
came the Nazis. Their attitude towards Bismarck was one of contempt because he had not completed the unification of Germany in
1866 when, according to their view, he had the chance. The Nazis
set out to rewrite German history from their point of view, and
one trembles to think what would have been the result had they
won the war. It is worth noting that they did not succeed in enlisting
many reputable historians for this job. One amusing incident is
worth recording. Hermann Oncken wrote a laudatory account of
Bismarckian and Wilhelmine Germany for the last volume of the
Cambridge Modern History, which was published in 1910. After
1918 he made his peace with republican Germany and was translated
from the University of Heidelberg to Berlin. When the Nazis took
over, Oncken wrote a biography of Oliver Cromwell which, because
of its praise of the Protector's dictatorship, was interpreted as an
effort to curry favor with the new order. But this was too much for
the Nazis; they called him a professional turncoat and dismissed him.

Another example of the precarious connection of history with
politics was provided by Russia. From 1917 to 1932 M. N. Pokrovsky
was director of historical studies in the Soviet Union and produced
works according to the best Marxian doctrine. But in 1932 Stalin
reversed his policy and called for genuine history, not socialist or
communist propaganda, and Pokrovsky was dismissed. When I
visited Moscow in 1935, I had several sessions with Communist historians, including the late Madame Pankratova, who ultimately became the grand panjandrum of Soviet historiography; they asked me
to believe that they followed the same rigid methods of historical
research and writing that prevailed in the West. I was not able to

verify their claims, but what I have seen of their publications in the sixth decade of this century dealing with diplomatic history is not history at all, but propaganda.

Still, Soviet propaganda masquerading as history is no worse than the jingoistic schoolbooks which used to be so common, both before and after the First World War. Between the two wars considerable effort was made in several countries to cure this evil, with some success, and the effort is still continuing. The incident most familiar to me was the meeting of French and German historians in 1936 in an attempt to agree upon a statement concerning the origins of the war of 1914; while it was not altogether successful, it produced more agreement than might have been expected. A similar meeting between English and German historians after the second war seemed to me less productive. So the problem is still with us.

Having been concerned all my life with recent history, I ask myself what is the duty of the historian in our troubled times? In 1914 it was not possible to find an adequate history of Serbia or of Austria-Hungary since 1867. In those days historians were chary of writing about recent events because it was extremely difficult to obtain accurate information and there was a genuine fear that anything written would savor too much of politics or propaganda. In 1918, when peacemaking was about to begin, there was no proper study available of the three great peace congresses of the nineteenth century, Vienna, Paris, Berlin (Wilson was contemptuous of Vienna and was determined that it should not repeat itself). Nor had the payment by France to Germany of the huge indemnity imposed by the treaty of Frankfurt been adequately analyzed. In fairness to historians who have not written up the latest incidents in a rapidly changing world, the danger involved may be well illustrated by two illustrations. After his dismissal in 1890 Bismarck revealed the existence of a "reinsurance" treaty between Germany and Russia, but gave no details. Endless discussion and speculation followed for years. Finally, in 1914 Count von Reventlow in his *Deutschlands Auswärtige Politik, 1888-1914* offered a version which appeared plausible—but which was made to look ridiculous in 1924 when Erich Brandenburg, having had access to the Foreign Office archives, published the true version in his *Von Bismarck bis zum Weltkrieg*. In 1931 Japan seized Manchuria from China, and the League of Nations attempted to deal with the problem. It was widely believed at the time that Secretary of State

Stimson had wished the United States to take more vigorous action than President Hoover approved of and that Great Britain had let the United States down. The publication in 1947 of the United States diplomatic correspondence in *Foreign Relations of the United States* showed how wide of the mark these hypotheses were.

Nevertheless, in spite of all the difficulties and dangers, I believe that it is the duty of historians to record what they can about recent history. Take Temperley's *History of the Peace Conference of Paris* or Bergmann's *History of Reparations,* published in the 1920's. They put together what was then known, and they are of great value to a historian writing a generation later when full documentation is available. We must never forget the dictum of Ranke that what people believe to be true is at any given moment more important than the truth itself. The same remark applies to the annual *Survey of International Affairs* issued by the Royal Institute of International Affairs. Strictly speaking, these papers constitute journalism, not history; but they do narrate what was believed at the time and what thus provided the basis for action.

As a professional historian, I was happy to serve for seven years (1945-1952) in the historical division of the Department of State, for I learned much about the way in which a foreign office operates. But I was also disillusioned. In the first place, I was shocked to discover how ignorant officials of the department often were. Frequently I was called up and asked questions which seemed elementary to me, and it was only too evident that in many cases officers charged with formulating policy had but the vaguest notions about the backgrounds of their subjects and were operating on a day-to-day hunch based on the latest telegrams. This, let it be said, was not always the fault of the persons concerned, for the practice in the department of constantly shifting people from one post to another makes it impossible for an individual to "stay put" long enough to familiarize himself with the problems assigned to him. Before 1939 many officers stayed on their jobs for years on end and learned them thoroughly. A return to that practice is greatly to be desired.

One of my assignments was to write a history of the San Francisco conference which drew up the Charter of the United Nations, the question of publication being deferred. I wrote a history in some 2500 typed pages, but it has never been published. The late Harold Temperley, who with G. P. Gooch edited the *British Documents on the Origins of the War, 1898-1914*, always insisted that they were not foreign office officials but scholars employed by the foreign office for a particular task. That was also my attitude during my years in the Department of State, although technically I was on the rolls as a regular member of the staff. I was and remained a historian. I never became a bureaucrat. In consequence my history of the San Francisco conference was written with complete detachment, and sometimes I criticized the policy of the State Department or the work of the American delegation. From the point of view of publication, this was a mistake, for the department was unwilling to admit—and I suppose it cannot admit—that it had ever acted otherwise than correctly and wisely. The kind of history required by the Department of State, if it is to be published, is the volume *Postwar Foreign Policy Preparation, 1939-1945* (Washington, 1949), a detailed record of what was done with the reasons therefor, but without any suggestion of criticism or evaluation. I feel no bitterness about the unwillingness to publish my history, on which I spent more than two years, for I thoroughly enjoyed writing it. I make my point to warn future historians that if they are asked to write official history from official documents, they must be prepared to conform to official standards. In passing, I note that the United States Army has a tougher hide, for the authors of the numerous volumes on the history of our ground troops in the Second World War have been free to criticize both the conduct of operations and the performance of individual commanders. The Navy has also given Admiral Morison, who was a historian long before he became a naval officer, a free hand, and he has used it.

I have great confidence in the future of history and historical writing. In the first place, people can and do learn from history. Consider the ratification of the United Nations Charter by the Senate in 1945 with but two dissenting votes—a complete contrast with the action of the Senate in 1929 when it failed to ratify the treaty of Versailles and the Covenant of the League of Nations. It is clear, to me at least, that the lesson of 1920 had been taken to heart. President Roosevelt had learned that Wilson made a ghastly blunder in not giving the Republicans adequate representation on the Commission to Negotiate Peace, and did not repeat that mistake. Secretary Hull saw to it that members of the Senate were taken into confidence during the preliminary conferences at Dumbarton

Oaks. Members of the Senate and of the House of Representatives, of both parties, were appointed to the delegation at San Francisco. The people rallied to the Charter, I think, because they realized that the failure of the United States to join the League of Nations and to play its part in organizing collective security contributed greatly to the outbreak of the second and more terrible world war. It is also clear to me that Britain, France, Germany, and Italy are all resolved not to repeat the mistakes made between the two wars.

Secondly, not only is better history being written than was the case fifty years ago, but it is being written more attractively, so as to appeal to a much wider audience than the professional historians. There is still enough unexplored ground to keep the next generation of historians more than busy, and happily the increase of college enrollments will provide jobs by which they may support themselves. If I were a young man looking for a professional career, I would ask for nothing better than to be a historian.

The Fashion and
Future of History

An address to the Graduate History Club of the University of Chicago in February 1933, after I had been appointed chairman of the department. The mood of the moment was one of deep discouragement resulting from the unending depression, of which the University was feeling the effects in a serious way. The department of history was being asked to reduce its offerings, while students who took advanced degrees found jobs difficult to get. The occasion for my speech was the annual dinner of the Graduate History Club, which was attended by both students and faculty, and I tried to offer some encouragement to the graduate students to persevere. The persons mentioned by name were colleagues in the faculty, Ferdinand Schevill, who had come at the founding of the University in 1892 and lived to be 86; William E. Dodd, soon to be appointed ambassador to Germany and elected president of the American Historical Association; and Avery Craven, Dodd's successor in the field of southern history and now, like myself, retired.

Rereading the paper after the lapse of nearly thirty years, I note with interest that I remarked that "much more attention must and will be paid to psychological influences and factors". This is just what William L. Langer, president of the American Historical Association in 1957, called for in his presidential address "The Next Assignment".

In 1933 few people could have been found who took seriously the possibility of another European war. That war came in 1939, and a new perspective is required. The years from 1914 to 1945 now seem to have been taken up in a single conflict, the period from 1919 to 1939 being an armistice between the two wars, and this is reflected in the latest historical writings.

In 1933 fourteen states occupied eastern Europe from the Gulf of Finland to the Adriatic and the Aegean, an arrangement based on the principle of self-determination, for each of the states represented a nationality. It was not generally recognized that the

15

situation was highly precarious, resulting from the defeat of both Germany and Russia in the First World War. As a result of the Russian victory in the Second World War, many of the independent states of 1919-1939 have now become Soviet satellites. Here again historians have to readjust their sights.

Finally, in 1933, atomic energy was not yet discovered. Historians of the future will obviously have to take this into large account.

In American history, a highly interesting development has been the willingness of many great business corporations to allow historians to have access to their archives and to write genuine history.

*   *   *

When, sir, you honored me with an invitation to speak this evening to the Graduate History Club, I accepted with pleasure and with a certain glibness, for I assumed that it would be easy to find a suitable theme. Actually it has not been altogether easy. For a time I toyed with the idea of discoursing upon things seen and heard at Geneva in this *annus terribilis* just passed [1932]; but reflection indicated that this might seem to imply too complete an acceptance of the famous dictum that "history is past politics and politics present history." Moreover, even the incidents of Geneva, striking and spectacular as they often were, presented themselves in a scale of diminishing importance as what Professor Toynbee has called the 'economic blizzard' increases its fury and ferocity. Nor, on an evening when historians, present and future, have gathered together in solemn recognition of their calling, did it appear altogether appropriate to dilate upon a subject about which, in spite of much information purveyed daily by the press, we are necessarily but partly informed and when that information is not readily subjected to the canons of historical criticism. Rather the instinct prevailed that on such an occasion one should choose a subject essentially historical or at least keep within the broad paths which History, with her all-embracing interests, allows her devotees to follow.

Curiously enough, it was the discarded epigram of Freeman which suggested the line of thought which I shall venture to expound. When the great English historian proclaimed more than half a century ago that "history is past politics," not only did his countrymen generally agree with him, but this philosophy was more or less accepted, at least in practice, by the professional historians. Yet because that idea is today a discarded shibboleth, it occurred to me that I might speak for a little while on the fashion and future of history, and ask what are the present and the possible conceptions of the task to which we have set ourselves.

Freeman's famous phrase and the adaptation of it by Sir John Seeley, "Without history politics has no root, without politics history has no fruit," were natural enough when they were coined. At that time, which was the mid-Victorian era, those who wrote history and those who read it belonged largely to the aristocracy and upper middle classes who controlled government and politics, people whose inherited wealth permitted them to ignore the ordinary economic processes and to rest happily content with the prevailing social order. Not only that: the famous histories handed down from the past, whether those of classical antiquity or the popular writings of the late eighteenth and early nineteenth century, had dealt primarily with politics, that is, with government and religion, diplomacy and war. And before we laugh off this somewhat narrow conception of the human process, let us recognize that these older histories were written with a style and a verve which few can equal today, that for this very reason such books were widely read, and, what is more important, they were weighed, pondered and cherished.

But this conventional view of history was hardly adequate when the industrial revolution, the enormous expansion of business and the opening up of our own West and the pampas of South America transformed not only the conditions of existence but of politics as well. And so the well-known economic interpretation of history made its appearance, and is still going strong.

More recently, however, a new fashion has been intruding itself, what may perhaps be called, loosely and not very accurately, the intellectual interpretation of history. This finds its most emphatic expression in the doctrine of a famous professor of this University[1] that history is only a method. Most of us were properly shocked to learn that what we had considered only a means was now the end of all our labors. But there is also Benedetto Croce, who, without going so far as our colleague, boldly proclaims that history is philos-

---

[1] John M. Manley (1865-1940), Chaucerian scholar.

ophy. To put it more drably, this school contends that what men
do is of less consequence than the reasons why they do it. And it
is a fact that some of the most original and most stimulating books of
recent years have been concerned with the history of ideas and the
effect of those ideas.

Lastly, we have to contemplate a biological interpretation of history.
This fills me with complete horror, for my mind, as I have demonstrated to my own lamentable satisfaction, is impervious to the facts
and formulae of science. By a biological interpretation I do not mean
the evolutionary thesis of history—that was popularized and put over
by the Romanticists a century ago—but the attempt to explain men's
ideas and intellectual processes by their physical condition and re-
actions. This is not so original as sometimes thought, for it has long
been asserted that Napoleon lost the battle of Waterloo because of
some intestinal disturbance on the fatal day. But James Harvey
Robinson was, I believe, the first historian of repute to advise his
colleagues of this approach to their subject. One of his pupils,
a well-known "revisionist," has been much taken by this new doctrine, and I have been told—I do not vouch for this!—that on one
exuberant occasion, he propounded the thesis that the Great War was
caused by the fact that Izvolsky[2] suffered from some kind of glandular
difficulty. Be that as it may, there is no doubt that the peculiar
mental make-up of William II, which more than one German medical
man has declared to have been pathological, had profound consequences for the world. This approach to history is so new and the
scientific data about historic figures so scant that we shall do well to
be on our guard and not adopt it blindly; but clearly, it is something
to consider.

What I have been saying must sound to you very much like commonplace, and you may properly ask why I am saying it. I am saying
it in order to remind you that there is fashion in history as there is in
clothes or cars. Each generation, in short, writes its own history
in accordance with its own ideas. Consequently most of you, who are
now presumably adjusting yourselves comfortably enough to the
ideas of history purveyed to you by us professors, will probably,
fifteen or twenty years hence, when you get into your stride, question

2 Russian foreign minister, 1906-1910; ambassador in Paris 1910-1914, considered
by some writers to be largely responsible for the war of 1914.

many of our most precious premises. You will be asking yourselves why we failed to see this or understand that, you will put the books of which we are so proud on your highest shelves—where I have buried those which seemed indispensable to me at Oxford—and when you encounter us at the meetings of the American Historical Association you will be publicly respectful and privately a bit patronising.

It can not and should not be otherwise. A static conception of history would be fatal to you and to history. The remorseless grubbing after new facts, which is the lot of so many of us, is futile *per se;* it is worth while only if it permits us to see old pictures through new spectacles. Unless we are continually drawing new patterns and weaving new clothes, history degenerates into sheer antiquarianism, which is the dullest of studies.

The future of history, then, is in your hands. What will you make of it? No one can say. But perhaps one may venture to guess at some possible lines of approach to this new "new history."

In the first place, much more attention must and will be paid to psychological influences and factors. Perhaps these factors will be measured by biological methods or the application of physics, perhaps not. But somehow they must be discovered and reckoned with. I can illustrate this by a reference to my own special field of study, diplomatic history. Read any manual of pre-war diplomacy or even full-dress presentations, and what do you find? Records of official negotiations, analyses of press opinion, estimates of results, and perhaps some pious moralizations. But what you rarely find is any attempt to link up momentous events with current feelings and prejudices. Since the war British policy has often run counter to that of France, and this attitude is usually rationalized by references to the balance of power, the economic necessities of Britain, reluctance to undertake new commitments, etc. Certainly these motives are important, perhaps even decisive. But what is back of these motives? Talk to Englishmen, and you will not be long in discovering that in spite of, or perhaps because of, the war, Frenchmen are still thought of in England as immoral, atheistic, dirty and light-headed, and large numbers of Englishmen wish to have as little to do as possible with such people. Similarly, before the war, one obstacle in the way of a Franco-German understanding was a certain Gallic repugnance for Teutonic manners. German travellers in France were notorious for making much noise, eating too much, and behaving generally like parvenus. French taste was offended—considerations which the *Temps* and the *Documents Diplomatiques Francais* consistently ignore. One final example—will the historians of the American election of 1928 record the fact that, as it would appear, thousands of women voted for Herbert Hoover for no better reason than that they did not wish to see Mrs. Alfred E. Smith in the White House? In other words, it is not sufficient to analyse newspapers, periodicals and books. Somehow, if we are to understand what has happened, we have to break through the crust of formalized opinion and discover what the people were thinking and saying, and why they did so. Just how this is to be done is not easy to say, for the more distant the period, the scantier the records of popular feeling and emotion. But a brilliant paper read at the Toronto meeting of the American Historical Association by a recent Ph.D. of this University on "Propaganda in the American Revolution"[3] gives a hint of what can be done. If it will frequently be impossible to discover what was being thought and said up and down the broad highways, at least the effort can be made to trace the action taken by governments and individuals to disseminate and popularize facts, alleged facts, and ideas. Perhaps no field of research offers greater opportunities to those who do not fancy the conventional leads.

But probably attention will continue to be concentrated upon the history of our economic and social structure. From this point I shall grow a bit reckless and I dare say even quite unhistorical. Suppose that Spengler is right in thinking that western civilization is on the decline and approaching a collapse. Or, to be more precise, suppose that fifty years hence the world has turned communist. Will not the historians then be demonstrating that the course of events for the last 200 years has led inexorably in that direction?

Which brings me to the very perilous question of law in history. For centuries the wish to predict the future of mankind from its actions in the past has been the *fata morgana* of historians. During a thousand years, from the disintegration of the Roman Empire to the end of the Middle Ages, the ecclesiastical historians saw everywhere and in all phenomena the hand and mind of God and believed in "one far-off divine event to which the whole creation moves." Within the last century Buckle thought he had found the clue in geographical

[3] Philip S. Davidson, now president of the University of Louisville.

influences and physical environment, and Auguste Comte essayed a *System of Positive Philosophy*. In our own day Professor Bury has written a book on the *Idea of Progress* and Professor Cheyney has addressed the A. H. A. on *Law in History*. Nor do these scholars have the last word. There is a professor in this University—I shall disguise him by inaccurately calling him a sociologist—who is manifesting much interest in the future of history. He was not always so enlightened, but, as I happen to know, he has been indoctrinated by Mr. Dodd and Mr. Craven. In a recent conversation with me he expressed the hope, and even the conviction, that in the course of the next few years—a decade, or perhaps a generation—a new school of history would arise, in this University of Chicago, which would seriously and consciously apply the study of history to the study, if not the solution, of contemporary problems. He believes that by a re-examination of historical processes, by the exact measurement of social phenomena, by a greater knowledge of the workings of the human mind and the organs of the human body, we can evolve a new science which, though it may not reveal the precise laws of history, will surely contribute profoundly to our understanding of the world in which we live. Just how this re-examination is to be made, my interlocutor did not know, nor, for that matter, did he greatly care. But he threw out one intriguing idea. The data of history, he asserted, have always been conditioned by chronology and geography, that is, the historian has been content to inquire what happened in a certain place and when. But may there not be some other factor, something analogous to the theory of relativity in the physical sciences? Only much research and prolonged reflection can answer this question, but it might be worth our while to accept the challenge. In any case, I personally agree with my friend that history ought to be a more useful and more practical subject of study, and I hope that we may discover the means for making it so.

I have already intimated that in my opinion historical research often degenerates into mere antiquarianism. Obviously the facts have to be gathered. There is also a certain legitimate curiosity about the past as such. This emotion, however, does not affect most people, for most people, at least in this country, are rather contemptuous of the past. (In England, on the other hand, there is too much reverence for the past!) If history is to be a vital study, it must do something more than stimulate intellectual curiosity or satisfy romantic crav-

ings: it must deliberately and unswervingly adhere to the idea that
"the roots of the present lie deep in the past," as Bishop Stubbs put it.
We all believe this adage—but how often do we apply it in our writings? In the last three years there has been considerable study of
the history of previous depressions, in the hope of finding comfort
and a cure. But, in the days of prosperity, did the historians or the
economists come forward with histories and analyses of past booms?
I am afraid they did not. Another kind of example: Before 1914
it was very difficult to find out what had been happening in the
world since about 1871, for the historians had refused to concern
themselves with contemporary history. Not that the historians could
have prevented the war! But if they had been on the job, at least
the world would not have been taken so by surprise when war
finally came.

If history is to explain the present, there will have to be much
more synthesis than we are used to. To be sure, we are always
hearing about synthesis, but we really get very little of it. So far as my
own reading goes, only the Beards' *Rise of American Civilization*
provides it. Since my knowledge of American history is derived
largely from attendance on Ph.D. examinations, I am not competent
to criticise the Beards' book. But who does not admire this brilliant
picture of the interaction of politics, economics, social forces, religion
and ideas? We are shown, in precise and clear-cut manner, how these
several factors did affect each other and can see the actual evolution
of a complicated civilization. This is the kind of history which I
hope you will write. And there is abundant opportunity if you are
students of European history. Consider any account of Europe from
1871 to 1914. There will be chapters on internal development, sections on foreign policy and imperialism, a general survey of socialism,
pacifism, etc., and then a narrative of the grand smash. But just how
internal politics reacted on foreign affairs and vice versa—this has
not yet been shown. No one has yet done for pre-war Europe what
Albert Sorel did for the Europe of the old régime in the classic first
volume of *L'Europe et la Révolution française*. Will one of you do it?

But whatever you may do, how will you do it? In other words, I
have to raise the eternal question whether history is a science or an
art, and I do this the more enthusiastically because, as I am informed,
the remarks on this same subject by Mr. Schevill at last year's dinner
provoked a lively exchange of views, and also because I should like

to air my own views. "Science," said the great Lord Acton, "is the combination of a great mass of similar facts into the unity of a generalization, a principle, or a law, which principle or law will enable us to predict with certainty the recurrence of like events under given conditions." Naturally, therefore, he denied that there was or could be a science of history. On the other hand, Professor Bury affirmed with great positiveness that of course history was a science. Evidently much depends on what you mean by science. A recent English writer has remarked that science does not cease to be science because it sometimes fails to formulate its laws or achieve the gift of prophecy. Thus meteorology cannot be denied the quality of a science because the laws according to which sunshine and storm succeed one another are as yet undiscovered and because weather forecasts are often wrong in exact ratio as they are precise. Science, in the mind of this writer, can be defined as "systematized, organized, formulated knowledge"; and history, the original meaning of which is investigation, is therefore a science if it is pursued with the sole purpose of ascertaining the truth, if all relevant facts are diligently searched for, if presuppositions and prejudices are eliminated, if the constants and the variables are noted and plotted with the same care that is the rule in the natural sciences. But do we really care whether the chemists and the mathematicians accord our study the title and dignity of a science? We believe that the critical methods which we use in the acquisition of historical information are every whit as scientific as those of the laboratory or the field expedition. For my part, I am willing to let the matter rest there.

At the same time, and I am now back on the main line of my thought, we must never forget that history, when we use the word in its second meaning of a record of our investigations, is an art. Certainly we must be as scientific as we know how to be in gathering and selecting our facts—but if, in presenting them we are only scientific, nobody will care greatly how many facts we assemble.

What has really been gained if you write a learned and dull book to be read by someone just as learned and probably just as dull as yourself? That such books are useful as works of reference to public officials, journalists, and writers of term-papers, may be admitted. The public, however, will not read them.

Unfortunately, it is currently believed by the professional historians that if an historical work is brightly written and easily read, it must be inaccurate and sloppy. In many cases this is true, but I fear that we teachers of history have laid too much emphasis on references and footnotes and too little on form to be exonerated from all blame. The enormous vogue of popular biographies indicates that the general reading public likes to read history. It is because properly-trained persons have been unable or unwilling to supply this demand with well-written books that hacks and sensationalists get a hearing. I have no intention of depreciating research. No one can be a sound historian who does not know how to do research and who has not actually done it. Perhaps style is a gift of the gods. But surely everyone can try to write as if he wished somebody to read what he wrote. Do you ever read Gibbon, Macaulay, John Richard Green, Francis Parkman or Trevelyan to discover the secrets of their style?

Of course a pleasing literary style is not the only ingredient of good historical writing. Often enough well-written books have no other historical merit. The *Journal of Modern History* has on hand at the moment a review of a new book by one of the best stylists among American historians; but the reviewer thinks rather unkindly of the book because of its defective organization, its lack of synthesis and its neglect of certain well-recognized canons. How often, in your own reading, have you not felt that the author was interested only in stringing together as many facts as possible without regard to effect on the reader? We can take lessons from the journalists whom we sometimes affect to despise. Very definitely, they write for their public, resorting to various literary devices and never forgetting that their mission is to impress. You may or may not like the style of the English historian G. P. Gooch; but you will have to admit that he always builds up his narrative in logical fashion, that he glides naturally and easily from one theme to another, and that at the end, you have a finished picture of the whole with every detail in its proper place and the wood visible in the trees. Here again, you cannot do better than to study the form of the great masters.

I have now invited you to reconsider your philosophy of history and have urged you to improve your technique: quite enough preaching for one evening. To conclude on a more cheerful note, let me indicate some fruitful fields of research, confining myself for obvious reasons to modern European history. The most generally neglected period is the seventeenth century, except in English history: which does not surpise me, for I could never arouse any enthusiasm about the Thirty Years' War, Louis XIV or the Spanish Succession. But the social and economic history of the age is very superficially known and will repay investigation. Or, if you want a geographical approach, Scandinavia, Slavic Europe and the Ottoman Empire call loudly for explorers. In these cases the problem of language does offer some difficulty, but you can certainly learn one language besides French and German, and you will have the great advantage of working an unfamiliar field and being able to lord it over ordinary people. It was this point of view that led Professor Seton-Watson many years ago to take up the study of Hungarian and Serbian history. Moreover, if you relish the notion of watching historical forces and traditions actively at work in the contemporary world, Eastern Europe is well worth your attention. History, and often very bad history, is invoked at every turn in such questions as the Polish corridor, agrarian reform in Czechoslovakia, Croatian separatism, Macedonia and Bessarabia. So, just as Horace Greeley used to bid young men go west, one can now say to young historians, go Slavic.

Still, your bent may not lie in that direction, so that some other roads may be suggested. You can break new ground by studying the history of railways with special reference to their political and social and even military effects, the growth of state policy towards industry, the history of social classes, or of societies and movements, or of minorities, and the changing code of morals and ethics. The reasons for European emigration have been frequently studied, but the reverse of the picture, the effects of emigration on Europe, remain to be investigated, and since emigration has largely ceased, there is some chance of doing a definitive job. Another highly interesting and important subject is legal history, which is just beginning to be taken seriously; along with this might be mentioned the history of administration. And I would even put in a word for military history. If I were not so deeply committed to diplomatic history, I should like nothing better than to try my hand at the military and naval operations of the late war. Or a most fruitful study can be made of the conceptions of strategy which rose and fell in the period from 1871 to 1914 and of the interactions of strategy and international politics. A friend of mine is writing a book on what he calls "The

Eastern Front, 1871-1914", and my guess is that it will throw more light on the origins of the war than most diplomatic treatises.[1] In short, there is no lack of themes which will repay investigation, provided you use your imagination and do not depend too much on us professors to find topics for you.

I do not know if there is any clear-cut idea running though my rather rambling remarks, but I have tried to do two things. First, to get you to think about the meaning and purpose and possibility of history. It is very easy to concentrate on the tasks immediately before us, whether preparing for next day's class or writing a book review, and in so doing, to lose sight of the larger aspects of our study, and precisely for that reason, so much of what is written is dull and uninspired. We need, every so often, to ask ourselves what it is all about and where we are going. Perhaps we cannot answer our own questions, but is not that all the more reason for asking them? In the second place, I have wished to encourage you. When I was a graduate student, I was often oppressed by the learning of my instructors (perhaps we modern professors are not so learned!) and wondered if ever I could scale such heights. Fortunately, my thesis lay in what was then—believe it or not!—an almost virgin field, namely, the diplomatic history of Europe since the Franco-German war, and one could feel quite superior because one's colleagues were so delightfully ignorant, including the professors. It may be different now, for your generation is not supposed to suffer from inferiority complexes. But if you are so afflicted, the way of salvation lies open: pick a field for study which is new or unpopular, cultivate it assiduously, and the chances are that by the time you have tilled it into bearing fruit, it will have been recognized as important or even urgent and lo! you will have arrived. Mere routine will not take you any farther in history than it does in business, but the rewards of imagination are infinite.

The other day I was irreverently asked if history had any future. Sometimes it does seem as if history is in danger of being squeezed out between the social sciences and the humanities. It is alleged on the one hand that the social sciences have no real interest in history and on the other hand that the humanities concern themselves only with its cultural aspects. I believe this view too pessimistic. Surely

[1] Alas! This book was never completed.

we have much to teach the economists, the political scientists and the sociologists. But we must teach them. It is not enough to assure them that they will profit by the study of history: we must show them that it is worth their while. We have, I submit, to link the past with the present much more definitely and purposely than we have hitherto done and to make the lessons of the past clear and helpful. Is it not rather humiliating that the most vivid interpretation of American history has been worked out by Charles A. Beard, who throughout his academic career was a professor of political science? On the side of the humanities there has been an artificial division between history and literature. Much literary criticism dealing with older writers has been divorced from the life of the time. But is not the fault partly, if not largely, our own? In the last few years several books have been published interpreting American literature in the terms of American life, but they have not been written by historians. I do not wish to imply that we should become literary historians; but it is, I fear, only too notorious that most of us know little about the literature and other cultural achievements of the periods which we study. I can say this because I am quite a sinner myself.

History, then, has a future, and a great future, if we exert ourselves to that end. But we shall have to adjust ourselves to changing times and needs and not be bound by customary and conventional approaches. What the new course is to be, is not for me to say, since the taste and temper of 1960[1] cannot be predicted in 1933. It is for you who are now on the threshold of your careers to blaze the new trail. Learn what we can teach you, but keep your minds flexible, and, I say it for the third time, don't be afraid to use your imagination.

[1] When I wrote this I did not dream that the paper would be published in 1960.

The Age of Extravagance

*A paper read to the Literary Society of Washington, D.C. in April
1959. The Society, founded in 1874, consists of forty members (like
the French Academy!) and meets eight times a year, the members
being accompanied by their spouses. The membership has included
presidents of the United States, cabinet members, justices of the
Supreme Court, members of Congress, and foreign ambassadors.
Obviously the papers should not be too heavy, and I have consciously tried for a light touch. Some one remarked that my age of
extravagance—the reign of King Edward VII of England—was now
as far behind us (and as unbelievable to contemporaries) as the ages
of Jackson or Washington.*

*I have described what I saw in the England of that day. A similar
picture, minus royalty, could be drawn of the United States. An intriguing question—unanswerable, of course—is, how long could
such an age have lasted had war not broken out in 1914? From
1919 to 1929 some effort was made to revive the pre-war world, but
it was not too successful, and after 1929 people were thankful if
they survived the great depression. Since the Second World War,
Edwardian England has become the "good old days," and the nostal-
gia is reflected in numerous plays and novels.*

*   *   *

To begin on a personal note: I went to England in October 1905
in the good ship *Haverford* out of Philadelphia, paying $42.50
for passage in the one-class ship. I was traveling without a passport—
for it was still an age of innocence in which nations trusted one
another. I was en route to Oxford University, where I had been
appointed a Rhodes Scholar.

This was a completely new world to me, for I had grown up in
Knoxville, Tennessee, a town of 40,000, and I had never been anywhere except to Washington. Not only was I very ignorant, but being

only 19, I was also very impressionable. I stayed three years in England without coming home. At Oxford I met Stanley Hornbeck, sometime ambassador to the Netherlands, who had preceded me by a year; Charles Mahaffie, until recently a member of the Interstate Commerce Commission; and the late Carol Foster, who spent thirty years in the Department of State and the Foreign Service.

Edward VII was king. A famous book describing the England of his day, *Edward and the English,* by Price Collier, appeared in 1909, shortly after my return. I have recently reread it, and find it much marked up with criticisms by myself and by Benjamin Bruce Wallace, another Rhodes Scholar of my time who was for many years a member of the Tariff Commission. Collier described England as "The land of compromise" and asked "Are the English dull?" I did not find them so, but I did find them different. (Twenty years later a Dr. Renier wrote a book entitled *The English: Are They Human?)*

In recent years there has been a spate of books on Edwardian England: Virginia Cowles, *Edward VII and his Circle;*[1] W. S. Adams, *Edwardian Portraits;*[2] Shaw Desmond, *The Edwardian Story;*[3] James Laver, *Edwardian Promenade;*[4] Ursula Bloom, *The Elegant Edwardians;*[5] W. Macqueen Pope, *Give Me Yesterday*[6] (a nostalgic comparison of the Welfare State with Edwardian England) ; and a composite volume, *The Age of Extravagance,* edited by Mary Elizabeth Edes and Dudley Frasier,[7] which provides the title of this paper. To the somewhat drab Britain of the nineteen fifties, Edwardian England, which lasted until 1914 (although Edward VII died in 1910) looks like a golden age, and very lovingly have these writers, most of whom remember it in person, recorded its glories and its failings.

Edward succeeded his mother in January 1901. For forty years Queen Victoria had denied him any part in the government, and his first act was to discard "Albert", his father's name, which he had been forced to accept, and to announce that he would be known

---

[1] London: Hamish Hamilton, 1956.
[2] London: Secker & Warburg, 1957.
[3] London: Rockliff, 1949.
[4] London: Hulton, 1958.
[5] London: Hutchinson, 1957.
[6] London: Hutchinson, 1957.
[7] London: Weidenfeld & Nicolson, 1955.

as Edward. This was not the only sign that a new age was beginning. Because of his exclusion from politics, the Prince of Wales had given himself over to pleasure and become the leader of Society with a capital S. He was named as the co-respondent in a divorce suit, and among his intimates figured, according to gossip, Skittles, a famous courtesan, Lily Langtry, a famous beauty and actress, and many others. The Prince was also something of a gambler and accumulated enormous debts. These "little wickednesses" as they were called, endeared him at once to the aristocracy, who imitated them, and to the masses, who looked upon them as a sign that he was human, a tribute further recognized by his popular name of "Teddy". A populace devoted at all levels to horse-racing rejoiced with the Prince when on three different occasions his horses won the Derby. Further evidence of the "common touch" lay in the fact that Edward was such a heavy eater, taking six meals a day, that Rudyard Kipling privately called him "a corpulent voluptuary." He was in fact shaped like a barrel, something that could not be concealed by the most elegantly-contrived clothes.

The truth is that the English people had become bored with the conventions and stuffiness of the Victorian age, and when the new king let it be seen that he was interested in amusing himself and in being comfortable, his people took up the cue, and Edwardian England proceeded to splurge as the Age of Elegance had done under George IV nearly a hundred years before. This was possible because Britain in the decade before 1914 was at the height of the prosperity which had begun with the industrial revolution at the end of the eighteenth century. It was the dominant commercial country of the world (although Germany and the United States were catching up), and the one country where prosperity depended on the excess of imports over exports, this excess being the dividends from overseas investments and the services of British shipping, which were larger than those of the rest of the world put together. The Edwardians were not always conscious of how the system worked, but the money rolled in and both the aristocracy and the middle classes spent it freely.

The aristocracy was typified by the Duke of Rutland, whose daughter was the famous Lady Diana Manners, later the wife of Duff Cooper, Viscount Norwich. It was she who made a theatrical sensation in the leading role of the nun in "The Miracle." She describes in her autobiography *The Rainbow Comes and Goes,* the servant problem at Beauvoir Castle. One ancient retainer "three times a day rang the gong—for luncheon, for dressing time, for dinner", and that was all, and "then there were the lamp-and-candle men, at least three of them", who did nothing but take care of the primitive lighting facilities. In addition there were water men, coal men, watchmen. Or take the Marquess of Bath. His seat at Longleat required 43 servants, and when the family moved to London for the season, 22 servants and 11 horses moved with him. The middle classes, on a less pretentious scale, also had their servants. One writer describes his family's house in London, with its 97 steps from basement to roof. Three servants were needed to take care of this establishment. Out of a total population of about 40,000,000 nearly two million were classified as domestic servants. They were, as a class, proud of their occupation, and passed their jobs on from generation to generation. On the other hand, ample service did not, in the eyes of visiting Americans, compensate for the general lack of bathrooms and central heating, even in the finest houses.

The coronation of Edward VII in the summer of 1902 was to be a spectacle outstripping Victoria's Diamond Jubilee in 1897, and royalties had already begun to arrive when the king had to undergo an appendectomy and the ceremony was postponed. When finally enacted, the coronation was somewhat subdued, but the daughter of Lord Esher, who had much to do with the exercises in Westminster Abbey, has provided an amusing account of how her father managed to smuggle into the crypt a crate marked OHMS ("On His Majesty's Service"), filled with sandwiches and champagne which were joyfully consumed after the ceremony. But the consumers made so much noise that they were raided by the police and were saved only because the Earl Marshal of England, the Duke of Norfolk, came along and was appeased by a glass of champagne.

The coronation over, King Edward replaced the dreary drawing-room receptions held by his mother with brilliant evening courts, to which he invited not only the hereditary aristocracy, but business men like Sir Thomas Lipton, Jewish financiers like Sir Ernest Cassell who took care of Edward's debts, American heiresses, and anybody who was interesting and amusing. These lavish entertainments naturally pleased the shopkeepers and all those who cater to pleasure and amusement. The king was fond of the theatre and for the first time actors received social recognition. Incidentally, the best seats—the stalls— cost 10/6 ($2.50), and evening dress—white tie and tails—was *de rigeur* (I used to sit in the pit, for 2/6 [60 cents]).

The king was fond of visiting the great country houses, and it was customary for the happy host to have his place redecorated for the royal visit. These hosts were not necessarily British, for one of his favorite haunts was the residence of Mrs. Willie James, who was an American. On such occasions, if you read the Court Circular, you would discover that the king's latest inamorata was always mentioned in the list of guests. These royal activities—as well as the doings of society in general—could be followed in the three society papers, *Tatler*, *Sketch* and *Bystander*, which appeared every Wednesday. It was from these papers that I became aware of the existence of a leisured class, people, that is, who never worked and often did nothing but amuse themselves.

King Edward was fond of travelling, and every year he visited the Continent, sometimes more than once a year. In the course of his short reign he called on almost all his fellow sovereigns except the Sultan of Turkey; incidentally, he had to spend a month at Marienbad to take the cure after a strenuous season! The only ruler with whom his relations were difficult was his nephew William II, but they managed to preserve the amenities. The Germans were fond of accusing the king of promoting the encirclement of Germany. Actually Edward had little influence on British foreign policy, except that he persuaded the Parisians in 1903 to cheer rather than to hiss him. He was always briefed by the foreign office before his interviews. What he did contribute was personal charm, and the resolution to refrain from making irritating speeches in the manner of William II.

The king happened to be at Biarritz in April 1908 when the prime minister, Sir Henry Campbell-Bannerman, resigned on account of ill health, and the monarch "sent for" (as the phrase goes) H. H. Asquith. I recall that some of the papers thought that the king should have returned to London for this solemn duty, because one of the few powers left to an English sovereign is to select his prime minister. Other papers, however, pointed out that the very fact that the king did not deem it necessary to return to London showed how powerless he was in fact, for the king's right to choose his prime minister is more apparent than real. It was probably at this time of Edward's visit to Biarritz that a French newspaper published pictures of the portly king walking by the seaside with a lady—whose face was carefully blotted out!

I myself saw King Edward and Queen Alexandra when they opened Parliament in January 1908, but I was not close enough to get a really good view. Edward's death in May 1910 came as a surprise, and he was genuinely mourned by all classes. But it is now evident that he never obtained the hold on his subjects that his son George V and his grandson George VI came to enjoy. History will not recognize that he accomplished very much for his country.

From early in May until August 12, after which date grouse could be shot on the moors of Scotland, London was the social capital of the world. Diana Cooper has described the doings, sometimes almost irresponsible, of the young set to which she belonged. Sir Osbert Sitwell, whose tyrannical father had insisted on his becoming an officer in a Guards regiment, devoted at least as much time to his social as to his military duties; you may read the details in the third volume of his fabulous reminiscences. Dinners, dances, receptions, garden parties (including those at Buckingham Palace) left no time for boredom. The West End was filled with fine carriages drawn by superb horses, and there was a daily parade of both equipages and their owners in Hyde Park. The high points of the season were the two race meets at Ascot and Goodwood, the Henley Regatta, and Cowes Week, where the most famous yachtsmen, including sometimes the Kaiser and the Tsar, came together. After August 12 society scattered to its country houses or to Scotland for the shooting or to the Continent.

Standard dress for men was the top hat and the frock coat (what we called a Prince Albert), with the inevitable umbrella; by 1914 the morning coat (or cutaway) was replacing the frock, but that irrepressible soldier, Field Marshal Sir Henry Wilson, always referred to the politicians as "frocks" because that was the costume they affected. This civilian uniform was adopted by middle-class men as well, and was worn even in banks and shops. I myself acquired such an outfit when I attended the opening of Parliament.

Of women's clothes, I speak with some hesitation. However, there are plenty of photographs in the books I have mentioned, photos of single women, of women in groups, and of mixed groups, so that a mere man can see for himself. Most obviously, clothes were much fuller than they are now, partly, no doubt because, as one writer remarks, there were at least five layers from the inside out. Next, skirts were bell-shaped and trailed the ground, so that innumerable crossing-sweepers had to be employed to keep the pavement clean. When dressed up for summer parties, women always wore boas and carried parasols, and their hats were enormous, "merry widows" I believe they were called, after the style set by the famous Viennese operetta. In general, women's clothes, like men's, were much more formal than they are today, and any evening function, not merely in high society but also among the middle classes, called for evening dress. One of the fashion experts I am following notes that country clothes were unknown, their being a development after the First World War; on the other hand, the matching of shoes, bags and gloves had not yet been thought of and the use of many colors in a single costume was highly regarded. In American eyes, however, English women were seldom smart, and even then it was well established that Americans, men as well as women, could be detected by their shoes.

In season and out of season, the week-end (which then meant from Saturday afternoon to Monday morning) was a national institution, and the most eloquent picture of the age of extravagance is the account of a week-end, as observed in the highest circles, written by Sir Harold Nicolson, the author of well-known books on good behavior and the English sense of humor. Its chief characteristic was that the week-enders "ate excessively and competitively". "No age, since that of Nero, can show such unlimited addiction to food", and the menus are set forth at length. "Who among us today would really dress for church and dress for luncheon and dress for tea and dress again for dinner? Who among us would possess the endurance to relish all those meals, to relish all that tittle-tattle? . . . The Edwardians were vulgar to a degree. They lacked style. They possessed only the hard glitter of their own electric light: a light which beat down pitilessly upon courtier, ptarmigan, bridge scores, little enamel boxes, and plates and plates of food."[8]

In this sophisticated society, sex was not talked about, although it had plenty of devotees, and certain words (not merely the four-letter words), but also others ("bloody" being the most famous, and "sick"

---

[8] "The Edwardian Weekend", in *The Age of Extravagance*, pp. 247, 252.

another) were eschewed. Divorce was unusual partly because it was very expensive, but also because a woman had to prove not only adultery but also cruelty on the part of her spouse. Young girls had to have chaperones, and "dating" was unknown. One of my Oxford friends—an American—called twice on a young lady and was immediately asked what were his intentions.

Thanks to the Atlantic Union, I was able to have a peek at this elegant world. The Union existed to extend social courtesies to Colonial and American visitors to England (its place is now taken by the English-Speaking Union), and every vacation—Christmas, Easter and summer—the Rhodes Scholars would receive invitations to various functions in London. I attended a large reception on almost the first evening spent in London, and as the night was very foggy, I made the acquaintance of the "runner", some unemployed person or waif who lighted your way and expected a few coppers. While I never went to a top-notch party, I did get inside some very nice houses. We repaid this hospitality by showing visitors around Oxford and giving them tea in our rooms. In later years I came to realize that the high-born and well-bred people one met in this fashion took it for granted that England was the first nation in the world and that they were entitled to rule it. What made the Germans so objectionable before 1914 was that they envied the English their poise, tried to imitate it, and failed completely. On the other hand, in spite of all the conventions and of the restraints which to Americans often savored of stiffness, there was room for individual personality and even for eccentricity to a degree we have never attained. If you did not wish to conform, that was your right, and you were not persecuted for being different.

Curiously enough, the age of extravagance was also an age of inexpensiveness. Good hand-tailored suits could be bought for three guineas, evening clothes for five, equivalent then to $15 and $25 respectively. Railway travel, third class, was a penny a mile, an inland telegram cost a shilling for twelve words; sixpence was a good tip. The books record two dinners unbelievable in 1959. A gallant soldier took an Italian princess to dine at the Carlton Hotel (which alas! was bombed out in the late war), an establishment patronized by Edward VII when he was still Prince of Wales. They had oysters, soup, filet of sole, noisettes, supreme of volaille, ortolans, salad, peaches, coffee and champagne, and the bill was £2 19s. 6d., less than

$15. The same gentleman too a prominent actress to lunch at Romano's in the Strand, and for £2 4s. (less than $11) they ate hors d' oeuvre (known in Oxford as "work-horses"), soup, fish, mutton cutlets, peas and potatoes, partridge, salad, artichokes, ice cream and coffee, the whole washed down with champagne and liqueurs.

At this time the automobile was just coming in. They were usually large affairs driven by chauffeurs, and they were, in 1905, still so few that as one writer put it, "it was very hard to get run over in London". In Oxford a few undergraduates—only one in my college— had cars. The rule of the horse was still maintained by 7200 hansom cabs in London, by the hundreds of horse-drawn buses, and by a post office bus which carried the parcel post every night from Oxford to London. But this was not to last. By the time the First World War broke out, there were only 300 hansoms left, and all buses had been motorized. The London streets were certainly less interesting after the fine horses had disappeared. Aviation was confined to military purposes, and very little of that.

Two other points must be mentioned. First, gold was in normal circulation in the form of sovereigns and half-sovereigns, which were generally carried in small silver coin cases attached to the other end of the watch chain, and this gold was accepted everywhere on the continent at practically face value. And there was no need for a passport. Second, the English trains were noiseless, smooth-running, clean and punctual. Oxford is 63½ miles from London. The standard running time for non-stop expresses was 70 minutes, which included getting started and slowing down.

Finally, a word must be said about the Empire Lounge, the most notorious spot in London, where ladies of the town could always be found impeccably dressed and to which Englishmen returning home after a long absence abroad instinctively repaired, for they were sure to find a lot of old friends. It was also visited by the undergraduates of Oxford and Cambridge after a great sporting event and made the scene of a "rag".

Looking back fifty years, James Laver has written an "Ode on a Distant Prospect of the Edwardian Epoch":[9]

> Ye distant times, ye vanished hours
> Thrice happy first decade,

[9] Cf. Thomas Gray's "Ode on a Distant Prospect of Eton College".

> Above whose ghostly people towers
> Great Edward's genial shade;
> We who used to frolic while 'twas May,
> And in a meaner epoch set,
> Look backward from our vale of tears
> And see across the gulf of years
> Your glory gleaming yet.

Then follow three stanzas describing the outdoor scenes in Hyde Park and elsewhere, with

> The men, frock-coated, tall and proud,
> The women in a silken cloud. . . .

And the final stanza:

> Ah, pleasant and primeval ways!
> Ah, times beloved in vain!
> Ah, good King Edward's golden days!
> They'll never come again. . . . . .[10]

There was of course another side to this picture. Benjamin Disraeli in his famous novel *Sybil* (1845) talked about the "two nations" of England, the rich and the poor, and it is of the rich that I have been speaking. But the poor were alas! only too much in evidence, wherever one went, and the prime minister in the Liberal government which took office shortly after my arrival, Sir Henry Campbell-Bannerman, declared that twelve millions, or nearly a quarter of the population, lived on the verge of starvation, a statement that anticipated the famous remark of Franklin D. Roosevelt about one-third of Americans being ill-fed, ill-housed and ill-clothed.

In the election of January 1906, the Liberal party won the largest majority in the history of the House of Commons and soon embarked on a program of social reform which was to lead, with many interruptions, to the Welfare State of today. During my stay the most important step was the introduction of an old-age pension for persons over 70 in the amount of five shillings a week, which was bitterly opposed by the Conservative party. This was followed by the Lloyd George budget and insurance for sickness and unemployment. There

---

[10] Laver, *Edwardian Promenade*, pp. 4-5.

was no obvious connection between the misery of the masses and the demand for votes for women, but the suffragette activity, although it failed to achieve success before 1914, was symptomatic of the restlessness of the age and the fading away of Victorian England. It is worth noting that at this time socialism made small appeal to Englishmen and that the drive for social reform came from Liberals and Radicals, not from the "Reds," as the Socialists might be called because they wore red neckties as the symbol of their faith. Two world wars were needed to give the Socialist party the mandate to create the England we know today.

It remains to say something about life in Oxford, in the midst of plenty and sometimes of extravagance. Our sitting rooms were heated only by grate fires and the bedrooms not at all. Hot water for shaving and bathing was brought in tin cans. Food was simple and cheap, two shillings (50 cents) being the price for dinner in hall. You were supposed to keep yourself fit by playing games in the afternoon. I confess that I was not much interested in sports, except in the spring, when I played tennis. I got my "ekker" (exercise) by walking and cycling.

The student body was drawn from the aristocracy and the upper middle classes. Scholarships were usually awarded for intellectual prowess rather than to meet financial needs. There were a few of the latter, but I do not recall any student who was working his way through the university. Many students were able to keep motor cars or horses and to entertain on a lavish scale. With few exceptions, the students rated as "gentlemen", and the contrast in manners, appearance and language between them and the shopkeepers of Oxford and the college servants was far greater than any social distinctions I had known in the United States. In recent years it has become fashionable to distinguish between U-speech and non-U, the language of the upper and lower classes respectively, and the distinction is real, not only in accent and pronunciation but also in vocabulary. On this point I may refer you to *Noblesse oblige*, edited by Nancy Mitford. Beyond a doubt, Oxford spoke U.

Not over half the students were interested in getting real education, and these read the honor schools. The others, typical of the times, came to make friends, to enjoy themselves, and to qualify as schoolmasters, for which a pass degree was generally considered adequate. But we Rhodes Scholars took ourselves seriously, and the education I received in Oxford was of incalculable advantage to me. Incidentally, the Rhodes Scholarships were at the time the only scholarships which enabled young people of one country to study in another country; today, according to figures quoted several years ago by Senator Fulbright, there are some 43,000 opportunities of this kind, taking in all the countries of the world.

One's social life at Oxford was carried on mostly within one's own college, although of course one knew people in other colleges. In my college, Merton, there were about 100 students, a few of whom were in their fourth year. We entertained each other at breakfast, lunch, tea and coffee, doing this in our rooms, for only hall dinner was taken in common. I belonged to two college societies which met several times a term to read papers or plays. When I arrived, I did not smoke or drink, but I presently decided to do both and found that relations with my fellow students were easier. It came as a shock to observe the chaplain taking his glass of wine.

Having attended a coeducational institution, I was accustomed to having women students present and to enjoying their company. At Oxford, male undergraduates left the women undergraduates severely alone. Young women appeared in Oxford from the outside at Torpids and Eights, the weeks of intercollegiate boat races in the winter and spring terms and at the balls given at the end of the summer term. It was highly dangerous to associate with the girls of the townspeople, for the disciplinary authorities of the university suspected the worst, and the penalty, if caught, was usually to be "sent down." For the ordinary student, his only contact with feminine society was calling on academic families in north Oxford on Sunday afternoon, for which one put on dark clothes, black shoes and a bowler hat. I may add that undergraduates were strictly forbidden to go to London in term time. Of course some did, and if they got back to Oxford after midnight, it was necessary to climb into college over high walls covered with spikes and glass.

There were six deliveries of mail a day, and it was possible to write a letter to London after breakfast and get a reply on the last delivery at nine in the evening.

This paper may well close with some quotations from a die-hard who looks back on Edwardian England with many regrets:

". . . . . The world of Yesterday was a better world than that of today. We had few cares and anxieties. We were allowed to keep nearly all the money we earned. We had beliefs and ideals and we cherished them. We believed that Home was a place to preserve and keep unsullied, that Marriage was a Sacrament and not an experiment. We believed in integrity and keeping our word. . . . . We believed in getting on, in making our way and in good workmanship. We also believed in work and we saw no harm in discipline. In fact, we were a strongly disciplined nation which disciplined itself. . . . . . We upheld the Conventions because they were only another name for Good Manners. . . . . .

"We had leisure and we had plenty. We had Peace and Security. War did not touch us—but we could fight when put to it. We had a golden sovereign worth its full twenty shillings, and we led the world. . . . . . A little money went a long way. For those of us who carried the main weight of it on our shoulders, the Middle Classes, it was a very good world indeed.

"I think the improvements we have experienced are much fewer than the happinesses we have lost. . . . . . We were the English, the British, and we lived in our own way—a decent way, a clean way, and all our own. It seemed that it must always endure. . . . . .

"Those days cannot come again. Today we are poor, we are weak, we are not world leaders. We follow and we are debtors. . . . . Today we live haphazard, not knowing what Tomorrow will bring forth. Science finds new ways of destruction—the old order changes, giving place to new. But those of us who lived in Yesterday know that it was better than Today. . . . . . what Tomorrow may bring nobody knows. Stability? Almost certainly not. Peace? Most unlikely. A contented world? Hardly a chance. . . . . . Give me Yesterday."[11]

I too am glad that I came to maturity before 1914 and remember that world so well.

[11] Pope, *Give Me Yesterday*, pp. 297-298.

Out of Their Own Mouths

A paper, under the title "Interviewing the Authors of the War", read to the Chicago Literary Club in March 1930, an organization founded in 1874 (like the Washington Literary Society, but limited to men and meeting forty times a year). At the time, the persons mentioned were still living, so the paper was printed privately and confidentially by the Club. All those interviewed are now deceased, there is no reason for keeping secret what they said, and the Club has graciously consented to the publication of the paper. The phrase "authors of the war" is a translation of the words used by the German government in the title of one of its official publications Deutsches Weissbuch über die Verantwortlichkeit der Urheber des Krieges.

My first book, published in 1916, was a study of the origins of the war of 1914: England and Germany, 1740-1914, *and this problem continued to be my principal interest. After the conclusion of the war various governments began to publish documents from their secret archives, and almost every politician, diplomatist, and military personage who had been involved in the great conflict published his version of what had happened. Many contradictions were to be noted in these narratives, which was not surprising, especially as often they were written in exile or without benefit of documentary support. After I had read the memoirs and the documents, I decided that it might be worth while to talk personally with the several authors, and in 1928 I succeeded in having interviews with quite a number of them. Being thoroughly familiar with the criticisms that had been made of each man, I asked him the most difficult questions I could think of. The paper indicates whether my probing was successful. Some men answered readily; some said that they had forgotten; some, I am sure, had really forgotten. I gathered some useful information and felt that the enterprise has been distinctly worth while; I am sure that my book* The Coming of the War 1914 *was better for it.*

It is worth noting that, thirty years after I wrote my paper and my book, many of the controversial questions which I discussed remain unsettled. In particular, there are still many mysteries about the

murder of Sarajevo, for the government of Yugoslavia has never pub-
lished whatever materials its archives may contain.

My interviewing the men of 1914 was a purely personal undertak-
ing. After the Second World War, the Allied governments made it
their official business to have important men among their late enemies
questioned at great length by competent persons, and the records of
these interviews constitute an importance source for the history of
the war.

*   *   *

As though it were only yesterday, I remember sitting on the veranda
of my old home in Knoxville, Tennessee, on Friday, July 24, 1914,
and reading on an inside page of the morning paper a dispatch from
Vienna summarizing the Austro-Hungarian ultimatum to Serbia. My
instant reaction, inspired by my studies of European diplomacy and
Balkan politics for some years, was, "It is the great war at last." A
second recollection is of Sunday, August 2. I was awakened prematurely by the thud of the Sunday paper as it was thrown on the porch,
and rushed down to get it. The first-page headline, in huge letters,
read: "European War Is On!" Finally, on Tuesday evening, 4 August,
I went into town to learn the latest news and read on the bulletins[1]
that Great Britain had, on account of the violation of Belgian neutrality, declared war on Germany. These incidents are indelibly en-
graved on my memory. So you will no doubt appreciate my emotions
when in the course of 1928 I was able to talk personally with many of
the principal personages who in July 1914 had plunged the old world
into war.

The occasion for the great struggle was provided by the murder of
the Archduke Francis Ferdinand at Sarajevo on Sunday, June 28, 1914,
by Gavrilo Princip, a Bosnian of Serbian race who had been outfitted
with the necessary weapons in Belgrade, the capital of Serbia. In its
famous ultimatum the Austro-Hungarian government charged Serbia
with the moral responsibility for the crime, on the ground that the
Serbian government had for years encouraged among its own people
and among the Serbian population of Bosnia-Herzegovina an agitation

---

[1] In 1914 radio broadcasting had not yet been imagined.

directed against the integrity of the Habsburg Monarchy. This could not in fact be denied. But what people wished to know was whether the Serbian government had been privy to or cognizant of the conspiracy. No light was shed until 1924, when a prominent Serbian politician, M. Lyuba Yovanovich, asserted that in fact the Serbian government, of which he was a member, had learned of the plot several weeks before its execution and had made unsuccessful efforts to stop it. Since then this allegation has been the theme of acrid controversy, which is not yet resolved. Unfortunately, when I attempted to make an investigation on the spot, both Yovanovich and his rival, Nikola K. Pashich, against whom he had brought the charge of knowing about the plot and who had denied it, were dead. So also was the person who is supposed to have sanctioned it, Colonel Dragutin Dimitriyevich, the chief of the intelligence section of the Serbian general staff in 1914. All I could do was to speak with friends of these three Serbs. From these gentlemen I learned much about the internal politics of Serbia before the war, but either they were not informed on, or else they would not speak precisely about, the question whether the Serbian government knew of the plot.

I was not more successful, and I had not expected to be, with the king, concerning whose connection with the conspirators numerous sensational stories have been told. King Alexander,[2] a vigorous, keen man of about forty, received me with great courtesy and talked readily about the problems of his country—this was six months before the proclamation of the dictatorship. But when I was bold enough to mention the name of Colonel Dimitriyevich, it was evident that I had touched a painful subject. His Majesty contented himself with saying that the colonel, who had been executed in 1917 for an alleged attempt to kill Alexander, had caused a great deal of trouble, and changed the subject. I had been told that the King was sometimes indiscreet and conceivably might say something; but I was disappointed. In general, my conversations with many Serbs left on me the impression that the moral indignation of the western world over the assassination of the archduke was not, perhaps could not be, comprehended by a nation which had lived for centuries under the Turkish yoke and had grown accustomed to violent methods as the only recourse against oppression.

[2] Assassinated at Marseilles in October, 1934.

According to one intriguing version, the plot against Francis Ferdinand was known to the Russian military *attaché* in Belgrade, and its execution had been finally determined upon only after the Russian officer had given assurances that if, in consequence, Serbia found herself at war with Austria-Hungary, she would not stand alone. As it happened, the *attaché*, General V. I. Artamonov, was living in Belgrade at the time of my visit, and it was not difficult to see him. Admitting his close relationship with Colonel Dimitriyevich, to whom he had supplied money for the procuring of photographic apparatus to use in getting military information from Bosnia, he denied that he had been cognizant of the Sarajevo conspiracy or that, as had been alleged by one writer, he had informed Dimitriyevich of a supposed plan of William II and Francis Ferdinand to begin an Austrian war against Serbia at the first opportunity. He said that he had received no such intelligence and adduced letters to show that his substitute—for he himself had gone on leave in the middle of June—had made no communications to the Serbian general staff. General Artamonov did not look the part of a conspirator or an accomplice in murder, and I was disposed to believe that he was telling me the truth.

But however doubtful it may be that Russia was aware of the Sarajevo plot, certainly the Austro-Serbian dispute would have remained localized had not Russia intervened to support Serbia. Of all the *apologiae* written by the actors of July 1914 that by Sergey Sazonov, the Russian foreign minister, is the least satisfactory, for it was composed in exile and without the aid of documents. It would, therefore, have been for me an experience of the greatest value to talk personally with the Russian statesman. Unfortunately, M. Sazonov died just before I started on my tour of investigation. I was able, however, to make the acquaintance of M. Peter Bark, the minister of finance in the Russian government, who is now a banker in London. M. Bark said frankly that after so many years, he had only a hazy recollection of details, and this proved to be the case. On one point, however, he was specific: the Russian cabinet had not been consulted about the general mobilization. That was an issue for the Tsar himself, and Nicholas II had decided after consultation with individuals without reference to the council of ministers. This prerogative of the crown in matters pertaining to the army and the navy was not peculiar to Russia, but was exercised as well in Austria-Hungary and Germany, and for this reason it is correct to describe those three states as military monarchies, in contrast with Great Britain and France, where such military decisions were taken by the civil government.

I was also able to see, in Paris, Baron M. Shilling, who was Sazonov's *chef de cabinet*. Like Bark, Shilling declared that his recollections were no longer clear; and he referred me to the Diary which he had kept during the crisis and which was published some years ago by the Soviet government. I was thoroughly familiar with the Diary, but some of its entries are difficult to reconcile with contemporary documents. When I pointed out some of these discrepancies, the baron replied that what he wrote down day by day was what was told him by his chief, Sazonov, or what he learned in the Russian foreign office. He admitted that Sazonov or other persons might have concealed things from him or that the information received in the foreign office might have been incorrect. But he insisted, and one could only agree with him, that his Diary described the situation as it was understood at the time, and that as a strictly contemporary document, it was to be valued far higher as a historical source than the post-war recollections of Russian generals and statesmen. Naturally, Baron Shilling asserted that Russia had not planned nor desired war; he emphasized the point that at the beginning of the crisis, M. Sazonov, recalling what had happened in the winter of 1912-13, had proceeded on the assumption that Germany would restrain her impetuous ally in Vienna. The Austrian declaration of war against Serbia, however, convinced him (Sazonov) that Germany not only stood behind Austria-Hungary but actually herself desired and contemplated war: wherefore Russia had no alternative but to prepare for this eventuality as fully and as promptly as possible. Shilling also maintained the accuracy of the notation in his diary that the French ambassador, Maurice Paléologue, had given the most unqualified assurances that France would support her ally, an assurance given before the Austrian declaration of war had rendered the situation hopeless.

There is no trace of any such incident in M. Paléologue's own memoirs. Consequently, I endeavored to see him. But it was midsummer, and the former ambassador left Paris on the very day that my letter of introduction reached him. What the French documents may have to reveal on this point,[3] when they are published, will be studied with particular attention.

---

[3] Published in 1937, the documents reveal nothing.

Not seeing M. Paléologue was, however, more than compensated for by a long conversation with M. Raymond Poincaré, who is represented by German writers as being, with the late A. P. Izvolsky, former Russian ambassador in Paris, the principal author of the war. At the time of my visit M. Poincaré was president of the council and minister of finances, so that he received in one of the pavillons in the Louvre instead of at the Quai d'Orsay. He is not an impressive person in appearance. Small, dressed without style—he was wearing the kind of cuff in vogue a generation ago—he looked, as someone has rather disrespectfully put it, more like an *épicier* than a great statesman. But the moment he began to speak, one was aware of a remarkable intelligence which commanded all the pertinent facts and reached conclusions intuitively and instantly. On all the minute points of the controversy concerning the responsibility for the war, he seemed as well informed as myself, and he answered my questions without hesitation or embarrassment. I will select three episodes.

1. When the crisis broke in July 1914, M. Poincaré was on a visit to the Tsar. As it happened, the British foreign secretary, Sir Edward Grey, had suggested that it might be desirable and possible for Russia and Austria-Hungary, the two Powers directly interested in Serbia, to hold conversations *à deux*, with the object of forestalling trouble between them when Austria demanded satisfaction from Serbia for the Sarajevo murder. When this suggestion was conveyed to M. Poincaré by the British ambassador in St. Petersburg, he had promptly rejected it as "dangerous." Why?—many commentators have asked. Does this not show, it has been argued, that the French statesman secretly desired an Austro-Russian quarrel? I put the question to him directly. Not at all, he replied. Such a procedure would be dangerous, he thought, because Austria and Russia would be likely to take stiff attitudes at once, and the difficulty of mediation would be greatly increased. What he wished to do was to organize the concert of Europe, as he had successfully done in 1912, and try to keep the peace by the mediation of all the Powers.

2. In the fourth volume of his memoirs, M. Poincaré published a telegram sent from Paris to St. Petersburg on Thursday, July 30, 1914. As there given it asked the Russian government to refrain from either general or partial mobilization. But the telegram had already been published in the *British Documents on the Origins of the War* (for a copy had been sent to London), and German writers had noticed that

the version given by M. Poincaré was inaccurate: by omitting the words, "which would give Germany the pretext for," he had, so they claimed, tried to make it appear that he had advised Russia not to mobilize, whereas in fact he had merely urged her not to give Germany a pretext for such action. The omission of the six words had been explained as a printer's error. Without indicating that I was aware of this explanation, I simply stated that I had noted the incorrect version given in his book. M. Poincaré repeated to me that the error was *"une faute d'impression,"* which I had expected. But he went on to say that the subsequent pages of his narrative, in which he referred several times to the telegram, proved that he had not been guilty of deliberate editing, for what he had written made clear that he supposed he had quoted the telegram correctly in his first reference. This statement was true, as I had noted when reading his book. But, not content with that, he asserted that when the error had been discovered, he had taken pains to see that the correct text was printed in the English translation of his book; and with that, he opened a drawer of his desk, took out a copy of the English translation, and leafed through it till he found the passage in question, which he showed to me. Later in the day, he sent me an autographed copy of the English translation.

3. On the evening of Friday, July 31, the Swiss minister in Paris called at the Quai d'Orsay to say that he had learned that the Austro-Hungarian ambassador had confided to their Romanian colleague that if Serbia were to address herself to Austria-Hungary, either directly or through friendly powers, perhaps the cabinet of Vienna would be willing to indicate certain "additional demands" which it intended to put forward as the price of peace with Serbia. It had been charged that M. Poincaré, in his eagerness for war, did not follow up this overture. He himself claimed in his memoirs that he had not heard of the incident until 1920. I pointed out to my host that the overture was mentioned in one of the documents in the French Yellow Book of 1914. The inconsistency did not faze M. Poincaré in the least. Of course, he said, he had heard of the suggestion, which had been communicated to the French Government by the Austro-Hungarian ambassador himself as a personal opinion: but he insisted that he had not known of the action of the Swiss minister, and a reference to his book would show that this was all he had said.

Our conversation lasted an hour, and many other points were

touched upon. As I rose to go, he asked me about Harry Elmer Barnes, who has been his chief critic in this country. Poincaré expressed his indignation that Barnes had had what he called the bad taste to request an interview with him. Fortunately, he said, he had another engagement at the time which Barnes had proposed, and there the matter had ended. Altogether M. Poincaré left the impression on me of a man absolutely convinced of the rightness of his conduct and prepared to defend it unreservedly.

The same thing could hardly be said of Sir Edward (now Viscount) Grey, the British secretary for foreign affairs. At any rate Lord Grey was prepared to discuss the hypothesis that he had made mistakes. Thus he spontaneously remarked that perhaps there was point to the criticism that during the July crisis he had tried to negotiate with Vienna through the medium of Berlin instead of turning directly to the Austro-Hungarian government. He had followed this course because he assumed that Austria would and could not move without the approval of Germany and because these tactics had been eminently successful during the Balkan wars of 1912-13; but he said he understood that Count Berchtold had in fact been annoyed by his (Grey's) procedure.

Of all my interviews that with Lord Grey was the most agreeable. The British statesman did not look his sixty-eight years, and although his eyesight is so poor that he does much reading in Braille, he gave the appearance of a man very vigorous physically and intellectually most alert. His handsome, clear-cut face, a rich voice, fine command of language, and perfect courtesy are perhaps only outward symbols of character. Yet one did not have to speak long with him to be aware that here was a deeply sensitive person devoted to the finer things of life, who hated war and the thought of it and was as likely to have worked for it as to have murdered his wife or sovereign. Grey was not, in my judgment, a diplomatist of the first water, for he understood little of the problems and peculiarities of other nations; but he was, I think, from the moment he assumed office entirely sincere in his efforts to adjust the differences of Great Britain with other countries and to preserve the peace of Europe. If he failed, it was assuredly not for lack of good will.

On two points he was most emphatic. In the first place, he insisted that he could not have determined the attitude of Great Britain at an early stage of the crisis. If, he explained, he had proposed to announce that Great Britain would remain neutral, as the German government desired and expected, one-half of the cabinet would have resigned. On the other hand, it was equally impossible to say that Great Britain would join in, as both Russian and French diplomacy urged, for then the other half would have resigned. He himself did not doubt that British interests required support of France, but he could not commit himself in advance, and I gathered that he thought such a course would have been unwise, for it would probably have aroused intense indignation in Germany and have aggravated rather than steadied the situation.

His second point was that Germany's refusal of a conference deprived him of any lever for bringing pressure to bear in St. Petersburg. Russia considered its interests threatened by the Austrian action against Serbia: if he was to ask Russia to take no action to protect those interests, he must be able to hold out some hope of diplomatic compromise. This Germany had forestalled by the abrupt rejection of his proposal.

I ventured to broach one delicate matter to him. On July 29 he gave his famous "warning" to Prince Lichnowsky to the effect that Germany must not count on Great Britain standing aside in all circumstances, a warning which had a devastating effect in Berlin. I asked Lord Grey why he had told the French ambassador of this warning. Would it not encourage France to believe that she could count on Great Britain? He replied, "No," for M. Cambon kept begging him for days for assurances that Great Britain would come in: an argument fully justified, I think, by the facts as we now know them.

Grey's colleague, Lord Haldane, whom death removed before I could see him, used to say to my friend, G. P. Gooch, one of the editors of the *British Documents on the Origins of the War*, that Grey was not anti-German, but the foreign office was. There is a great deal of evidence in the British documents, in the form of departmental "minutes," to support this thesis. Consequently when I went to see Lord Carnock, who as Sir Arthur Nicolson had been the permanent under-secretary of the foreign office from 1910 to 1916, I expected to find what the Germans call a *Deutschfresser*.[4] He proved in fact to be a very mild gentleman with very little rancor toward the Germans. Indeed he went so far as to say that in his judgment Anglo-German

---

[4] This interview occurred some years earlier.

rivalry, which seemed the dominant factor in pre-war politics, would not *per se* have led to war. He argued, and I believe that historians are coming more and more to agree, that the *fons et origo malorum* was the Austro-Russian antagonism in the Balkans. The friends and allies of the two Eastern empires could restrain them perhaps at a given moment, but in the long run they were bound to escape control. The First World War, in short, was an Eastern war, not a Western one.

Lord Oxford and Asquith also died before I had arranged to see him. Mr. Winston Churchill was so busy with making a budget that he begged off; nor did I see Mr. Lloyd George, though had I known then some things I later learned, I should have made an effort to talk with him. I learned much from long and intimate talks with the editors of the British Documents, who, I am convinced, know much more about British policy, from having read all the materials, than do Grey and the other statesmen who directed it during the pre-war years.

But you are probably more interested in hearing what our former enemies had to say for themselves, and my experiences in Austria and Germany were in fact highly interesting. They began in Budapest, where I sought information about Count Tisza, who was Hungarian premier in 1914 and had been assassinated in October 1918 because he was held primarily responsible for the war. Actually, Tisza at the beginning of July 1914 had opposed making the murder of Sarajevo an excuse for war against Serbia, but later he changed his mind and sanctioned that course. Why? Various reasons have been suggested: personal indignation at the conduct of Serbia in not proceeding to an investigation of the crime and at the language of the Serbian press, the excitement of Hungarian public opinion, pressure from Germany, Tisza's love of office and his inability to dissuade Francis Joseph from the warlike policy. I spoke with a number of persons who had known Tisza, who had discussed this very problem with him, and from each I received a different explanation. Nevertheless, in spite of their admissions that Tisza could have prevented the war had he stood up for his original position, these same Hungarians contended that the war had been Austria's and not Hungary's war, and that Hungary had been most unfairly punished in the peace settlements.

It is true, however, to say that the driving force for war had come from Vienna and not from Budapest. Foremost in the advocacy of this policy had been the chief of the general staff, General Conrad von Hötzendorf, as his memoirs abundantly prove, and he died in the conviction that this had been the only possible policy. I was anxious to ascertain if the civil authorities also remained similarly convinced. The first of such persons whom I saw, Dr. Friedrich Ritter von Wiesner, had not changed his opinion. Wiesner is rather a tragic figure. In July 1914, he was sent to Sarajevo by the Austro-Hungarian foreign office to report on the investigation being conducted there into the circumstances of the murder. He was expected to find, if possible, proofs of the complicity of the Serbian government. He had not found them, at least he had found no evidence that clearly established the point, and had so reported to Vienna. After the war his telegram was published. Furthermore, it seemed that, in spite of this telegram, the Austro-Hungarian government had gone ahead with its deliberate aim of seeking war with Serbia. Thus Herr von Wiesner's position had not been an enviable one. In speaking with me, he said that his telegram had been misunderstood. Personally he was at the time quite convinced, by the evidence secured at the investigation, of the moral culpability of the Serbian government for the Sarajevo crime, but as the evidence was not of the kind which a court of law would accept, he had been unwilling to have it used in the formal case against Serbia. He had, he said, made this clear on his return to Vienna, and the charge that the government had deliberately disregarded his exculpation of the Serbian government was, he argued, unjustified. Wiesner was the most bitter of all the people in either camp with whom I spoke.

On the other hand, Count Alexander Hoyos, who was the *chef de cabinet* of Count Berchtold, took a rather philosophical view of the problem. Hoyos intrigued me more than any other figure. After the murder he had been sent to Berlin as the special emissary of the Austrian government, bearing documents the consideration of which took place at Potsdam on 5 July. On his return to Vienna, Hoyos made a report of his mission in the presence of Berchtold, Tisza, and the German ambassador in Vienna. According to the latter's account of the conference, Hoyos had read a memorandum, which appeared to be a document rather compromising for Germany. But it was not contained in either the German or Austrian collections published after the war. I was unusually keen, therefore, to see Hoyos and secure positive information about this document. To my disgust I was told in Vienna that he was in the country for the summer. At the suggestion of the American minister, whose personal friend he was, I rang him up on the long-distance telephone. In my best German I announced myself as a professor in the University of Chicago and the bearer of a letter of introduction from his Excellency the American minister. Count Hoyos answered in perfect English. (I later learned that his mother was an English lady, Miss Whitehead, a member of the family which manufactured torpedoes for the Austro-Hungarian navy at Pola.) The count readily agreed to see me in the country and the next day I traveled to Schloss Schwertberg in the Danube Valley, where I spent a delightful afternoon with the Hoyos family Hoyos, I might add, is not a Magyar noble, as his name seemed to imply, but of Spanish descent, the family having come to Austria during the Thirty Years' War.

When I mentioned the memorandum, Hoyos laughed. It had never existed! At the conference he had read from some hastily-made notes. He had intended to prepare a formal record of his conversations in Berlin, but in the crowded days which followed, never did so, and ultimately his notes had been lost. So my brilliant hypothesis was exploded, and one had a new illustration of the danger of trying to reconstruct history solely from documents. Count Hoyos admitted, however, what I had deduced from other documents and what has been generally overlooked by most writers: that he had explained to the German government that Austria-Hungary desired war with Serbia and that Germany, in agreeing to support its ally, did not do so in ignorance of what was planned. The count also said that a mistake had been made when the Austro-Hungarian minister in Belgrade was instructed to break off diplomatic relations in case the Serbian reply did not follow the Austrian ultimatum word for word; and when I suggested that if Austria-Hungary, instead of rejecting the Serbian reply as unsatisfactory, had put Serbia to the test of living up to it, the Habsburg Monarchy would have taken an unassailable diplomatic position which the other Powers would have been compelled to support, Hoyos said that perhaps I was right.

After my visit to Count Hoyos, I proceeded to Paris. While there I received a letter from a lady whom I had met in Budapest. She said that she had talked with her friend, Count Berchtold, about me, and the count had expressed a desire to meet me; indeed, if it would be convenient for me, he would be pleased to entertain me at his castle in Moravia. As it happened, I was going to Berlin later in the summer, so I at once intimated that I should be happy to accept an invitation from Count Berchtold. The invitation was awaiting me when I reached Berlin.

Buchlau, the seat of the Berchtold family, is extraordinarily interesting. There are two castles. One, built on a high hill eight hundred years ago, was never captured even in the palmiest days of feudal warfare, and has been uninterruptedly occupied by a Berchtold throughout the centuries. It is a veritable museum of costume and household goods actually possessed by the family and carefully preserved from generation to generation. Count Berchtold personally conducted me through the countless rooms and recited the history of each piece. I never spent a more interesting morning. The newer castle, now used as the residence of the main branch of the family, was built at the beginning of the eighteenth century by a famous Italian architect. The salon is a magnificent oval-shaped room two stories in height, with a gallery about half way up the sides, and overlooks a charming formal garden. On either side are the living quarters, and in the rear a handsome building once a stable but since the coming of the motor car converted into guest-rooms. Count Berchtold has allowed the servants' quarters to be fitted up with electric light, but in the dining-room candles are still used and elsewhere kerosene lamps—which fit very well with the exquisite eighteenth-century furniture and the long line of ancestral portraits. Buchlau, I may remark, has long been famous for the meeting between Baron Aehrenthal and M. Izvolsky, Austrian and Russian foreign ministers respectively, in September, 1908, where they discussed the annexation of Bosnia-Herzegovina and the opening of the Straits. There has been endless controversy as to what was said. Count Berchtold gave me his version, as he had received it from each of his guests—but that is too long a story. He has placed a tablet on the wall of the room in which the conference took place.

My host was as charming a gentleman as I ever met. Elegantly attired, lively of speech, full of art and literature and horse-breeding—which interested him far more than politics—wearing his sixty-five years with grace and ease, properly attentive to each of his dozen guests, to whom he spoke in German, French, Magyar, or English (he also knew Czech and Italian), he made one feel welcome; and to me, a complete stranger to him, he was courtesy personified. Although I disagreed with many of his political views, I was warmly attracted by the man and understood his popularity in the elegant world of pre-war days. Nor should I fail to mention the Countess Berchtold, a gracious lady much interested in the poor children of Vienna, or the elder son, Count Louis, whom his father was thinking of sending to the United States to complete his education. The family estates in Czechoslovakia had been largely lost as a result of the agrarian reform in that country, but those in Hungary had been saved, so that there was still, so one had to conclude, an ample fortune for maintaining the old manner of life. It was interesting to learn that the Czechoslovak government had for some years been very suspicious of Count Berchtold and had refused to let him live at Buchlau. But he had so fully demonstrated his complete retirement from politics that in 1928 he was given permission to spend four months there.

Off and on for two days, I discussed with Count Berchtold various phases of his policy as Austro-Hungarian foreign minister. It was not always an easy task, for he was prone to go off on a tangent and a conversation which began with politics might end with architecture. But I finally wrote out a little memorandum which I read to him and corrected in accordance with his suggestions. The document is too long to read here, so I state briefly only the essential points.

1. Immediately after the murder at Sarajevo he would have liked to take military action against Serbia, without waiting for mobilization—a procedure blocked by the opposition of Hötzendorf on military grounds and by Count Tisza for political reasons.

2. In the days following he was repeatedly urged to military action by Germany—of which, it may be remarked in passing, there is abundant documentary evidence.

3. He had desired Serbia to accept the ultimatum. This statement I challenged, citing the remarks of the German ambassador in Vienna to the effect that the ultimatum had been so drafted as to make its acceptance out of the question; to which Count Berchtold replied that he had not read the German documents to which I referred! I did not believe that Berchtold was deliberately trying to deceive me: rather after so many years he had simply convinced himself that he had not deliberately provoked war with Serbia.

4. He admitted that his plan had been to partition Serbia among

her neighbors, without, however, taking any part of her territory for Austria.

5. He thought it a great pity that Sir Edward Grey had made his successive proposals for mediation to Berlin instead of at Vienna. He himself, he contended, had accepted the German view that Great Britain would keep out of the war, and he was the more inclined to believe this because the British ambassador in Vienna, who was personally sympathetic with Austria, was not instructed by Grey to make representations which would have caused him (Berchtold) to take another view of British policy. Personally, I doubt if the situation in 1914 was what Berchtold described it to be in 1928; but there may be something in his argument.

6. He insisted that he had accepted Grey's final proposal of mediation, which had been overtaken by the Russian mobilization. What the contemporary documents show is that Berchtold sent a note to London accepting British mediation on paper, but he attached to it conditions which would render that mediation illusory: for the Austrian advance against Serbia was to continue and Russia was to stop all her military preparations.

Count Berchtold expressed to me his lively desire to meet Sir Edward Grey, and said that he had intended to invite his great antagonist, M. Sazonov, to visit him; but unfortunately the latter had died. In my room I discovered a copy of the memoirs of Prince Lichnowsky, the German ambassador in London, with many highly interesting annotations by Berchtold. He told me that he was writing his memoirs—when he had nothing else to do! Recently their completion has been announced, and they promise to offer instructive reading.[5] Unlike his subordinate, Count Hoyos, Count Berchtold could not appreciate the objections raised elsewhere to his policy; he embodied in his person the essence of the Habsburg Monarchy which went blindly to its doom.

Turning at last to my adventures among the Germans, I may say that although I spoke with very many scholars and propagandists, I was less successful in seeing the men of 1914 than I had hoped. Thus I was not able to meet Herr von Jagow, the foreign minister of 1914, Dr. Zimmermann, the under-secretary, or Admiral von Tirpitz. In part, this was due to the fact that I reached Berlin in

[5] They have never been published.

midsummer, and I was told that these gentlemen were away on their holidays. In the case of Herr von Jagow, however, I have some reason for suspecting that he was unwilling to talk with me, for I had published in *Current History* a sharp reply to an article by himself, in which article I had, in polite language, accused him of lying; so that I was really not surprised when he evaded an interview. I suppose I was as indiscreet as Mr. Barnes!

But one very interesting conversation I did have—with General von Haeften, who in 1914 had been the adjutant of General von Moltke, the chief of the general staff. Most writers have condemned Moltke for his effort to bring about an early German mobilization, in opposition to the policy of the chancellor, Bethmann Hollweg, who wished to delay that step in order to saddle Russia with responsibility for the war. Haeften denied that the chief of staff favored a preventive war and had tried to bring it about. But he (Haeften) became excited and overeloquent, and said, I fancy, rather more than he realized. For he practically admitted that Moltke believed a general war unavoidable and therefore demanded the military measures which the political situation required. What I could not ascertain was whether Moltke had, as is usually charged, gone behind the back of Bethmann in inciting the Austrians to action and refusal of the British proposals of mediation. The statement which interested me most was that Moltke was quite terror-stricken on learning that England was coming into the war, raising his hands toward heaven and exclaiming, "England will attack us, England will attack us!" The point of the story is that while Moltke, according to the available evidence, expected England to take the side of France, he did not believe that it would be able to make up its mind promptly and would arrive on the scene of action too late, that is, not until the German armies sweeping through Belgium had rolled up their adversaries and rendered France *hors de combat*. Throughout our conversation General von Haeften denounced the incompetent Bethmann Hollweg in vigorous language, and I must confess to considerable sympathy with his point of view.

While in Berlin I was the guest of honor at a luncheon given by one of the numerous societies interested in relieving Germany of responsibility for the war. In a brief speech, I remarked that I was making the rounds of the different countries involved in the war, and stated that I had seen Grey, Poincaré, etc. After the luncheon, a former general asked if I was going to visit the Kaiser, I replied that I did not have the *entrée* to His Majesty. The general, who, I learned later, is a personal friend of the fallen monarch, said that he could arrange it, and took my address. About three weeks later I received, in London, a letter from the Hofmarschall at Haus Doorn, saying that His Majesty would be pleased to receive me and that if I would telegraph the hour of my arrival at Utrecht, the nearest station, *"ein kaiserliches Auto"* would be sent to fetch me to Haus Doorn. So on Tuesday, August 28, 1928, I arrived at Utrecht, and there, sure enough, I found a handsome gray limousine awaiting me. It bore no coat of arms and the chauffeur did not wear livery; a quiet turn-out such as any successful American might maintain. A half-hour's drive brought us to the porter's lodge of Haus Doorn. This is a new structure built by the exile to house the officials of his tiny court and his guests, who are seemingly rather numerous. Only the presence of a Dutch policeman suggested that it was not the property of a private person. I was ushered into a suite of rooms decorated with paintings, photographs, and other memorials of the old regime, and was served the usual Dutch breakfast. After an hour the adjutant on duty appeared, in plus fours, to notify me of the arrangements for the day. I would be received by the Empress at eleven and by the Emperor at noon, after which luncheon would be served, and for the rest, whatever circumstance might suggest; I was asked to wear a dark suit.

Shortly before eleven the house doctor came to escort me to the imperial residence, which is a house of fourteen rooms built something more than a century ago by a prosperous merchant. Since the Empress's five children have to be accommodated, the house is none too large; it impressed me as being more comfortable than the palaces inhabited in the days of power. The fittings were elegant, most of them brought from Germany, but in keeping with an unpretentious establishment. The servants wore dark blue uniforms, and there were no guards about.

The Empress—as she is called, though she has no right to the title—received me in her sitting-room. She is rather a plump woman, motherly and devoted to her present husband. She talked first of Woodrow Wilson, toward whom she seemed to feel rather bitter and about whom she believed the scandals which were once current. She then denounced the Dawes Plan which, she insisted, was driving

Germany toward Bolshevism and ruin. Finally she came to speak of the Emperor. She explained that he kept himself from growing morose and despondent by omnivorous reading and that, in talking with him, I should find him prone to discourse on many topics. But since I had come to speak of particular things, I should not hesitate to interrupt and bring him back to what I wished to know. By this time an hour had passed, and the servant entered to say that His Majesty was now ready to see me. So I withdrew, descended to the ground floor, and was taken into the Emperor's study by the adjutant.

It was hard to believe that I was about to face the person who has probably been the most excoriated man of our time. But before I could give myself over to meditation, the door opened and in walked William II of Hohenzollern, once German Emperor and King of Prussia. Dressed in a gray suit with a pink tie adorned with a pin of the Prussian order *pour le Mérite,* brown shoes, white spats, and a straw hat, his eyes flashed as he came forward with outstretched hand to say, "How do you do, professor? I am very glad to see you." I bowed slightly, and he invited me to be seated. Then, "What can I do for you?" I explained that I was investigating the origins of the war and had talked with many of the survivors of 1914.

"Well," he said, "the answer is very simple. Cecil Rhodes made the war." Whereupon he descanted for a quarter of an hour on the iniquity of Rhodes, who as far back as 1895—the time of the Jameson raid—had planned to destroy Germany, because Germany stood in the way of his African ambitions. Whether His Majesty knew that I had been a Rhodes Scholar did not come out. He declared that Edward VII (his own uncle) and Edward Grey were merely the instruments of Rhodes, and when I remarked that most German writers were now disposed to absolve England of deliberately plotting the war and laid the blame on Poincaré and Izvolsky, he waived these suggestions airily aside and repeated his original proposition. He seemed also to attach credence to the tale circulated years ago by R. G. Usher of an Anglo-Franco-American alliance directed against Germany; to prove this he produced a sensational pamphlet by an American woman whose name I have forgotten. To these astonishing theories I really had no answer. But when I remembered that several years ago, in speaking with another American, he was said to have laid the blame for the war on the Jews, I realized that William II possessed the capacity to believe at any moment what pleased or suited him, that he was a highly emotional personality whose reflexes could not be gauged by ordinary standards, and that I was not likely to secure from him any positive or satisfactory information. I also appreciated that he must have been an exceedingly difficult problem for his ministers and advisers, who, it is well known, were sometimes greatly inconvenienced by his sudden actions and consequently did not scruple to conceal from him information the effect of which on him might be disconcerting. Later His Majesty essayed to prove that the Russians had been secretly mobilizing for months before the July crisis and that the British army had secret stores of supplies in Belgium. But I should add that there was no bitterness in what he said. Finally, he presented me with an autographed picture, on which is written: "Nothing is too improbable to be true. Every once in a while all the circumstantial evidence in the world seems to get mobilized to down an innocent man." I supposed then that the inscription was his own composition, but I have since learned that it is taken from a book by the late C. E. Montague.

It was now one o'clock, and luncheon was announced. The company was assembled when the Emperor and myself came out of his study—about twenty persons in all. The Empress and her five children, a couple of tutors, the court officials—that is, the marshal, the adjutant, and the doctor—three generals of the old army who had come to present His Majesty with a silver cup from members of the regiment in which he had performed his first military service, and two or three others whom I can no longer identify. All were somewhat dressed up, the generals in morning coats to which they did not seem accustomed. The Emperor made the round of the company and presented me to each, after which we went to table. The two royalties sat at the center of a long table facing each other; one general was on the Emperor's right, myself on his left, and he conversed alternately with us. The glassware bore the monogram of Frederick II and dated from his time, so the Emperor said. The meal was simple: soup, main course, dessert, followed by coffee in the Emperor's study. There seemed to be no constraint, and I had ample time to observe two large portraits of William and Hermine at either end of the dining-room. The Emperor's portrait was evidently made at Doorn, for he is represented with the Van Dyck beard he has affected since the war; none the less, he is painted in the full uniform of a field-marshal of the German army. I may say that this was the only visible sign of unrepentance anywhere about the place. As we were taking our coffee, the Emperor came up to me and asked if I would care to walk with him in the late afternoon, to which, as they say in the House of Commons, the answer was in the affirmative.

Before this little expedition, the Emperor's doctor took me over the estate, which consists of only twenty-two acres, and talked about his patient, if one may so describe a man of nearly seventy whose health was obviously excellent. By dint of wood-sawing and work in his garden, His Majesty has really kept himself quite fit, and by entertaining a constant stream of guests avoided being utterly bored. There are no legal restrictions on his movement, and he does a certain amount of motoring; but, said the doctor, in order not to arouse excitement, he does not often visit the larger towns and avoids going toward the German frontier. The marshal, the doctor, and the adjutant are all friends of the old days; they change every few months, so that the exile need not have to see the same faces for too long a period. The settlement with the Prussian government has left the Emperor in comfortable financial circumstances, though for a while just after the war there was a real shortage of cash. But when all was said, one could not doubt that life at Haus Doorn was rather dull, and that the punishment thus meted out to William II was far more effective than anything which the Allied and Associated Powers might have decreed if they had succeeded in bringing him to trial "for a supreme offence against international morality and the sanctity of treaties," as they were pleased to express it in Article 227 of the Treaty of Versailles.

At 5:30 P.M. I joined the Emperor again for our walk. He showed me the beautiful rose garden which he has presented to the town of Doorn, and then we strolled along some country lanes. Passers-by saluted him respectfully, and their greetings were scrupulously returned. I endeavored to interrogate His Majesty about the war. I addressed him simply as "You"—the days of "Your Majesty" were over. He said he had been most unwilling to go to Norway, but that the chancellor had insisted, fearing to disturb the European bourses. As to the famous conferences at Potsdam, he declared that he had understood that "the Austrians intended to give the Serbs a good hiding," and that they would do so promptly; but I could not pin

him down to a more exact statement. And when I tried to speak of
mobilization and the details of the July crisis, he referred me to his
books, copies of which he had sent around to my room. So I came to
the conclusion that I was not likely to get much information from
him, partly because he could not remember specific points, partly
because he had formed his own picture of events. I therefore let him
talk his own line.

He proceeded to talk with great animation about the politics of the
moment—Russia, China, the League of Nations, and his own beloved
Germany. In his opinion, there was no prospect of overthrowing the
Bolshevist régime by force, and the situation would have to work
itself out. As for China, he was greatly pleased by the American
treaty just negotiated,[6] which had put a spoke in the wheel of
the British, whom he dislikes as much as ever. For the League of
Nations, he showed a rather amused contempt. But most of his talk
had to do with Germany. The Germans, he argued, are not a western
but an eastern people: that is to say, they require an autocracy
or a dictatorship. The present rulers were all reds, or at least pinks,
and were ruining the country, driving it steadily toward Bolshevism.
I ventured to ask if he did not think that Dr. Stresemann had been
conspicuously successful in the conduct of German foreign policy.
"Stresemann," he exclaimed, "Stresemann! He's the greatest scoundrel
unhung!" In his opinion, the time would come when the United
States would appreciate the help of Germany against great Britain,
and if he were back in Berlin, he would see to it that this support
was given. We would yet regret the day when we insisted on his
abdication. For, he said, shaking his fist in my face, "You—meaning
the United States—are responsible for my being here, and it is your
duty to see that justice is done." To which there was nothing I
could say.

The Emperor speaks excellent English, with a keen appreciation
of idiom, and his language is always vigorous, not to say picturesque.
In spite of everything, I could understand how it was that for
thirty years he captivated all who knew him. Convinced as he
is of the rightness of his course and conduct, he will go to his
grave thoroughly unable to understand why, after long years of

---

[6] Treaty of July 25, 1928, by which China acquired, so far as the United States
was concerned, complete national tariff autonomy.

hate, he has been repudiated by his own people and forgotten by the rest of the world.

The hour drew near for my departure. His Majesty graciously accompanied me to the lodge, where the gray limousine was waiting. My bags had already been loaded. The Emperor asked for my address, so that he might send me any subsequent writings of his about the war, and I gave the adjutant my card. The Emperor himself opened the door. I took my seat. The great car got slowly under way, and as it rolled under the gateway, I beheld William II, hat in hand, bowing low to a citizen of the country which he had declared was chiefly responsible for his presence there that day.[7]

[7] I sent the former Emperor a copy of my book. He was reported to have said that "of all the books written about the origins of the war, that by Bernadotte Schmitt was certainly the worst".

Modern European History in the United States

A paper read at the Sixth International Congress of Historical Studies, Oslo, in August 1928. In the thirty-two years since Oslo American interest in the history of Europe has increased enormously, and particularly since the close of the Second World War. The number of books published in recent years is so large that it would be invidious to single out only a few for mention. In my own studies, I have been pleased to note how often American books on European history are cited by European historians.

For American historians, the principal difficulty at the present time is to cope with the languages of eastern and southeastern Europe. It is most important for American scholars to read the historical works put out under Soviet auspices. If those which I have been able to read in translation (alas! I do not know Russian) are characteristic of Soviet historiography, I fear that there is little common ground between Russian historians and those of the west.

* * *

Ninety percent of the population of the United States is of European extraction. A considerable proportion has landed on our shores within the last fifty years, and a still larger number is but a single generation removed from European traditions and environment. Moreover, in order to preserve some kind of connection with their European homelands, many groups within the American people maintain newspapers in their native languages, create singing and social organisations for the observance of Old-World customs which are dear to them, and in a variety of ways endeavor, while submitting cheerfully to the process of Americanisation, to retain something of the individuality characteristic of the nations of Europe. One would expect, therefore, the history of Europe to make a wide appeal to Americans, and it does so. At any rate the historian is favorably impressed by the wide range and the quite passable quality of books of history which are offered for sale in any good bookshop. Nevertheless, it is easy to exaggerate, and the real fact appears to be that until rather recently the American people were not greatly interested in the history of Europe.

This state of mind was quite intelligible. In spite of our European origin, the past was of less interest to us than the present and the future. We had a huge country to develop, and that task absorbed both our energy and our enthusiasm. Only slowly did there arise a cultivated and leisured class with time or inclination to be curious about its European origins. If history made any appeal to the American people, it was its own history, of which we were very proud; to many, in fact, Europe was something to forget. The result of this state of things was that until comparatively recently historical studies in the United States were very little concerned with Europe and that only a few works by American writers commanded recognition in Europe. Prescott, the historian of Spain, Motley, of the Netherlands, Lea, of the Inquisition, and Mahan, of sea power, proved that Americans could write European history, but they and a few lesser lights did not make a very impressive list.

Yet another circumstance must be mentioned. Precisely because so many Americans were recently arrived from Europe, it was deemed imperative, for obvious political and national reasons, to emphasise the teaching of American history in the public schools. The newcomers themselves were anxious to be instructed, and European history was accordingly discounted or belittled. Not that European history was not taught, for it was; but, as I well remember from my boyhood days and as I am sure my contemporaries will agree, the books used were not interesting and the teaching was often indifferent.

Within the last generation a tremendous change has come about which gives great encouragement to the cause of European history in the United States. In the first place, the general interest in history has steadily expanded, as I am quite ready to testify after twenty years' teaching and observation. This is not to be explained merely by the fact that there is now a large and ever-growing class in America which has time and taste for intellectual interests. There are particular reasons why history is coming into its own. For one thing, the immigration of millions of people from all parts of Europe and the necessity of fitting them into the American scheme has compelled a certain attention to the background of these immigrants. Why did they leave Europe? What did they bring with them?

These and other questions could be answered only by reference to the history of these people, and to their history we have gone. Not all the researches have been made by professional historians; indeed the work has been chiefly by economists, sociologists, and students of government, but much of what they have written has been history. Another factor has been the ever-increasing habit of Americans to travel in Europe. No doubt a fair proportion of these travellers go to amuse themselves, but the great majority are serious-minded, and to some extent they try to equip themselves before starting by learning something of the countries they intend to visit. I myself am often asked by prospective tourists to recommend books of history.

But most important of all has been the shock of the Great War. Europeans, unless they have visited the United States, cannot appreciate either the feeling of incredulity with which the American people greeted the events of July 1914 or the extent to which they were ignorant of the issues involved. The process of education, however, was not long in beginning. Those authors who were fortunate enough to have written readable books on European history began suddenly to enjoy large royalties, and many new books were offered to an eager public. It would be easy to draw up a quite respectable list of books written by Americans dealing with the various belligerent countries and the historical backgrounds of the struggle. The interest thus aroused has not flagged since. One English historian told me recently that more of his books were sold in the United States than in his own country. My own conviction is that if historians, whether American or European, will write interesting and attractive books on European history, the American public will buy and read them. At the moment historical biography is very much in vogue, and there is no reason why straightforward history, if attractively presented, should not become equally popular.

Another cause for satisfaction is that the teaching of European history has improved enormously of recent years. So far as the primary and secondary schools are concerned, this is due in large measure to the American Historical Association. That body, whose foundation in 1884 marked a turning-point in the development of American historical studies, has devoted much time and energy to the problem of teaching history, and numerous committees, whose work has extended over many years, have pointed out in a series of reports, what should be the content and the method of the history curriculum.

On the whole, the educational authorities of the country have been not unwilling to follow the advice of the historical experts. Thanks to this co-operation, the textbooks of European history used in the schools provide our young boys and girls with a sympathetic and intelligent view of the Old World which was quite lacking in the books which I had to study; moreover, the very fact that our population is an amalgam of all the races of Europe compels authors to deal fairly with the several nations of Europe, that is, if they wish to sell their books to school authorities!

But even good textbooks do not do away with the necessity of good teaching. On this score also much progress can be observed. It used too often to be the custom to give over the teaching of history to the least-occupied members of the staff, the theory being that history was a matter of kings and battles and dates and that no special preparation was necessary for imparting this information to young minds. Well, the custom has not entirely died out in small communities, but generally speaking, our high schools, which correspond roughly to European *lycées* or *gymnasien*, entrust the teaching of history to persons who have made some study of history. So well recognized is this principle that numerous societies of teachers of history exist in various parts of the country.

It cannot be said that in our high schools excessive attention is paid to the history of the United States. The four-year course is usually arranged as follows: in the first year, ancient and medieval history; in the second, modern history; in the third, English history; in the fourth, American history. Thus modern European history fares very well. Of late years, chiefly as a result of the interest aroused by the Great War in the recent history of Europe, the tendency can be observed to include the Renaissance and the Reformation in the work of the first year, and to let modern history begin with the Age of Louis XIV, in order to gain time for studying the last fifty years. Occasionally the complaint is heard that too much attention is devoted to the nations of western Europe and that eastern Europe, from which so many of our recent immigrants have come, is neglected.

Sometimes ambitious politicians propose that a certain kind of patriotic history shall be taught. Fortunately little attention is paid to such vaporings, and by and large the modern history taught in our schools is history and not politics or propaganda.

If from the secondary schools one turns to the colleges and universities of the United States, one is again struck by the preponderance of attention given to the history of Europe. The introductory course, which is often a prerequisite for more advanced work, usually deals with medieval and modern history, not with American history, and the emphasis is upon the modern end. Among the advanced courses the most popular are almost invariably those relating to the French Revolution, the history of Europe since Waterloo, and pre-war diplomacy. The expansion of Europe is also a much-studied subject. In the large universities, the history of separate countries—France, England, Germany, etc.,[1] is often presented, and of recent years the question of the Near East has been taken up in a number of institutions. Perhaps the clearest indication of interest is the fact that there is a greater demand for teachers of modern European history than of any other branch.

To provide these teachers of history is the function of our graduate schools, and our universities from the Atlantic coast to the Pacific, are doing their best to discharge it. There are at least twenty institutions of learning which offer advanced instruction in history, using the most modern methods of research and the seminar. Even so, they find it difficult to meet the demands made upon them, for more and more teachers in secondary schools are being required to pursue advanced studies as a condition to promotion, and particularly in summer are the graduate schools of history overwhelmed by the number of would-be apprentices of Clio. If not all these aspirants measure up to an exacting standard, nevertheless the general result is worth while, for at least some are stimulated to make the study of history a life work. Only a few of the very largest universities are able to provide instruction in all fields of European history, but it can be safely said that in some university or other, one can study any branch of European history under the direction of a highly-trained specialist. I do not wish to be indelicate, but I may say that the universities of the United States offer more facilities for the study of European history than European universities do for the study of American history.

So far, I have been speaking of the study of modern European history in the United States. When I turn to the other aspect of

---

[1] Since the Second World War, increasing attention has been paid to the history of Russia.

this paper, the writing of history, the picture is perhaps less satisfactory. It must be confessed that we Americans do not contribute, certainly not so much as we should like, perhaps not so much as we should, to contemporary historical literature. There appear to be three main reasons for this. First of all, most of our historians are teachers in the colleges and universities to a greater degree than is the case in Europe, and in our educational institutions more time has to be given to teaching and to administrative duties than in European universities. Furthemore, the academic year is longer. The consequence is that our historians, by and large, have little leisure for the slow business of research. It is not always possible for them to reserve even the summer holidays for study, for many of them feel the necessity of earning extra money by teaching in the summer sessions which practically all large universities now maintain. But the average American historian is not lacking in the will to contribute to historical knowledge, and most of them, in spite of the handicap of too much teaching, manage to keep some kind of research, if only a modest one, on the stocks and to publish an article from time to time.

A second, and more fundamental, difficulty arises from the lack of materials, that is, the documents and other sources from which history is written. It is true that in our large universities one will find practically all the printed collections in the chief languages of western Europe, and a few of the largest also possess the sources for the history of eastern Europe. The files of historical periodicals are likewise fairly complete. But the colleges and the smaller institutions do not have the money to buy expensive series, and are fortunate if they can procure an adequate collection of secondary books and a few of the more important sources. Thus, unless a scholar is a member of a large university or lives in close proximity to one, he finds it difficult and frequently impossible to surround himself with the documents and books of reference and other tools necessary for a sustained piece of research; many an ambitious young student, placed by circumstance far away from libraries and fellow-historians, has been unable to write the book of his desire, and some succumb to discouragement and do not even keep their hand in by writing articles.

In this connection it may be noted that naturally few manuscript materials of European history are available in the United States.

Occasionally a great collection of private papers crosses the Atlantic, such as the Shelburne Papers, which have been acquired by the University of Michigan; but such instances are rare, and American opinion does not unanimously approve of the transfer of such precious records from their native country. Now I do not wish to suggest that all possible subjects of investigation in printed materials have been exhausted; the annual production of doctor's dissertations amply proves the contrary. But the prospect of using unpublished materials is always a strong inducement to a historian, and in this respect our European colleagues have the distinct advantage of us. The number of Americans who have made use of European archives is considerable, and is increasing; but a visit to Europe is a costly enterprise, at least for a student dependent upon his academic income.[2] So we shall for the most part have to be content with what the printed sources offer us.

A third reason for American backwardness is the matter of language. Our scholars learn French and German as a matter of course, and many add Italian or Spanish. But very few of us have any acquaintance with the Slavonic languages, which is most unfortunate, because the history of eastern Europe offers unlimited opportunities for investigation and presents the kind of problems which naturally appeal to Americans. It may also be noted that the knowledge of Latin is on the decline in the United States, and the state of Greek is even worse. Thus the field open to most American researchers is the history of the western nations, the field which has been most assiduously cultivated for decades and which does not make easy the finding of an uncultivated patch.

Nevertheless, in spite of these handicaps, American writers have in recent years made contributions to the modern history of Europe. Not to make too long a list, I shall mention only certain books published since the close of the Great War. The strong appeal which English history, for obvious reasons, has always made to us, still continues. So we note Conyers Read's *Mr. Secretary Walsingham and*

---

2 This is not so true in 1960 as it was in 1928. The Fulbright Fellowships, and grants-in-aid from the American Council of Learned Societies, the Social Science Research Council and the American Philosophical Society (to mention only the most notable sources of funds) now make it possible for American scholars to visit European archives fairly easily, and there is now a steady stream of historical works based on extensive research in foreign archives.

the Policy of Queen Elizabeth, P. V. B. Jones' *The Household of a Tudor Nobleman,* E. P. Cheyney's *History of England* from 1588 to 1603, Wallace Notestein's publication of the diaries of Stuart parliaments, and the first two volumes of E. R. Turner's *The Privy Council.* For the eighteenth century, there is A. H. Basye's *The Board of Trade and Plantations,* only the latest in a long series of books and monographs by American historians which have greatly extended the knowledge and revolutioned the conception of the British colonial system before the American Revolution. F. J. Klingberg's *Abolition of the Slave Trade* and Paul Knaplund's *Gladstone's Imperial Policy* throw light on the working of that system in the nineteenth century; while L. H. Jenks' *The Investment of British Capital Abroad* provides exact historical information on a rather elusive subject. Miss Violet Barbour's biographies of late Stuart statesmen and Miss Frances Gillespie's *The Rise of the English Working Classes* indicate that women as well as men make good historians.

In the field of continental history, quite a little has been done with economic problems. Witness F. C. Palm's *The Economic Policies of Richelieu,* F. L. Nussbaum's *Commercial Policy in the French Revolution,* F. C. Melvin's *The Continental System of Napoleon,* W. F. Galpin's *The Grain Trade of England during the Napoleonic Wars,* and C. E. Hill's *History of the Danish Sound Dues.* But other interests are represented by Preserved Smith's *Life of Erasmus,* Albert Hyma's *The Brethren of the Common Life,* F. W. Albion's *Forests and Sea Power,* L. R. Gottschalk's *Jean Paul Marat,* and E. D. Adams' *Great Britain and the United States during the American Civil War.* In spite of our intense interest in social and economic history, we do try to keep it in its proper perspective.

An aspect of modern history which greatly interests American historians is the question of pre-war diplomacy and the problem of responsibility. R. H. Lord's *The Origins of the War of 1870,* which made use of and published documents from the Prussian archives, and J. V. Fuller's *Bismarck's Diplomacy at its Zenith,* which was the first book to make use of *Die Grosse Politik der Europäischen Kabinette,* have been much discussed. E. M. Earle's *Turkey, the Great Powers and the Bagdad Railway* is the fullest account yet written of that enterprise which loomed so large in Near Eastern politics; another problem of that area is treated in Miss Edith Stickney's

Southern Albania in European Affairs 1913-1923. Both of these books were awarded the George Louis Beer Prize offered annually by the American Historical Association for the best monograph dealing with European international relations since 1895. W. L. Langer will soon bring out a study of Caprivi's policy and the Franco-Russian alliance. Sidney B. Fay's long-expected book on *The Origins of the World War* will be published in September. Ultimately American historians may be expected to interest themselves in the history of the war itself, for they possess in the Hoover War Library at Stanford University, the gift of the present Republican candidate for the presidency, a very complete collection of published books, pamphlets and documents, and not a little unpublished documentary material. In fact American writers have already begun on the war. Charles Seymour's *The Intimate Papers of Colonel House* and R. S. Baker's *Woodrow Wilson and World Settlement* are perhaps the most informing books yet written about the war and the peace. We like to flatter ourselves in thinking that we take a more objective view of the great conflict than can Europeans, but I suppose that we are hardly able to decide that question.

To sum up: American historians are not discouraged and look forward to ever greater activity. So bright, in fact, are the prospects for the advance of modern European history in the United States that the University of Chicago has recently established *The Journal of Modern History*, the first issue of which will be published in 1929. Although the *Journal* will be edited by American scholars, it will welcome contributions from European historians, and on behalf of its board of editors I extend to the members of the International Congress of Historical Studies a most cordial invitation to submit articles, documents, reviews of books or any other material relating to any phase of the history of Europe since the close of the middle ages. The *Journal* will also be glad to receive books for review and bibliographical notes; and, I need hardly say, it will be very happy to receive subscriptions. Our hope is that the *Journal* may be an organ of intellectual co-operation between Europe and the United States and help to remove the reproach often heard of recent years that history has become mere propaganda in the service of exaggerated nationalism. The *Journal*, one should add, is not to be the rival but the complement of *The American Historical Review*.

Some Reflections on a Revolutionary Age

*An address to the Phi Beta Kappa Society, Indiana University,
June 1927. It was a commonplace that the nineteenth century began
with the fall of Napoleon and the Congress of Vienna (1814-1815)
and extended to the outbreak of the First World War in 1914.
Often the eighteenth century was considered as covering the period
from 1715 to 1815. I did not like this periodization, for it seemed
to me that the collapse of the Ancient Regime in Europe began,
not with the events of 1789 in France, but with the American
revolution of 1776, the partition of Poland in 1772, the invention
of the steam engine in 1769, and the publication of Adam Smith's
The Wealth of Nations in 1776. In about a hundred years these
circumstances and forces produced a relatively stable Europe, the
like of which had never been known in modern times—the Europe
of 1871-1914. The theme of this address was, then, that of a century
of revolution, 1770-1871, followed by an aftermath of synthesis
which was interrupted by the war of 1914-1918. In 1927 the synthesis
appeared to have been renewed. Europe had recovered from the
worst effects of the war, the Great Depression was not foreseen,
Mussolini seemed to be of little importance, Hitler of even less.
Russia was still in economic confusion and no longer interested in
promoting world revolution. The withdrawal of the United States
from European politics, while regretted, was not taken too seriously.
Japan had not begun to overrun China, even though the chaos in
China invited such action. European colonies in Asia and Africa
gave no sign of their revolt twenty years later against their white
masters. In 1927 Europe looked as stable as it had been in, say, 1900.*

*Were I to rewrite the paper in 1960, I should not change the
first and second parts, that is, up to 1914. But the years from 1919
to 1939 I should treat as a period of armistice between the two
world wars, and the years from 1914 to 1960 as a period of violence,
the end of which is not in sight.*

*The basis of the territorial settlements of 1919-1920 was the prin-
ciple of nationality or self-determination (although it was violated
in detail from place to place). This basis was not seriously changed*

in the settlements after the second war. To be sure, Poland was shifted somewhat to the west, and the Soviet Union, as the successor of the former Russian Empire, reabsorbed the Baltic states and Bessarabia; and a few other rectifications of frontier took place. Germany is at present partitioned: whether permanently, no one knows. The territorial revolution which began with the partition of Poland may now have well come to an end.

*   *   *

Y ou, young ladies and gentlemen, who have just been inducted into Phi Beta Kappa, average, I fancy, twenty-two years of age. Though you may not realise the fact—unless you have sat at the feet of my friend Professor Benns[1]—your life has been passed in an age of revolution. In the year of your birth occurred what is commonly called the First Russian Revolution. When you had reached the age of three, the Young Turks rose against the Red Sultan, Abdul Hamid; when you were five, Portugal indulged in the first of its twenty-three revolutions. At nine, you might have been excited by the prospect of Ulster rebelling against the British government which was proposing to establish Home Rule in Ireland. The habit of revolution was not, however, peculiarly European. In 1905 Persia imposed a parliament upon its autocratic Shah and a few years later forced him to take the road to exile. The winter of 1911-1912 saw the Manchu dynasty toppled over by Chinese republicans. In that same year Porfirio Diaz was driven out by Francisco Madera, who himself mounted to the presidential chair of Mexico only to be supplanted presently by Victoriano Huerta, who in turn gave place to Venustiano Carranza. In Venezuela the famous General Castro maintained the reputation of Latin America, and of Central America it is hardly necessary to speak.

The Great War gave a brief pause to such tendencies, for every people, no matter how discontented, rallied to its government and, in the expectation of victory, nobly endured privation and suffering of the direst sort. But when victory proved elusive and the promised rewards could not be paid, war-weary and maddened nations rose

[1] F. Lee Benns, professor of history in Indiana University.

one after the other to dispense with rulers who had led them first into war and then into disaster. In 1917 Russia passed from Tsarist autocracy to inchoate democracy and thence to full-blown Communism. At the end of 1918 the Habsburgs and the Hohenzollerns were unable to survive the defeats of their armies. The return of peace has not destroyed the fashion. Sinn Fein terrorized the British government into recognizing the Irish Free State, and that same government has made concessions to Egypt and India that were the alternate to, if not the equivalent of, revolution. In Turkey Mustapha Kemal Pasha has overthrown the Sultanate and the Caliphate, and in Persia Riza Khan Pahlavi has deposed the House of Qajar in favor of himself. At this moment the Chinese Revolution has flared into renewed vigor. Even so well-ordered a state as Chile has recently witnessed several upsets. Nor are the exploits of Benito Mussolini and General Primo de Rivera to be forgotten. One may well ask whether revolution is not endemic in the modern world.

As a matter of fact, the sensational picture I have drawn gives an entirely false perspective. Our age is impressed by this riot of revolutions because the last quarter of the nineteenth century was a singularly quiet and peaceful epoch in which the most startling events were the occasional assassination of some chief of state. But our grandfathers and their fathers lived in one of the liveliest periods in the history of the world, and I propose to show that the excitements of our day are merely the belated manifestation of forces long at work, forces which may be traced back to the early days of your society.

As a point of departure, let me summarize our Western civilization as it exists in the first quarter of the twentieth century. The unit of world organization is for better or for worse, the nation, and in a rough way the frontiers of states correspond to the identity of peoples.

In politics fundamentals are: freedom of personal movement, freedom to follow any trade or profession, freedom of conscience; equality before the law, equality of opportunity so far as the law can provide it; democratic methods of government, achieved by most peoples or recognized as the goal to which they aspire. Materially, life is dominated by machinery. Men and goods are transported by machinery; information is transmitted by machines; the commodities of daily existence are made almost exclusively by machinery, and if food is not actually grown by machinery, the land is able to produce the necessary quantity of food only by the aid of machinery. Fabulous wealth, however, has not solved, but rather intensified, the age-old problem of poverty; with the result that millions of men and women, convinced that the existing economic system is unjust, ask if it is necessary. Indeed, no institution, political, social, economic or religious, is now regarded as sacrosanct, and man refuses to accept any barrier to his imagination or enterprise.

These are commonplaces which it is almost insulting to your patience to repeat. But if Voltaire were to return to earth, he would scarcely recognize the European landscape. In 1778, the year of his death, there were scarcely any nation-states, for the idea of nationality had hardly germinated. In politics despotism, or occasionally oligarchy, as in Britain or Holland, was the rule. Socially, privilege was the fortune of the few, serfdom the lot of the masses over large sections of the old world. The hand-worker still furnished the only kind of labor, industry was monopolized by the guilds. There were many barriers to intellectual freedom, and religion was the most potent spiritual influence in the lives of the overwhelming majority of mankind.

These again are commonplaces. The point I wish to make is that these conditions had obtained for centuries. Germany had been a mosaic of minute states for five hundred years, Italy a geographical expression for a thousand; the Turks had been established in the Balkan peninsula for four centuries. In spite of innumerable small changes of territory, the map of Europe had altered little in essentials since the early Middle Ages. The prevailing political philosophy which lauded the benevolent despot was not radically different from that which had inspired the best Roman emperors. The methods of industry and agriculture showed but little improvement since the days of Charlemagne. In matters of the mind, age-old tradition was still strongly entrenched. If science was beginning to plot a new course, religion was not, for Protestant and Catholic alike appealed to the ideas, as they respectively understood them, of the early centuries of the Christian era. Apart from a handful of intellectuals, there was, in most parts of Europe, little disposition to challenge historic institutions or change existing conditions; it could not have been otherwise, because for centuries the masses had been ignorant and were supposed to remain so. If Voltaire would be surprised, and perhaps not altogether enchanted by the spectacle of the twentieth century, the Emperor Frederick II (1215-1250) would have easily comprehended the age of Louis XV (1643-1715).

The picture is not radically different for the New World. In the English-speaking areas, the social system was freer for white men than in Europe, but slavery still flourished; democracy was by no means an universal creed; industry was hardly born; nationalism was but a frail plant. Latin America was still controlled by Spain by the methods and in the spirit of the sixteenth century. Africa was almost beyond the ken of Europe, and Asia lived its own life, disdainful of Europe, and except in the case of India, hostile to intercourse with it. The separation of continents was not a mere fact of geography, it was sanctified by barriers of ignorance and prejudice.

In the last century and a half, then, society and civilization have undergone a greater transformation than in the previous thousand years. They have, in short, been revolutionized, not merely in the sense that overt acts have changed the form and fabric of states, but they have been transformed in character and spirit. The process has been accomplished in three phases. First of all, there is a period from ca. 1775 to ca. 1875, which may be described as a century of revolution; revolution political, social, economic, colonial, territorial and intellectual. During these hundred years the various forces which govern the world of today are generated, chiefly in Europe, and begin to do their work; but they remain to some extent isolated phenomena, or at least, their relation to each other is not fully understood. They gain momentum; but they do not come into their own, so to speak, and exercise preponderating influence until the generation or half century preceding the Great War. This second period I venture to call, for lack of a better term, fifty years of synthesis. Lastly, the Great War reveals a fact obscured by the great material prosperity of the second period: the fact that the work of synthesis was not complete, that the constructive ideas of the mid-nineteenth century had been kept in check in certain regions by conservative forces which rested on the support of tradition and military power. The effect of the Great War was to give new life to the revolutionary impulses and, by the destruction of the military caste which opposed them, to make possible their fuller application. It is their renewed expression which has created at once the seeming confusion of the past ten years and the hope for the future.

The political phase of the century of revolution begins with the revolt of the American colonies. The complicated causes of that struggle and its effects on our own country do not concern us here. What I wish to point out is that it succeeded and that its success unquestionably hastened the great French convulsion of 1789. That event may fairly be called the beginning of a new era, for it proclaimed and to some extent established two great principles: (1) control of government by a representative assembly and (2) universal manhood suffrage. Henceforth European political history is the record of the advance of these ideas, in constant conflict with absolutist tradition and often at odds with each other. Nearly a century has to pass before the victory is won, but by about 1870 the principle of self-government is definitely accepted as the basis of European constitutions. In France itself, it was not effectively secured till 1875. In Italy it went along with the achievement of unity in 1861, and Spain finally got a liberal constitution in 1869. The year 1867 witnessed the establishment of constitutionalism in Austria and Hungary and the creation of a national diet in Germany. The Balkan states reached the same goal in the sixties and seventies. Universal suffrage made slower progress, being restored in France itself only in 1848; but its adoption in Germany in 1867 may be said to have made it the norm towards which political progress would henceforth move. In the same year, the second Reform Act gave England a democratic franchise for the first time.

The social revolution, without which the political revolution would have been meaningless and impossible, was likewise in large measure a product of France, although it is fair to remember that both Joseph II and Frederick the Great did something towards abolishing serfdom in their respective dominions. The famous night of August 4, 1789, provided a program for French armies to carry with them in their conquest of Europe; but beyond the reach of those armies the process of reform was slow. Although serfdom was formally abolished in Prussia in 1807, a generation had to pass before all the details of the new order were worked out. Efforts were actually made to reestablish serfdom in Sardinia after 1815. The last remnants of feudalism disappeared in Austria only in 1848. Bondage right lasted in Romania until 1864 and in Russia until 1861. The abolition of slavery by the French Convention in 1793 and by the British Parliament in 1834 set examples which the United States was constrained to follow, albeit a generation later and at the cost of civil war.

In similar fashion, the guild system, though destroyed in France by the National Assembly, withered slowly elsewhere; it survived in Prussia, except for a temporary abolition in 1846-1849, until 1869.

The economic revolution began in England at about the same time as the political and social revolution in France, and it kept pace, in the rest of Europe, more or less with political progress and social reform. English farming was put on a modern basis in the latter half of the eighteenth century, but it was not until the third quarter of the nineteenth that scientific methods were generally adopted throughout continental Europe; as late as 1861 the flail was still being used in some parts of France. Progress in this direction depended in no small measure upon the disappearance of feudal methods of landholding, and advanced as the latter were abolished.

Industrially, there is the same story to tell. The great inventions which inaugurated the industrial revolution were made in England chiefly between 1770 and 1800; in the next quarter of a century they are systematically applied, and by 1825 England has been pretty thoroughly industrialized. On the continent the new processes begin to be experimented with after 1815, and by 1850 they have been generally adopted in France and Belgium. Germany takes them up in earnest in the following twenty years, the sixties being a kind of boom period, and by 1870 the spade work had been achieved. About this same time Italy and Austria begin to fall in line. In general, therefore, it may be said that nearly a hundred years elapse from the time when Englishmen begin to demonstrate the possibilities of machinery until the continental peoples grasp its necessity. Our own country was nearly as backward, for it required the impetus of the Civil War to start the North on the path of large-scale industrial development.

The political consequences of this economic transformation need only be mentioned. The effective demand for popular participation in government increases *pari passu* with the adoption of the new industrial methods, and aspirations to unity in both Germany and Italy receive much stimulation because the material disadvantages of disunion are for the first time clearly appreciated. These facts, however, illustrate my argument that the democratic idea did not enjoy general recognition until three quarters of a century after it had been launched in France.

The colonial revolution has several aspects. Most obviously, the independence of the United States and the South American peoples doomed the old colonial system as a means of exploitation; and the somewhat paradoxical consequence was that when the New World became free to work out its own political destiny, its economic relationship with Europe became closer with each passing decade. A second aspect of the colonial revolution is equally important. The economic changes in the United Kingdom were directly and immediately responsible for a huge emigration from that country in the first three-quarters of the nineteenth century, and in so far as this emigration went to British colonies, it brought about a complete change in British colonial policy. In spite of what is often asserted, that policy was not greatly affected by the American Revolution which was a protest against it. It is true, of course, that the exploitation symbolized by the Navigation Acts was abandoned, but the control of the mother country was maintained well into the nineteenth century. When, however, Canada and Australasia began to fill up (the expression is not accurate as a statement of fact!) with Englishmen who insisted on governing themselves, England grasped the logic of the situation and granted self-government, all the more readily because imperial sentiment was at a low ebb. But not till 1859, nearly a century after the Townshend Acts, was tariff autonomy granted, and the colonies were made responsible for their own defence only about 1870, more than a hundred years after the Stamp Act. Once again it is evident that the change from the old to a new system is spread over nearly a century, and it may be noted that there were few new developments until the Great War.

About the same time that Great Britain lost its American colonies, it began to find compensation in India. Clive's victory at Plassey in 1757 was followed by the famous India Acts of 1773 and 1784, which established the beginnings of effective control and thanks to these arrangements, India became a most valuable market for British goods. But England had a third commodity for export besides men and goods — capital. Between 1848 and 1856 large amounts were invested in India for the construction of roads, canals, telegraphs and railways, and the transfer of the functions of the East India Company to the Crown is to be explained as much by the desire to control the economic development of the country as by the incident of the Great Mutiny. The system set up in 1857 was not modified until the present century.

Farther east, China and Japan were objects of increasing interest, for their products were in great demand and it was thought only reasonable that in return they should, willy-nilly, open their doors to European goods. Between 1839 and 1860, under the leadership of England, China is forced to enter into regular relations with the western nations; similar treatment is meted out to Japan between 1853 and 1864, with Great Britain again playing a leading, though not the instigating, role. But once contact is established, the policy of Europe and America in the Far East becomes quiescent till the very end of the century. These mid-century trading activities were mutually profitable and must be carefully distinguished from the land-grabbing and concession-hunting imperialism of our own day. Before leaving this theme, it may be noted that French colonial policy was also breaking with tradition. The decision to incorporate Algeria into France and to regard its inhabitants as Frenchmen was a new departure, inspired however, not so much by economic necessity as by political idealism.

The territorial revolution begins with the partition of Poland, 1772-1795, which excited considerable indignation at the time. It was in fact a body blow at the doctrine later described as historic right, and set a precedent which was promptly utilized by the French Directory to seize the Rhineland and the Netherlands and by Napoleon Bonaparte to reorganize Italy and Germany. These achievements are often looked upon as merely so many things to be undone by the Congress of Vienna. Actually they were revolutionary acts of the greatest moment. No doubt Napoleon's manipulations of the map were dictated by his own political necessities, but they also pointed the course of the future. His kingdom of Italy, incomplete though it was, provided patriots of the Peninsula with an ideal for the future; his reduction of the number of German states facilitated enormously the work of Bismarck, and his later oppressions aroused German national sentiment from the torpor of centuries. The diplomacy of Metternich might restore the old arrangements and prevail for a time, but the imponderables were against him and his successors. In the revolutions of 1848 the primary aim of the Italians was national unity; in the Frankfort Parliament, the principal topic of debate was the area to be included in a German national state, and the decision was revolutionary, for it was against the inclusion of Austria, which had been part of Germany for 800 years. Germans and Italians both failed in 1848-9, but the very fact of failure made them the more determined to succeed by other methods. So the actual work of unification by Cavour and Bismarck, heroic as it was, was only the logical conclusion of the work begun in 1797 and 1803. And it may be observed that our Civil War, though it involved no territorial changes, nevertheless symbolized the victory of the American national idea over the doctrine of particularism and separatism; it was, in a very real sense, the counterpart of what was happening in Europe during the same decade.

During the same period, a similar process was at work in the Balkan peninsula. As far back as 1780, Joseph II and Catherine II had elaborated their "Greek project" for the destruction of the Ottoman Empire; their aims were essentially dynastic, and they met with scant success. But the signal had been given, and the influence of the French Revolution commenced to tell.

From the beginning of the Serbian revolt in 1804 to the Treaty of Berlin in 1878, the trend is ever the same. One people after another secures emancipation from the Turkish yoke, and by the latter date four independent states and one practically independent principality have been established. The map of Europe took the form it was to retain till the eve of the Great War; in comparison with the changes effected, in the name and interest of the idea of nationality, the innumerable shufflings of territory that went on before 1789 seem of small consequence. For this reason it seems proper to speak of these great events as constituting a territorial revolution.

In this connection a word must be said about the new conception of international relations. In the eighteenth century the only principles had been the self-interest of monarchs and the balance of power. The first of them had induced many rulers to compromise with Napoleon, who was able thereby to dispense with the second. So in 1815 an attempt was made to organize Europe for peace. The experiment of the Holy Alliance — to use the conventional, if inaccurate term — was successful for only a short time, but the idea of a Concert of Europe remained. In a Ph.D. examination I once asked the candidate what he understood by the phrase "Concert of Europe". After some hesitation, he replied, "Well, there is concert only when the powers don't play"; a shrewd observation, for obviously if one power sounds too strident a note, there is little chance for accommodation. This was proved in the two most important episodes of the century, the unification of Italy and Germany, when Cavour and Bismarck went their ways regardless of the rest of Europe, which, for that matter, showed little disposition to intervene. The Concert also failed to prevent both the Crimean war and the Russo-Turkish war of 1877; but it did succeed in asserting the principle that the settlement of Near Eastern questions, no matter how they might arise, was the concern of all the Great Powers. In view of the events of 1908-1914, it is well to recall that the independence of Greece in 1830, the settlement of the Egyptian question in 1840, the convention of the Straits of 1841, and the recognition of Romania were determined upon by the Concert, and that after the Crimean War Austria and Prussia were invited to the Congress of Paris, although they had not been belligerent. In 1878, most important of all, Russia recognized that it must submit its treaty with Turkey to the judgment of the Powers. The principle of the Concert was apparently well established, if not in the public law, at least in the public practice of Europe.

Finally there was an intellectual revolution. In the first place the authority of religion was steadily undermined. Protestants and Catholics differed on most points, but on one thing they were agreed: the infallibility of the Bible. Nor, in 1789, were there many persons who did not believe in a personal God or regard religion as essential to a well-ordered and proper life. Seventy-five years later, the picture is radically altered. Sir Charles Lyell's new geology (1830-33) has played havoc with Archbishop Ussher's calendar, and the co-called "higher criticism" has denied the literal accuracy and even the divine inspiration of Holy Scripture; Alexander von Humboldt has drawn his picture of the Cosmos as a natural phenomenon, and Charles Darwin has proclaimed the theory of evolution. To such teachings the Roman Church replies with doctrines which from some points of view are equally revolutionary—I mean the pronouncements of Pius IX on the Immaculate Conception and Papal Infallibility. By 1870 the conflict between science and religious dogma is in full swing, just as in that very year the Pope could be deprived of his temporal power without any serious protest being made even from Catholic countries. Practically speaking, religion had lost considerable ground. The masses in the towns, seeing in their Sundays the only day of relief from their factory work, were becoming more indifferent, while the intellectual classes discovered in nationalism a more than adequate substitute for religious devotions.

The second great change intellectually had to do with social and economic problems. From time immemorial it had been assumed that poverty was inevitable, and only rarely had an agitator dared to question the sanctity of private property. But the revolution in France confiscated the estates of the nobles and clergy, and in 1797 Baboeuf was ventilating the first of modern socialistic schemes. Both Fourier and Saint-Simon, it may be noted, were writing before the new industrial methods had made much headway in France. Real socialism was of course somewhat later in manifesting itself, but by 1870 the Marxian program was fully developed, and a socialist party had been formed in Germany, which meant that millions were demanding that private property be no longer respected if it was a barrier to social reform.

Thirdly, a new conception of human society gradually developed in the first half of the nineteenth century. Hitherto regarded as static and subject to immutable laws, it now came to be looked upon as dynamic, a point of view that was perhaps borrowed from the treatment of matter at the hands of the chemists. Mankind was no longer to be left helpless in face of the prejudices of the past and the problems of the present. For this iron law of inevitability there was substituted the doctrine of human perfectibility. Just as the individual, condemned before the French Revolution, with rare exceptions, to the status to which he had been born, was now according to the principles of 1789, free to rise as high as chance and talent might carry him, so there was no limit to the possibilities of social development. Scientific research might even discover the formula for controlling it. At any rate, the philosophical radicals in England, the followers of Comte in France, and the socialists in Germany, elaborated their several laws of progress. Common to all of them was the horror felt for human suffering, a feeling which was displayed in the late eighteenth century and which sank deep in the popular mind as the evils of the new industrialism were gradually revealed. The humanitarian legislation of Victorian England and the genuine sympathy of Napoleon III for the working classes of France show that this new philosophy left its impress upon practical politicians. In short, it was now accepted by thinking people that progress was not only a theory but a fact. Finally, under this heading should perhaps be mentioned the new notion that the education of the masses was both desirable and possible. It was natural that revolutionary France should proclaim this precept: it was more significant that it should be first practically applied by conservative, absolutist Prussia. But not until "the German schoolmaster had won the battle of Sadowa" (according to the contemporary saying) and Robert Lowe had said, as an opponent of the Reform Act of 1867, "We must educate our masters", did England take the lesson to heart and manage to put through the Education Act of 1870, more than seventy-five years after Condorcet had persuaded the Convention to approve his generous plans.

By 1871, to take a familiar date, the century of revolution had had been supplanted by constitutional, and in some countries had been supplanted by constitutional, and in some countries democratic, government. Distinctions at law between classes had disappeared, and personal rights and liberties were tolerably secure. The new industrial system had been generally adopted. The problem of capital and labor had become familiar, and various proposals were being advanced for its solution. In international politics, the principle of nationality had been recognized as a proper basis of state organization. In religion churches had been brought under civil control. In short, the foundations of contemporary civilization had been firmly laid.

From 1871 to 1914 there were few new developments. Protective tariffs, which became the rage, were certainly not new, for they had flourished in the days of mercantilism. The movement toward separation of church and state, evident in a few countries, was new to Europe, though long since accomplished in the United States. The one original contribution was the idea that the State, without becoming socialistic, should nevertheless undertake to deal with the problem of poverty by intervening between capital and labor and by setting up schemes of social insurance. This, it may be noted, was the reply of capitalism to that socialism which was appealing more and more to European workers.

In general, the period is one of synthesis: the various forces cast up in the first half of the century are, so to speak, thrown into a crucible and fused together. The new political machinery, once an end in itself, is used for the solution, or attempted solution, of economic and social and religious problems. Conservatives and radicals dispute the control of parliaments for very practical reasons. Socialists attack religion and the churches as bulwarks of the existing economic order. The problem of education is seen to involve all the issues: fitting men and women to discharge their political duties as citizens, preparing them to make their living, instilling into them religious precepts, indoctrinating them with patriotic traditions and nationalist sentiments. Politics, economics, social problems, and religion become more and more interrelated, and it is no longer possible to separate them in water-tight compartments as was possible to a considerable extent in the early part of the nineteenth century.

The details of the picture vary from country to country, for the new ideas and forces are combined in different proportions. Great Britain is seen as a highly industrialized, democratic state; France is perhaps even more democratic, but agriculture remains the basis of its economy; Germany becomes almost as industrialized as Great Britain, but resists the democratic pressure; Austria-Hungary continues to be both conservative and agricultural; Italy resembles France, and the United States took its cue from England. I omit Russia, for my formula clearly does not apply to that vast country, which though lying in Europe was not of Europe and went its own way, resisting as far as possible the penetration of European ideas and contributing little or nothing to the solution of Europe's problems. The revolution of 1905, an attempt to introduce Western ideas into government and politics, was not understood or really appreciated by the masses, and was, on the whole, a failure.

Western and Central Europe, in spite of differences of race and political forms, constituted a fairly homogenous entity; in the New World a similar conception found expression in the gospel of Pan-Americanism.

Thus, outwardly at any rate, the process of synthesis had been highly successful. There was no war between the great European powers; a longer period of peace was enjoyed than at any time, says the German historian Stern, since the days of Hadrian and Antoninus Pius. Even the Russian upheaval of 1905 did not seriously disturb the general calm. For these reasons the era was one of unparalleled material prosperity, in which the working classes shared to some extent. Social reform was in the air, and freedom of speech and liberty of conscience were not seriously contested. At long last, Europe seemed to have secured stability, so much so that towards the end of the last century it could not find within its own confines a sufficient outlet for its energies and turned to the task of spreading its civilization throughout the world.

Actually this apparent stability was that of the calm before the storm. It was, in fact, being undermined by two forces which were the logical, though one hesitates to say inevitable, consequences of the process of revolution already referred to,—nationalism which was born of the political revolution in France, and imperialism which was the child of the economic revolution in England.

The French Revolution laid down the doctrine that people should govern themselves. But what should be the unit of organization? The same revolution gave the answer—the nation. I shall not attempt to define the criteria of a nation beyond saying that a nation exists when a group of people with common traditions and aspirations consider themselves to form a nation. My point is simply that the demand for self-government and the desire for national unity and independence developed simultaneously; the achievement of the latter was only the natural application of the former. Hence the idea of nationality, in the first three quarters of the last century, appeared to be constructive and helpful, and united Italy, the new German Empire, and the emancipated Balkan states were welcomed as stabilizing and proper entities. But as time went on, nationalism became a disturbing factor. However political in its origin, it acquired more and more an economic tinge. In an age of protective tariffs and intense commercial competition, it was quite natural for governments and peoples to seek security for their own interests, regardless of others, but this state of mind did not promote the comity of nations. Each became a law unto itself, and the Concert of Europe grew more and more fragile; if the eighteenth century was dominated by dynastic interests, the twentieth thought only in terms of national interests, about which it was deemed traitorous to compromise.

Another danger lay in the fact that the principle of nationality was not thoroughly applied. Many irredentist areas were created or left by the wars of 1859-1878, and the Habsburg Monarchy remained a bundle of unrecognized peoples. It was perfectly natural that the ever-increasing force of the democratic dogma should stir and make restless those races or groups of races whose aspirations had not been satisfied, and when their reasonable demands were refused, in the interest of the nationalism of the ruling races, the only recourse was conspiracy, terrorism, and revolution. Alsace-Lorraine and Trentino, Bohemia and Poland, Bosnia and Macedonia were so many elements of poison seeping through the body politic of Europe. And the great military monarchies to which these disputed and discontented provinces belonged could think of no other cure for the disease than to try to maintain their titles by force. Hence, in the first place, the heaping-up of land armaments, and secondly, the conclusion of alliances and counter-alliances. For a generation, this system seemed to provide guarantees of peace; in fact, it made concessions and changes difficult or impossible, yet the longer they were postponed, the more likely were the chances of an explosion.

Contemporary imperialism developed because the industrial nations of western Europe could not find at home food for their people, raw materials for their industry, employment for their workers, markets for their goods and capital. The impulse to seek for these things beyond the shores of Europe was very strong. No doubt a good deal of the impulse came from individuals who were over-greedy for the profits to be made by exploiting undeveloped lands and backward peoples. But the commodities of imperialistic enterprise were more and more in demand, and apart from its excesses, the movement was an ineluctable economic necessity. And just as political nationalism put on an economic dress, so economic imperialism became the football of politics. It is not altogether clear whether the imperialistic rivalries had much direct bearing on the outbreak of war in July 1914, for the sundry disputes about colonies and concessions which had been plaguing Europe for some years had been adjusted by diplomacy; the African and Bagdad slates were clean. But these rivalries had bred naval armaments, and it was fear of the German navy that took England into the war, just as it was partly unwillingness to resume colonial wrangling that made it refuse to sacrifice the ententes with France and Russia as the price of an agreement with Germany. Furthermore, the attitude of Russia toward Serbia and of Germany towards Austria was inspired in part by their conflicting plans for the future of Turkey. Whatever the exact truth about 1914, imperialism contributed powerfully to making the international atmosphere full of hatred and suspicion and fear, so that when the final crash came, no government entirely trusted another and some distrusted each other so deeply that compromise was out of the question.

Personally I am inclined to think that nationalism and imperialism, more particularly the former because of its excesses, did make a general European war almost inevitable, in spite of the fact that most statesmen wished to avoid it. Be that as it may, it is futile for the historian to bemoan their existence or to berate their protagonists. Both are phenomena which developed normally out of the circumstances of the age and whose historical provenience is quite respectable.

If the Great War was, in the last analysis, produced by revolutionary forces which had escaped control, its consequences were equally revolutionary. What began as a Balkan conflict developed into a world-wide struggle: the United States, certain states of Latin America, India, China and Japan were drawn in. Four ancient monarchies were overwhelmed; in one of them a new social order was established, and in the other parliamentary governments were set up. In the making of the peace, the map of Europe was redrawn with a thoroughness not equalled since the barbarians destroyed the Roman Empire. Finally a League of Nations embracing all continents was brought into being. This League was the particular contribution of the United States for the solution of the European anarchy; we remained, shall it be said by an accident, outside our own creation, but we discovered ourselves as the richest nation of the globe. The Romanian statesman Take Jonescu, claims to have foreseen much of this in August 1914; but for the rulers whose action precipitated the war, these results were utterly unexpected. To those of us who have witnessed them, the spectacle is overwhelming. Likewise, the effort of Asiatic and other non-European peoples to modernize their institutions and to become masters in their own houses fills certain circles with dismay.

Yet these cataclysmic events are in large measure only the logical result and working out of the ideas whose origin and development I have been tracing. The substitution of democratic for autocratic government in eastern Europe had been desired and striven for by its peoples for three quarters of a century. The reconstruction of the map of Europe on the principle of recognizing each and every nationality, which is so bitterly denounced under the name of "Balkanization", is nothing if not the corollary of self-government. Both derive from the principle of 1789. So also does that trend to the Left which has been so evident in Europe in spite of the fact that at the moment liberalism is at a discount in more than one country; even the most despotic governments feel the necessity of legislating in the interests of the masses, and the men who govern are more than ever men of the people, after the fashion of 1793.

The most vivid illustration of this tendency is to be seen, of course, in what was and still is in popular parlance, Russia. The temptation is great to discourse on the Soviet regime, for it connotes an upheaval more stupendous than even the French Revolution; it has, in fact, achieved revolution literally, by elevating the lowly and depressing the mighty. A few observations must suffice. The Communist philosophy is that of Karl Marx, but it has been applied in conditions never imagined by its founder, for Russia had not passed through the industrialization of western Europe. For that reason, Bolshevist rule has been experimental, and has been compelled in recent years to depart more and more from the canons of socialist orthodoxy. And precisely because the whole system is still on trial, one may be spared from passing judgment. It is well to remember that the social formulae of the French Revolution, which now command general acceptance, were as bitterly denounced a century ago as Bolshevism is today. A century hence, Moscow may serve as the model of all progressive societies.

Even the participation of non-European nations in the affairs of Europe, which I suggest is the real significance of the League of Nations, is not surprising. In the generation before the Great War, the world, without very fully realizing what was happening, became more and more an economic unity. That was in part a result of the much-decried imperialism, and that circumstance is becoming more and more the governing factor in the life of the world. What more natural, then, that the world should seek political union as well? Just as nineteenth-century nationalism was enormously stimulated by economic advantage and necessity, so world unity grows as the nations find that they cannot live alone. It is the fashion nowadays to decry the excesses of nationalism, but we owe it to that very nationalism that we perceive the possibility and the desirability of a world society, and we ought also to remember that the League of Nations owes not a little to the Concert of Europe, inadequate as was that organ of international action. If my contention is sound that twentieth-century Europe, as moulded by the forces of the nineteenth, though afflicted by growing pains and sundry sicknesses, is sound in body, we should not despair if the peoples outside of Europe exhibit an enthusiasm for the paraphernalia of western civilization for which they may not be altogether prepared. Rather it is only when all nations have adopted the great principles of the French Revolution and acquired the technique of modern business that the world order can be firmly secured. It is our privilege to live in an age of revolution which began a century and a half ago and which has moved inexorably from one triumph to another; you who are about to venture from these academic walls may reasonably expect to live and play your parts in a still better world.

Germany in the Reign of William II

A lecture given at Western Reserve University in January 1914. It created a local sensation, not only in the German press of Cleveland but also among my colleagues in the faculty, some of whom had studied in Germany and though of it in quite different terms. Six months later, when the war broke out, the lecture was remembered, and I was hailed as a prophet. Many of the judgments given were indeed confirmed by later events.

*   *   *

The new German Empire is the most perplexing quantity in the modern world, and as unavoidable as it is perplexing". This statement of an English observer, whose candor reflects his distrust, will perhaps not command general acceptance. The average American, at any rate, has a well-defined conception of Imperial Germany. He thinks of a country grown rich and powerful almost as rapidly as our own; of a state where universal military service and a rigid educational system generate discipline and efficiency; of cities clean, uncannily well-governed, and progressive; of a people whose pleasures are indissolubly connected with beer and tobacco and whose personal appearance is expansive and heavy. These elements are held in solution, he will add, by an autocracy thinly covered with parliamentary whitewash, an officious bureaucracy regulating every detail of the national life, and a wide-spread cultivation of the military spirit. The deluge of books dealing with the Kaiser, his capital, his people and his works testifies to great popular interest, as do the thousands of magazine articles and the despatches which figure in even the newspapers of Cleveland. It is safe to say that the best-known picture in the world today is that of Kaiser Wilhelm and his heaven-trained mustaches, and that few persons are so hated or more admired. It is not my purpose to present a bird's eye view of Imperial Germany, but rather to examine from an historical point of view some of the main tendencies of the last twenty-five years, or the reign of William II.

95

His Majesty became King of Prussia and German Emperor on June 15, 1888, under circumstances tragic and painful. Just one hundred days previously, the old Emperor, William I, *der greise Kaiser,* who had seen service against Napoleon, died in his ninety-first year, loved, honored and respected. His son and successor, Frederick III, was mortally ill, and harassed by the brutal attitude of the Iron Chancellor, Prince Otto von Bismarck, and Prince William, the heir to his crown, both of whom detested his liberal aspirations. The untimely death of this noble and unassuming gentleman, *der weise Kaiser* as he was often called, brought to the throne a young man of twenty-nine who disappointed his subjects by a considered neglect of his father's memory and by a bombastic proclamation to his army. He was known as an ardent German and a man of resolute will, but a succession of costly state visits and holiday jaunts to Norwegian waters were regarded with popular disapproval, and William II began his reign amid indifference in Germany and disgust in Europe. Twenty-five years have wrought a profound change. *Der reise Kaiser,* or the travelling Emperor, has proved to a doubting world that he is a man of considerable ability and a factor to be reckoned with on all occasions. He has come to be recognized as the embodiment of a new German spirit, as a man who has identified himself so completely with his subjects that in the minds of most men William II and Germany are synonomous terms. Even to Americans this astonishing monarch is interesting. But admitting that the Kaiser has scored a great personal triumph, it is, I believe, possible to demonstrate that the position of Germany is relatively less secure and its condition less sound than at the beginning of his reign.

By 1888 the new Empire, then seventeen years old, had completed the formative period of its development. The problems arising out of a united Germany had been disposed of, the foundations of a great national life had been deeply laid. An efficient government, a superb army, and an economic advance which had already raised Germany to the second rank among commercial states—all these insured the permanence of the new order and glorified the genius of Bismarck, whose handiwork they chiefly were. Any defects in the body politic were held to be remediable through the agency of universal suffrage, and social discontent was to be cured by means of a thorough-going system of state insurance. Above all, the foreign policy of the Empire had been conducted with marvellous success.

Not only did Germany not fear a foreign attack, but it bestrode the European situation like a colossus; the isolation of France was complete, and Bismarck could view with amusement the intrigues of General Boulanger to bring on a war of revenge.

The future historian may not improbably decide that the Bismarckian system required a Bismarck to direct it, and signs were not wanting that a "new course", to quote the Emperor William himself, was being plotted. Though William II had in his earlier days regarded Bismarck with boundless enthusiasm and at the beginning of the reign had assured the Chancellor that his services would be retained, in reality the two men had little in common except a dislike of Frederick III and his liberal ideas. Bismarck was now an old man in tolerably feeble health, who displayed no appreciation of the new forces agitating an industrial society. To social progress he presented an attitude of resolute opposition: the insurance schemes were designed simply to euchre the Socialists, and at heart he was an individualist. Moreover twenty-eight years of well-nigh autocratic power had convinced him that Bismarck and Germany were identical. That an inexperienced stripling should desire to evolve a personal policy was unintelligible to the old giant. Less wise than Moltke, who resigned six weeks after the new dispensation began, the Iron Chancellor clung passionately to office, though on every side there were signs that the Kaiser was asserting himself. For the latter the situation was not unlike that of Louis XIV on the death of Mazarin. The officials and courtiers had asked, "Who will now show us the way?" and they received the reply, "I". As in 1661, so in 1888. It was a question whether the Bismarck or the Hohenzollern dynasty should rule, for the chancellor had laid plans for his son to succeed him.

The crisis began in January 1890, and on March 20 the founder of modern Germany resigned as imperial chancellor and president of the Prussian council of ministers. The clash was precipitated by the reluctance of the Emperor to renew the anti-socialist law even in a milder form, for the latter proposed to solve the social problem by means of an international labor conference. This Bismarck called "great phraseology," and spurned to the extent of refusing his signature to the imperial rescript. The unpleasant fact that the Socialists promptly polled more than a million votes added fuel to the fire. In the domain of high policy, the Emperor was unwilling to renew the secret treaty with Russia, on the ground that such conduct was disloyal to his ally, the Emperor Francis Joseph, whom Bismarck was apparently quite willing to desert. Yet personal power rather than public policy was the deciding factor. The Emperor insisted on entering into direct relations with his ministers, a practice unknown in the days of William I and legally contrary to a cabinet order of 1852, which prescribed the minister president as the medium of communication between king and ministers. Several interviews followed; both monarch and minister would seem to have lost their temper, and finally William demanded the chancellor's resignation. As a sop the old man was offered the dignity of Duke of Lauenburg, which would have made him one of the sovereign princes of the Empire, but which was declined because he desired only the name and title he had always borne.

So fell the remarkable statesman, who in his own words had "cut a certain figure in the history of Germany and of Prussia". Even his iron will could not withstand the fervor of youth, and his passing was unregretted save in the narrow circle of his intimate friends. The exact measure of responsibility to be borne by each of the principals and their subordinates cannot be determined at this time because the readjustment in German policy caused by the crash has not yet been completely worked out, and because men still dispute as to the merits of the "new course". Indeed, it has recently been alleged by a famous German historian that Bismarck's real offence was a plot to destroy universal suffrage as a means of crushing the Socialists, to which the Emperor refused his assent, and that the other disputes were unimportant. Without dissecting this statement, I would point out that the Emperor was hardly justified in saying, as he did in his letter to the prince that "the reasons advanced for your decision convince me that further efforts to induce you to withdraw your proposal would be fruitless": it was the Emperor, not Bismarck, who demanded a change. In the second place, William II, while never persecuting the Socialists in Bismarckian fashion, had constantly declared that they are not worthy to bear the name of Germans, and like King James and the Puritans, had threatened to harry them out of the land. Incidentally, the Socialists increase *pari passu* with the imperial denunciations. And finally, the abandonment of the Bismarckian foreign policy, though its methods have been retained, has seriously compromised the international position of Germany and has entailed a burden of armaments, which, whatever the effect upon the people, has thrown the finances of the state into considerable confusion. The retirement of Bismarck was probably inevitable, but his premature dismissal by an inexperienced master has reacted with disastrous consequences upon Emperor and nation alike. The four chancellors who have succeeded Bismarck, General von Caprivi, Prince Hohenlohe, Prince Bülow, and Dr. von Bethmann Hollweg, need merely to be named, for they have one and all been the servants rather than the advisers of the Emperor.

The monarch who in 1890 began to rule as well as to reign is the most enigmatic individual of our time. Restless in his physical make-up, singularly endowed by nature in mind and imagination, possessed of a tenacious memory, and imbued with boundless self-confidence, William II combines an ardent belief in medieval political doctrines with an enthusiastic devotion to every phase of modern life. There would seem to be no branch of human knowledge or activity in which His Majesty does not participate and indulge his ordinate love of speechifying. In addition to the ordinary vocations of an emperor and king, he has shown an intense interest in the development of German commerce, preached stirring sermons on land and sea, criticised severely the national education system, and attempted to dictate styles of architecture. He has designed boats for the Kiel yachting week which he himself created, directed productions in the royal opera house, conducted an orchestra, composed music, painted pictures, and discussed archaeology with learned professors. To illustrate, there is the Siegesalle in Berlin, with its rows of marble horrors, and publicists still occasionally refer to his cartoon depicting the yellow peril. The latest exploit is a rescript forbidding officers to lean on the arms of ladies in public places! Even after twenty-five years the world is alternately amused and alarmed by the vagaries of the royal arbiter. Outside of Germany he is generally considered a harmless dilettante, but thousands of his subjects regard him as a genius who unites in his own person the myriad talents of the nation. At least no one will deny the interest and appeal of this many-sided activity, which is probably explained by a feverish desire to lead the German people to yet higher things and to impress them, if that be necessary, with a sense of their greatness. Let us add that the Emperor William has a deep-seated feeling of responsibility, that by precept and example he preaches moderation in eating and sparingness in drink, and that his personal charm is universally admitted.

On the other hand William II is the greatest living champion of reaction and militarism. His first official act as king was to issue a proclamation to his army, which he regards as the chief prop to his throne, and on every occasion he has caressed and flattered the military spirit. In harmony with this tendency is his positive encouragement of duelling. His political philosophy is summed up in an unswerving allegiance to the divine right of kings, as evidenced by innumerable speeches. Two examples will suffice. In 1890 he declared that "it is a tradition in our house to consider ourselves as designed by God to govern the peoples over whom it is given us to reign". In August 1910, he exploded with these words:

> "My grandfather by his own right hand placed on his head the royal crown of Prussia, once more declaring with emphasis that it was bestowed upon him by God's grace alone, and not by Parliaments, national assemblies or the popular voice; so that he regarded himself as the chosen instrument of Heaven, and as such performed his duties as ruler. . . . . Looking upon myself as the instrument of the Lord, regardless of the views and opinions of the hour, I shall go my way, which is devoted solely to the well-being and peaceful development of the Fatherland".

On a par with this antiquated belief, which reveals the earlier Hohenzollerns in a sorry light and which even Thomas Hobbes, the great apologist of monarchy, did not care to defend, is his intolerance of opposition. His most famous utterance is perhaps this: "There is but one master in this country; it is I, and I will bear no other." He has proclaimed that "an opposition of the Prussian nobility to their king is a monstrosity", and transformed an old Latin expression into *Voluntas regis suprema lex*. William II has relentlessly disposed of every official who refused to bow the knee — Bismarck is merely the most illustrious example — and has persecuted so far as the law allows all who dare to criticize him or offer unwelcome advice. Convictions for *lese-majesté* have become so common that the press has ceased to notice them; it is said that most German newspapers maintain "sitting" editors whose pleasant duty it is to serve out the sentences imposed for obnoxious references to exalted personages.

Much might also be made of the Emperor's singular ability, as a Protestant monarch, to rule his empire with the help of a Catholic priesthood, and to cultivate an advantageous friendship with the Caliph of Islam. That he is too fond of publicity and is for all the world like a junker cavalry officer; that he talks too much and interferes in every branch of the government—these are natural criticisms which will only be recorded. But when all is said, there remains the fact that William II is the greatest of the Hohenzollerns, with the possible exception of the great Frederick, and that by his unflagging energy and ardent patriotism he has conquered the affections of his countrymen and is entitled to the respectful consideration of other people. I confess to little love for the Kaiser or his people, but in this day of flabbiness and mediocrity, it is refreshing to find some one who knows what he wants and strives with all his might and power to get it.

It is the economic advance of Germany in the last twenty-five years which has made it the cynosure of all eyes and the wonder of the world. In 1888 the population of Germany was 49,000,000; at the present time it is not less than 66,000,000, an increase of nearly 35 percent. Most of these new Germans have been absorbed by manufacturing and commerce: thus in the earlier year 43 percent of the population still lived by agriculture, while today only 32 percent are so occupied. In 1890 there were 26 towns of more than 100,000 inhabitants, today there are 48, where live nineteen millions of the people. In the early eighties more than two hundred thousand Germans left the Fatherland annually for the United States, Australia, and Brazil. In the early 'teens not only has emigration practically ceased, but seven hundred thousand Poles and Russians are imported every year to harvest the crops consumed by the town-dwelling Germans. The national wealth is estimated at some $16,000,000,000, a truly astonishing accumulation for only a generation of industrial life, for it is approximately equal to that of England, where the industrial revolution occurred seventy-five years earlier. The foreign investments of Germans run into the hundreds of millions. The imports for 1887 were $781,175,000; for 1912, $2,530,140,000; the exports stand at $778,825,000 and $2,175,111,000. The shipping which is intimately connected with this expansion tells the same story. The 664 steamers of 420,605 tons in 1886 have increased to 2098 with 4,380,343 tons. The Hamburg-Amerika Line is the largest steamship company in the world, its Brobdingnagian "Imperator" the largest steamer for the moment, and its liners, together with those of the Norddeutscher

Lloyd, are considered by many travellers the most comfortable and luxurious afloat. The production of pig iron, which stood at 3,600,000 tons in 1885, had reached 10,000,000 in 1912, so that Germany stands second only to the United States in the iron and steel trades. The consumption of coal has increased fourfold. The chemical industries of Germany enjoy almost a monopoly of the world market, and their output is not less than $300,000,000 annually; they supply about ten percent of the total exports of the Empire. Even agriculture, which has had to meet the competition of the virgin soils of America, Canada, and Argentina, has flourished, thanks to a high tariff and other governmental measures. In short, there is not a single phase of German economic life which has not shown a development without parallel. It is all the more creditable because Germany has had great odds to contend against — the long-established industries in England, its inferior communications with the outside world, and an unfavorable location of its coal and iron supplies. That Germany has become the second industrial and commercial state and has threatened to demolish the century-old supremacy of England is notorious: some have explained the miracle by the adoption of a high tariff, and unquestionably the Bismarckian protection did enable innumerable industries to get on their feet. But their later triumphs are due rather to the lack of encumbering traditions, to a relentless scientific method and attention to detail, and above all to a discipline and energy which her rivals have been somewhat slow to imitate.

It is now time to ask whether Germany has secured a corner on prosperity and whether the great progress of the present reign has created a sound economic framework. In the first place, other nations besides Germany have expanded their industrial and commercial girth, if indeed in lesser degree. The imports of the United Kingdom increased from $1,749,317,360 in 1888 to $4,071,818,495 in 1902; exports rose from $1,343,335,085 to $3,220,716,975. Our own country has also done considerable foreign business. The distinction of Germany has been the rate of increase, and here is the point: that rate is rapidly falling. The Germans had to catch up with the start of seventy-five years obtained by England and of half a century by France and ourselves. Now that they have done so, the race will be much more even. British trade ceased to expand about 1890, while Germany's began, with one exception, the most remarkable period of its development, which continued until after 1903. By 1900 England was feeling the effects of the Boer war. 1907 was a banner year the world over, but ended in panic, from which a complete recovery was not effected until 1911. Let us study the following figures, which refer to millions of dollars.

Year	UNITED KINGDOM				GERMANY			
	Imports	Percent. increase	Exports	Percent. increase	Imports	Percent. increase	Exports	Percent. increase
1890	2100		1315		1120		790	
1899	2425	15	1320	0	1360	21.5	1000	27
1903	2710	12	1450	10	1580	16	1250	25
1907	3225	19	2130	47	2250	42	1770	41
1911	3400	6	2270	6	2385	6	2025	11.5
1912	3820	10	2435	7.5	2530	6	2185	7.9
1890-1903		30		10.2		36.6		58.5
1903-1912		37.5		68		60		74.6

From this table it is quite clear that the advance of Germany in recent years, while still more rapid than that of England, is relatively much slower than in the period before 1903. But other considerations enter in. From 1890 to 1910 the population of Germany increased some 26 percent, that of the United Kingdom only 18 percent. Notice the following table showing the exports per head of the population.

	United Kingdom	Germany
Average 1900-1904	$31.81	$19.78
1907-1910	44.32	25.81
1912	52.01	31.66
Increase	20.20	11.87

The advantage is apparently on the side of the English worker. Then there is the question of the rise of prices, by which free trade England has been less affected than any other country. But the figures for foreign trade are calculated according to the prices of their respective countries, and since prices have risen more in Germany, it follows that a mere comparison of figures does not furnish an accurate test of the commercial advance of the two countries. Not that England has effectively nullified the competition of Germany, but as a result of this very competition, slow-moving and conservative John Bull has at last bestirred himself and is holding his own. Leaving figures aside, this much is abundantly clear. In the early years of this century England was suffering from lassitude and the number of unemployed was increasing so rapidly that protection was felt by many to be its only salvation; Germany, on the other hand, seemed to be capturing the old markets of British trade the world over. Today the unemployed in Germany are numbered by the hundreds of thousands, whereas in England there is work for all who will work, the trade boom of the last few years shows no sign of abatement, and the foreign commerce of the United Kingdom increased in the year 1913 by the enormous sum of $302,500,000. In other words Germany must look to its laurels, and it is the opinion of some competent observers that a financial panic of the old-fashioned kind cannot long be delayed.

Should such a calamity come about, and in the interests of the United States let us hope that it does not, it will have been caused by an undue expansion of credit. In their desire to acquire wealth rapidly, Germans have resorted to the familiar methods of the boom. The profits of one venture are immediately invested in another, and the balance of the required capital is raised abroad, usually in France. The dangers of this abnormal expansion were clearly seen in the Morocco crisis of 1911. When it became apparent that the German government proposed to press its claims to an extreme point, the French bankers called in their short-time loans to German industrials and a panic was threatened which would not only have prevented war but have undone the splendid achievements of forty years. At the crucial moment a delegation of German business men waited upon the Kaiser and practically forced him to choose between war and national bankruptcy. From that moment the negotiations with France were conducted in a more amicable spirit. Furthermore German banks are not required to keep large reserves, and no less than 55 percent of the deposits of the savings banks are locked up in mortgages upon which it would be impossible to realise in a time of crisis. Within the last year two governmental loans, one Prussian, the other Imperial, amounting together to several hundred millions of dollars, have been ignored by the investing public. In England these would have been taken up immediately by the savings banks, but in Germany the ready money was not to be had, or else German patriotism has suddenly displayed an astonishing independence of government.

The next point to which I wish to advert is the relation of economic progress to the welfare of the people. No one will question that the nation as a whole has prospered enormously. The growth of the population, the increased consumption of commodities of all sorts, and the accumulation of nearly five billions of dollars in the savings banks attest the fact, were it not evident in the transformed face of the country, the improvement in dress and housing conditions, and the gratification of the desire for travel, in which the Germans are surpassed only by the English. The average American, returning from a summer's tour in England and Germany, will probably assure the reporter that he was appalled by the poverty of Whitechapel and amazed by the solid comfort of the German workingmen. In some respects the comparison is true enough. But there is, I think, a widespread impression that modern Germany has succeeded in avoiding the evils of modern industrialism and large-scale enterprise without foregoing its advantages. Do not most of us believe that the German tariff is scientific and impartial, that the cartels and syndicates, as German trusts are called, are kept in order by an all-powerful government, and that the majestic fabric of social insurance erected by Prince Bismarck is a panacea for all the ills to which the flesh of workingmen is heir? It is this presumption which I wish to challenge.

As for the tariff, it may as well be admitted at once that it is as impartial and scientific as any tariff can be, with or without a tariff commission. It imposes duties which are not abnormally high on foodstuffs and manufactured articles, and leaves raw materials on the free lists. None the less the last five years have witnessed an extraordinary revolt against the protective system. Within a year of its formation the *Hansabund*, the purpose of which is to break down the present tariff, comprised 450 branches and its members are numbered by the million. The cost of living has increased nearly fifty percent in the last fifteen years, whereas in free trade England the advance has hardly averaged twenty percent. The cost of collecting the duties runs into hundreds of millions of dollars, and the State is said to receive only 25 percent of the increased cost, the rest going to the producers. A majority of the present Reichstag is committed to an immediate reduction of duties, and the Socialists, who represent one-third of the voters, wish to abolish them at once.

Then as to the trusts. Only a few of the German syndicates have reached the American stage of development, in which the ownership of a large number of establishments is merged in a single corporation, but the distinction is academic. As long ago as 1905, there were more than 400 trusts in the Empire, and in 1906 the Austrian consul in Berlin reported to his government that fifty men controlled absolutely the economic life of the nation. The German syndicates have probably gone farther than our trusts in the development of profit-sharing schemes, and the law against stock-watering is rigidly enforced. But it has been conclusively proved that the syndicates have raised prices unduly; that they have sold raw and half-manufactured materials abroad cheaper than at home, to the prejudice of both German producers and consumers; that under the aegis of protection they have deliberately kept production below national requirements in the interests of higher prices; and that they have reduced dealers and middlemen to a state of complete subjection. Ever since the cartels began to be formed, public opinion has been suspicious of them and the Reichstag would pass with alacrity a law subjecting them to state control. But the German government, unlike our own, does all in its power to encourage the trusts. It gives them preferential rates on its railways, it regards combination as an economic advantage and necessity, and it consistently declines to interfere in any respect, in spite of the fact that the Prussian state coal mines and potash deposits have been seriously injured by the respective trusts.

With the details of the social insurance schemes it is not necessary to deal. Under the laws passed by Prince Bismarck, 25,000,000 workmen are insured against accident, 16,000,000 against old age and invalidity, and 14,000,000 against sickness. In the last two the state stands part of the expense, but otherwise it is divided between the employers and the workmen. The total cost since the beginning has been $1,800,000,000, and the annual payments now amount to $190,000,000. The burden upon employers is now some $36,000,000 annually. In 1908 the Krupps paid out 13.6 percent of their net profits for this purpose, and some employers as much as 22 and 47 percent.

What is there to show for this terrific expenditure? Assuredly life has been prolonged and health protected, though the death rate is 17.2 per thousand as opposed to 14.6 in unregenerate England. Also factory conditions have been improved and medical science has been considerably advanced. But state insurance has failed lamentably in three respects. It has not brought social peace as Bismarck predicted. Social democracy has increased *pari passu* with the extension of insurance. In 1910 there were 2109 strikes and 1121 lockouts affecting 687,000 persons. Poverty has not been eliminated. There are still five thousand tramps in Germany, and in 1912 over one million persons were accommodated in the night shelters of Berlin alone. Lastly, social insurance has not brought about a better condition of health among the German masses. The percentage of conscripts fit for military service declined nearly ten percent between 1902 and 1910. In the last thirty years the population has increased forty percent, but the number of those who suffer from heart disease and rheumatism by 600 percent. Finally, in addition to the immense army of state officials required to administer the insurance schemes, the national character has deteriorated sadly. In 1907 the number of new pensioners was 380,819, but the days of sickness paid for by the authorities increased to the tune of 26,219,632. In other words, German workmen have discovered that it is highly profitable to be ill or to be disabled by accident. The late head of the Imperial Insurance Office, who retired after twenty years' service, has stated in a fifty-page pamphlet that social insurance as practiced in Germany is a hotbed of fraud and abuse and a positive breeder of pauperism. If the efficient Germans cannot devise a satisfactory system, the task must be hopeless, and social reformers would do well to think twice before they impose upon American workingmen a species of nostra which will make them the sport of a meddling government.[1]

The socialistic enterprises of German governments are very interesting, such as the taxation of unearned increment by municipalities; or the state railways, which are supposed to be very efficient and are certainly profitable, but which are often complained against by shippers and do not hesitate to grant differential rates. We must pass on to a very brief survey of German finances. At the beginning of the present reign the expenditures of the imperial government stood at $183,000,000, and the debt, all of which had been contracted since 1877, at $145,000,000. Today the figures are $800,000,000 for expenditure, $1,131,000,000 for the funded debt, an increase of nearly 6,000 and 1,000 percent respectively. Likewise the separate states and the municipalities have increased their expenditures and borrowings. The total debt of all the governments in Germany in 1910 amounted to $6,420,000,000, practically all accumulated since 1870, and actually larger than the total indebtedness of the United

---

[1] In 1960 I feel differently about Social Security!

Kingdom, which includes the cost of all the wars waged by the British Crown since 1694. It is quite true that the German governments have bonded themselves for state railways and various enterprises, many of which bring in handsome returns. But even if all such loans are written off, the remainder is sufficiently large for a young nation. Two facts cannot be ignored. First, for the past twenty years, there has been a constant excess of expenditure over revenue, and the deficit had been met by borrowing; and second, the last attempt to float loans has been unsuccessful. Not even the United States government could go on indefinitely under such a system. A country which is increasing in wealth as rapidly as Germany can bear considerable new taxation, but it is not agreed as to who shall be taxed. The Socialists and Radicals would like to tap the fortunes of the rich by increasing the income tax and by a progressive inheritance tax, but the Conservatives and Clericals, from whom the government takes its majority, are firmly opposed to such proceedings. Their plan is to increase the import duties. Meanwhile nothing has been done except to add new taxes upon liquors of all kinds, tobacco, matches, railway tickets, and other necessities of the masses. The situation was revealed a year ago when the government determined upon an increase of the army. The problem was to find $312,000,000 with which to equip the new troops and an annual revenue of $50,-000,000 to support them. It was proposed to raise the former by a tax of one-half of one to two percent on the capital value of all property above $2,500, and the latter by a poll tax of thirty-one cents per head. The Reichstag made some modifications, but the tax is downright confiscation, and there are 136,000 fewer men to help replace the loss. No wonder that the Bavarian premier has dared to raise his voice against further increases of armaments.

If it be added that increased taxation, the high cost of living, and the spread of luxury have led to a marked decrease of the birth rate, our survey of economic conditions is finished. Whether the imperial government will be able to ensure to the Kaiser an increasing supply of soldiers remains to be seen, but Germans are evidently worried by the problem, and we may leave them to wrestle with it.

The political situation is as unsatisfactory as the economic. Bismarck, says an English publicist, "found his country politically anarchic, but morally united; he left it with a semblance of political union and a plague of moral anarchy that has become increasingly apparent since the veil of his personality has been removed from the facts". With all allowance for the prejudice which inspired the remark, we are bound to admit the truth of this indictment. Fifty years ago men were willing to sacrifice everything to German unity: today, after forty years of the new Empire, sectionalism is rampant and ill-concealed by the gilded trappings of the imperial edifice. Germany, like ancient Gaul, is divided into three parts. East of the Elbe lie the Mark of Brandenburg and the provinces taken from Poland. Won by the sword and retained by the energies of German colonists, these lands are the heart of the Prussian monarchy. They are thinly populated, given over to agriculture, backward in development, and dominated by the landed nobility, who exercise rights handed down from the middle ages. These gentlemen were described by Bismarck himself, who was one of them and knew the breed, as "the most reactionary class in Europe". Devoted to king, army, and church, whether Lutheran or Catholic, they are the pillars of the autocracy, they almost detest the Empire lest Prussia should be absorbed in Germany, as promised by Frederick William IV in 1848, and they look with bitter contempt upon the ravages of modern industrialism. Along the Rhine are the provinces secured by Prussia after the Napoleonic wars. Here are located the great industries which are the glory of modern Germany. The teeming population is a whirlpool of social democracy, and the eternal enemy of junker privilege. Then there is South Germany, which is best described as non-Prussian, if not anti-Prussian. It joined the Empire reluctantly, and finds the Prussian spirit distasteful to its liberal and democratic ideas. Several years ago a friend of mine entered a café in Munich, where he found a seat with difficulty. A fire-eater at the table accused him of being an Englishman. Confessing his American origin, he remarked that his interlocutor must be a Prussian. The most uproarious applause greeted this sally, and my friend was the guest of the company for the evening.

This lack of any real unity among the people of Germany is at the bottom of the autocratic régime imposed upon them from above. The history of England teaches that self-government and national unity go hand in hand, but German statesmen, recalling the long centuries of disunion and weakness, are afraid to test the new-born unity by experiments in self-government. They have yet to learn that unity is most quickly achieved in this progressive age by an appeal to the orderly instincts of men, and that sectionalism is perpetuated precisely because the non-Prussian elements distrust the Prussianising policy of the imperial government. Hence it is that the Reichstag sits powerless in the palace guarded by the statue of Bismarck. Elected by universal suffrage and endowed with the right to pass laws and levy taxes, it is little more than a debating society. Five times has it learned that resistance and opposition to the Imperial will is countered by a dissolution, and that in the election of a new assembly the malcontents will be pilloried as traitors and bidden to leave a country they cannot appreciate. Germany is governed by the Bundesrat or Federal Council, which is an assembly of diplomats representing not the people, but the governments of the federated states. This body originates all legislation, directs policy, and is dominated by Prussia. Since the fall of Bismarck the imperial chancellor has been a mere tool of the Emperor, to whom alone he is responsible. Likewise the ministers are simply heads of departments and have no contact with the Reichstag except when they choose to address it. There is, in short, no way for the people of Germany to limit the action of their government except by open rebellion, which would be futile against an army of nearly a million men.

If further support for this mailed fist rule were needed, it would be found in the bureaucracy of two million officials, which regulates the life of the German people to the last detail, even to the point of inspecting bedticks and the prohibition of whistling in public. Its latest exploit is to prosecute a man for sneezing in the street. No meeting may be held without police supervision, the press is zealously censored where it is not inspired, and more things are forbidden by ubiquitous notices than are dreamed of in our philosophy. That the people exist for officials to govern is the maxim of this omnipotent and omniscient machine, the higher ranks of which are recruited almost exclusively from an aristocracy to whom decorations and titles are the staff of life. It cannot be denied that the German people as a whole accept this deadening tradition without a murmur. But what a commentary upon their education! The far-famed German schools turn out walking encyclopedias who are exceedingly proficient at obeying, but whose character-formation is left entirely to accidental influences. Not even in Russia are individuality and independence so dwarfed, and in no country in Europe do the people count for so little. It is significant that there is no national sport, and that the military classes receive reduced rates on the railways. Once in Constantinople I saw a group of dogs in front of the German post office: their alignment was perfect, and they were indifferent to exhortation. So it is with the German people.

I have examined the institutions of modern Germany with some care because they explain why the progress toward a solution of the four great political problems has been negligible in the reign of William II. First, there is the question of the four disaffected provinces, Posen, Schleswig-Holstein, Hanover, and Alsace-Lorraine. Posen was Prussia's share of the loot in the third partition of Poland. Since 1886 enormous efforts have been made to destroy Polish nationality by forbidding the use of the Polish language and by settling German colonists in the land. It has cost $120,000,000 to establish 110,000 people, and the natives are still bitterly anti-German. Schleswig-Holstein and Hanover were annexed by Prussia in the wars against Denmark and Austria. Their delegates to the Reichstag are consistently anti-Prussian, and despite the revival of the Duchy of Brunswick for the Kaiser's new son-in-law, the Guelf family have not renounced their rights and claims. In Alsace and Lorraine, taken from France in 1871, the Gallic spirit remains unquenched. Official policy has alternated between repression and conciliation, but to no avail. The constitution granted in 1911 leaves the reality of power in Berlin, and had better been refused. The Kaiser himself admitted the failure of the Prussian regime by recently threatening to incorporate the provinces in Prussia, as if that were the worst punishment imaginable.

Any friendliness which may have grown up will be extinguished by the Zabern episode. Several months ago an ardent lieutenant made disrespectful remarks about the inhabitants of this garrison town because of their attachment to France. The populace began to pester him with similar compliments, and the gallant officer took to shopping with an escort of soldiers with fixed bayonets. One day he struck with his sabre a lame shoemaker who brushed him in the street. An uproar followed, the colonel of the regiment proclaimed martial law, and threatened to "shoot up" the town. A man was arrested for laughing, and also several governmental officials who protested against the suppression of the civil authority. The climax of this ridiculous episode was a court martial which exonerated the officers, and formally sustained the pretensions of the military. Now the dashing colonel has received the Order of the Red Eagle. Thus on every hand the Prussianizing policy has failed, as every such policy must fail which sins against the eternal facts of national life and character, and these provinces which contain one-eighth of the population continue to be a permanent centrifugal force.

The next problem is that of the Prussian franchise, which even Bismarck admitted was wretched and absurd. There is manhood suffrage, but the voters are divided into three classes according to the amount of taxes they pay. The largest taxpayers who together pay one-third of the taxes form the first class; the next largest class paying another third form the second class; and the mass of the people the third. As each class chooses the same number of electors who in turn choose the representatives, the well-to-do and rich control the Prussian parliament. The following table illustrating the election is more eloquent than any words of mine. Despite the liveliest discontent on the part of the Prussian people this system remains from generation to generation, and the laws of the Medes and Persians were not more sacred than this hypocritical franchise in the eyes of the privileged voters.

PARTY	VOTES	SEATS EARNED	SEATS OBTAINED
Social Democrats	598,522	113	7
Catholic Centre	499,343	94	104
Nationalists	404,802	76	19
Conservatives	354,786	67	152
National Liberals	318,589	60	65
Radicals	120,593	22	36
Free Conservatives	63,612	11	60
	2,360,247	443	443

Then there is the antiquated distribution of seats. In 1871 the population of Germany was 39,700,000, and one representative was accorded for every 100,000 people. Since then the population has grown to 66,000,000, and what is more important, has shifted. The Rhineland is thick with artisans, the eastern provinces are thinly populated by the agricultural element. Yet there has been no rearrangement of seats. Thus Berlin has only six representatives instead of the twenty which its two million inhabitants deserve. One Berlin district contains as many as 800,000 people, while some in the country as few as 14,000. As the rural constituencies always return conservative deputies, the government is opposed to any change, and the Reichstag is powerless. In the election of 1907 the Social Democrats secured one seat for every 75,000 votes, the National Liberals one for every 30,000, the Centre for 20,000, and the Conservatives for 18,000. The government does not deign to notice this grievance; it simply ignores it.

Finally the question of ministerial responsibility is still on the tapis. Bismarck was confronted by it in 1877, and succeeding chancellors have had it dinned into their ears by orators galore. But all of them have calmly ridiculed it. It is really the most pressing of all questions, for if the chancellor were responsible to the Reichstag, the present institutions of Germany could be made over by vote of that body. Only out-and-out revolution, I venture to think, will bring about this change.[2] The commons of England had to cut off the head of one king and drive his son from the throne before they secured even partial control of the executive. France indulged in three revolutions for the same end. In Germany the ascendancy of Prussia is secured only by making the chancellor irresponsible to the Reichstag and the tool of the Prussian king. Let the Reichstag choose the chancellor, and that mouth-piece of the Emperor may very easily be his bitterest opponent. The Prussian army will have to be humbled before the parliamentary system is established, and it is more likely that the Emperor will follow the advice of a well-known conservative and send a lieutenant with ten soldiers "to close up the Reichstag".

Under such conditions of political life it is obvious that political parties, with the exception of the Conservatives, who have a perpetual lease of power, cannot pretend to the same importance as the great organizations of England and America. They can not change one jot or one tittle of the law of custom; they can merely "wait and see", as Mr. Asquith has put it, what the government intends to do. But in spite of this unreality it would be a profound mistake to suppose that party struggles and general elections are void of significance. Once every five years the public opinion of the Empire finds a free outlet, and its trend in the reign of William II has been unmistakable. Not only has there been a distinct verging to the left, but in the

---

[2] Five years later it came about, on October 1, 1918—just three days before the German government appealed to President Wilson for an armistice.

present year of grace the Socialists are the largest, wealthiest, and most highly organized party in the country. At the elections of January 1912 they polled 4,250,000 votes and returned 110 out of 397 members.

It must not be thought, however, that a third of the German people are advocates of Socialism. The Social Democratic party is not an engine of revolution, but a party of protest, which is milder in its demands than our own progressive party of happy memory. There are about one million genuine Socialists who pay dues to the party organization, but even they are content to advocate political rather than social reforms. A parliamentary system, a redistribution of seats, reform of the Prussian franchise, freedom of speech and of the press, disestablishment, free, compulsory and secular education, woman's rights, and control of peace and war by the Reichstag—these are the main planks in their platform. Free legal proceedings, free medical attendance and burial, and the raising of all revenue by progressive income and inheritance taxes are the only points which can by the wildest imagination be connected with socialist propaganda. Marxian socialism may be the ultimate goal, but at present little is said about it, because otherwise the millions of well-to-do who vote the Socialist ticket would be alarmed. When the Conservative party issues election manifestoes against "the red peril of socialism" and government newspapers speak of "a peril for the national unity of our people", they are talking the most arrant nonsense. At the present time the Social Democrats demand little more than the control of the German government by the German people, a control which will do more to consolidate the nation than all the soldiers and all the Dreadnoughts demanded by the military classes. In 1890 the Emperor William told Bismarck to leave the Socialists to him: he knew how to deal with them. Here are the results of His Majesty's tinkering.

YEAR	TOTAL VOTE	SOCIALIST	PERCENTAGE
1890	7,228,500	1,127,300	10.11
1893	7,674,000	1,786,700	19.74
1898	7,757,700	2,107,076	23.30
1903	9,495,586	3,010,771	31.71
1907	11,262,800	3,259,000	28.94
1912	12,206,806	4,250,329	34.82

Owing to special circumstances there was a relative decline in 1907, despite an increase in votes, but the loss was more than repaired in the elections of 1912.

The Centre or clerical party is not a political party of the usual type. It developed during the Bismarckian persecution of the Catholic church, and has been maintained to protect the interests of that church. It cuts across the ordinary political animosities, for it is agrarian, semi-socialistic, particularist, or nationalistic, according to the locality. In the present reign it has never sent fewer than 91 representatives to the Reichstag, and has always combined with the Conservatives to furnish the government with a majority. It is essentially opportunist, but as long as the Socialists are beyond the pale, it holds the whiphand.

The disruption of this Blue-Black Block was one of the issues of the elections of 1912. Others were the whole protective system, especially the duties on foodstuffs and the prohibition of foreign meats; and the question of armaments. The foreign policy of the government was bitterly criticised, but only the Radicals and Socialists opposed an increase of armaments. The following table will show not only the results of the elections, but the course of party fortunes since 1890.

	1890	1893	1898	1903	1907	1912
Conservatives	93	98	79	77	84	59
Anti-semites	5	20	24	17	28	15
Clericals	106	96	102	100	104	91
Nat'l Liberals	41	53	48	50	54	55
Radicals	79	49	53	38	53	44
Nationalists	38	36	35	34	31	33
Socialists	35	44	56	81	43	110

Even the Socialists themselves were astonished by their success, which would have been greater but for the distribution of seats.

Yet the new Reichstag has proved as complaisant as all the others. It has obediently voted large increases of the army, the appropriations being secured through the help of the Socialists, who declined to let slip an opportunity for taxing capital even though the working classes must suffer most from the additional military burdens. The truth is that the Social Democrats have not learned practical politics. An alliance between them, the Radicals, and the Nationalists would create a block of 187, or almost a majority of the Reichstag, and they would draw many National Liberals to them. But the Social Democrats decline to co-operate with any representatives of the black-coated white-collared classes, and the government marches serenely on. Perhaps the time will come when the Socialists will secure an absolute majority of the Reichstag, but before that the government will probably restrict the suffrage in such a way that only those who accept the existing regime will be allowed to vote. France would speedily find a solution for the problem, but Germany's one experience with revolution in 1848 was such that this expedient will be postponed to the Greek kalends. Personally, I can see no hope for a more liberal regime in Germany until tyranny and oppression have made over the German character.

The foreign policy of Germany in the Guilelmian era is a topic bristling with controversy and full of pitfalls for the student. In economic matters one may reckon from the official figures; domestic politics are also intelligible enough to a perservering observer; but in the domain of high policy it is almost impossible to get beneath the surface. The motives which animate and the ambitions which dominate not Germany alone but all the nations of the world defy accurate analysis, for the simple reason that the said nations do not proclaim their intentions from the housetops, and any responsible statement is subjected to such meticulous criticism by foreign publicists as to be almost useless. Even the very course of events is disputed. The following account of German diplomacy is therefore a tentative one, which may be revised at any time in the light of new information.

Its main currents in the reign of William II would seem to have been (1) a maintenance of the Bismarckian tradition; (2) the rise of the Pan-German movement; (3) the emergence of a world policy; (4) an inability to reconcile these somewhat conflicting aspirations; and (5) as an inevitable corollary, a reckless and inhuman piling-up of armaments.

With respect to the Bismarckian tradition, it is necessary to distinguish between policy and methods. Bismarck was too clear-headed not to see that the older nations regarded Germany as a parvenu, and that nothing was to be gained by a policy of bluster. In his eyes, the best guarantee of German hegemony in Europe lay in the division of its enemies, and especially in the diversion of French energies away from a war of revenge. He utilised the Balkan situation to intensify the traditional hostility between Austria and Russia, the opening up of Africa to sow distrust between Italy and France and to breed animosity between France and England (and troubles in Central Asia to make bad blood between England and Russia.) In addition, he contracted a strict alliance with Austria, which later included Italy, kept the wire open to St. Petersburg by a secret convention, and co-operated with England by accepting its maritime supremacy. Thus France was isolated, and Germany secured its share of the good things in Africa.

The first act of William II after the dismissal of the Iron Chancellor was to repudiate the convention with Russia, whereupon the Tsar promptly came to terms with France and rescued the Republic from twenty years of isolation. The Dual Alliance counteracted the Triple, to the intense chagrin of Bismarck, whose work since 1871 was thus largely undone. William II has since flirted now with the Tsar, now with France, but the Dual Alliance remains unshaken.

On the other hand, the German foreign office has sedulously endeavored to imitate the methods of Bismarck. That is, it has created situations in the hope of fishing in troubled waters, it has developed a splendid capacity for ignoring or twisting treaties in the best Bismarckian style, and it has attempted to dictate the public law of Europe, without, however, recognising the limitations which the old chancellor deliberately imposed upon himself. This attitude of the Wilhelmstrasse, coupled with a fearful lack of good manners, is in no small degree responsible for the bad reputation which Germany has earned for itself in recent years. The constant fear of a second Bismarck can be dispelled only by a frankness and honesty which has so far been a detestable hersey with the fussy bureaucrats of the German foreign office.

The Pan-German movement starts from the fact that of the eighty-odd millions of Germans in Europe, fewer than seventy millions enjoy the blessings conferred by the new Empire. Ten millions reside in Austria, a few more in Bohemia, where they are intermingled with the Czechs, and some others in the Baltic provinces. Then the Dutch are of the Teutonic race, and their fertile lands not only once belonged to Germany, but actually control the mouths of the German Rhine. Why should not these peoples and these lands revert to their ancient allegiance, and thus complete the union of all Germans in one Fatherland? Various overseas possessions, such as Dutch South Africa and southern Brazil, might conveniently be added if the cards were properly shuffled. The little detail that the present possessors of these regions might object was of no concern to the apostles of militarism who conceived this enchanting picture of a greater Germany. Rattle the sabre, and use it if necessary, became the axiom of these paper strategists, who made up in vociferation what they lacked in popular enthusiasm. Bismarck was wont to declare that Germany was "saturated": the Pan-Germanists insist that he stopped half way.

For various reasons, Pan-Germanism is hardly a practicable issue. The people of Germany have never displayed much sympathy with the idea, the government has now and again repudiated it, and its fallacies are self-evident. Is Bohemia to be included in Pan-Germany, and the Czechs added to the number of Slav irreconcilables, or if only Austria proper is taken over, are the Germans of Bohemia to be left to the tender mercies of Russia, towards whose orbit Bohemia would inevitably gravitate? But there can be little doubt that most Germans would welcome the incorporation of Holland and perhaps the Flemish provinces of Belgium, which would be a declaration of war against France and England. It is obviously difficult to estimate the real strength of a movement which is only one of many political issues agitating the Fatherland, but two tendencies may be noted.

First, the Pan-German propaganda is carried on spasmodically, but each outburst has been followed by militant proceedings at the foreign office, and a period of great tension between the European Powers. This would seem to indicate more sympathy with the movement in high places than is commonly admitted, but such a conclusion is frankly inferential.

Second, the German army has been repeatedly increased without provocation from its neighbors, until today its peace strength is not far short of a million men. The armies of other states have indeed been augmented, but in every case the increase has been a reply to the German initiative. The German Emperor may be perfectly sincere in his peace profession, and he has kept the peace for twenty-five years. But why constantly add to an army already superior to its rivals, not one of whom would dare attack it? The statesmen of Europe cannot help believing that some day, especially when the the chauvinistic Crown Prince becomes Emperor, efforts will be made to realise the Pan-German program, wholly or in part, and they are bound to prepare for every emergency. If there is any one man who above all others has forced Europe to turn itself into a vast parade ground, that person is His Majesty the German Emperor. And before disarmament can become a reality, a great prophet must arise from beyond Germany who shall convince the Kaiser and his henchmen, intrenched as they are in a citadel of privilege, that militarism is incompatible with a healthy national life.

The third and by far the most spectacular phase of German diplomacy has been the development of a world policy, which shall ensure the nation its "place in the sun", as the Emperor never tires of repeating. The motives of German imperialism were genuine enough. The economic system produced a surplus of goods which must be marketed abroad, and created capital faster than domestic industries could absorb it. The demand to share in the partition of Africa was quite legitimate and was recognised by the other Powers. But the acquisition of German South-West Africa, German East Africa, and the Cameroons whetted the national appetite, for which the imagination of the Kaiser and the zeal of innumerable pamphleteers has conjured up a great colonial empire comparable to that of France or England. Unfortunately for Germany, and just here is the rub, there are no lands left for Germany. By 1890, when *Weltpolitik* had become popular with the masses, practically the whole of Africa had been occupied or staked off, and there were left only those regions of Asia and Africa where non-Christian peoples live under feeble governments and decadent civilizations—China, Persia, Turkey, and Morocco. It is now evident, though Germans will not admit it, that Bismarck over-reached himself: he played England against France so successfully that together they appropriated the very lands which Germans had ear-marked as their own. Now the patriots attempt to visit the sins of their hero upon the very countries which profited by them, and loudly declare that on every hand Germany is being restricted by the jealousy of France and England. All this is solemn flapdoodle, but no amount of arguing or evidence to the contrary will cure the national jaundice of a disappointed people. One can only state the solemn fact that in these half-barbarous lands invaded by European capital and adventurers in the last twenty years Germany has filched quite as much as any of her rivals.

Thus in China the port of Kiaochou was secured as an indemnity for the murder of two missionaries. Samoa was the subject of considerable argument with Britain and ourselves, but in the end Germany got two out of five islands. Various other islands in the Pacific were acquired by arbitration or occupation, and the British government made no objection to a German establishment on the island of New Guinea. Lastly in the final settlement of the Morocco question, the French government ceded to Germany an enormous tract of land in West Central Africa which will make an excellent spring board for further leaps. The total area of the foreign dependencies of Germany is now 1,130,000 square miles with a population of 15,000,000. Compared with the far-flung dominions of Great Britain, France and Russia, overseas Germany is of course a mere bagatelle, but thirty years ago there were no German colonies, and its great rivals have been in the game for three hundred years, during most of which Germany was a mere geographical expression. If we add that part of the Portuguese colonies is destined to become German and that Mesopotamia will be bagged in the final extinction of Turkey, it is clear that the effulgence of imperial Germany is scarcely as dim as we have been asked to believe.

German *Weltpolitik* has achieved its greatest success in the lands of the Sultan, that sick man whose mortal illness has lasted some sixty years since it was first diagnosed by the Tsar Nicholas I. Bismarck used to declare that the Eastern Question was not worth the bones of a Pomeranian grenadier, but William II has thought differently. In 1897 the famous Baron Marschall von Bieberstein was sent as ambassador to Constantinople, where he reigned supreme for fifteen years. German concessionaries were royally treated, German goods began to supplant those of England in popular estimation, regular lines of German steamers linked up the Turkish ports, German officers were called in to rejuvenate the Sultan's army, and above all the concession for the Bagdad railway was secured on terms perhaps disastrous to Turkish finances, but very profitable to German shareholders. It is not possible here to discuss the merits of this particular concession, which has so alarmed the French and the British; the world, however, has a lasting interest in its success. The line is to run from Constantinople across the Anatolian plateau to Bagdad and ultimately to the Persian gulf. Branch lines will be built to Alexandretta on the gulf of Adana, and to the Persian system when that is constructed by the Russian government. The regenerating influence of the iron horse will bring life again to this quondam garden spot of the earth, especially when the irrigation schemes of Sir William Willcocks are completed. In spite of many obstacles the line is being pushed forward, and the future historian would probably regard its completion as the brightest ornament of the reign of William II.[3]

A few words as to Morocco. The last independent state of Africa Minor, the Shereefian Empire, had long been the arena of European intrigue, without falling a prey to it. But in April 1904 France and England signed a convention which recognised the English occupation of Egypt and the predominance of France in Morocco. The German government accepted the arrangement cordially, but as it put an end to the long hostility of the contracting parties, the Emperor William II suddenly landed at Tangier in March 1905 and declared formally for the independence of Morocco, which was ostensibly taken under German protection. War nearly followed, but in the end an international conference turned the country over to France and Spain as the agents of the great Powers. The German government seemed to accept the *fait accompli,* for in February 1909 it signed a convention with France which distinctly admitted the political interests of France and guaranteed to Germany equal treatment in economic matters. France now adopted an aggressive policy that culminated in tribal revolts, which in turn led to a French occupation of Fez. This proved too much for Germany, which asserted that its economic interests were threatened, as probably they were, and a cruiser was despatched to Agadir, where, incidentally, European ships had no right to be, as it was a closed port. Three months of crisis, during which war was averted only by the resolute intervention of England, led to a settlement which it is devoutly to be hoped will be lasting. France secured its protectorate over Morocco in return for the cessions in Central Africa already referred to, and Germany was given guarantees for the maintenance of the open door, a principle consistently championed by it. Many well-informed persons believe that Germany's real ambition was to share in a partition of the Morocco whose independence and integrity it had promised to maintain, and that it has not yet given up its designs;

---

[3] Not completed until after the First World War.

but the evidence is conflicting, and for the moment all is quiet. The Moroccan disputes have neither improved nor aggravated the relations of France and Germany. For more than a thousand years, which are but as yesterday in their sight, the two nations have fought over the valley of the Rhine. Germany did indeed dismember France in 1871, but even Alsace and Lorraine do not atone for all the sins of France, and in my humble opinion, "a firm and lasting peace", as the language of treaties has it, will not soon be established between the most persistent enemies in the long history of Europe.

The quarrel of Germany with England, on the other hand, is but a passing phase of contemporary politics, which has well-nigh if not altogether run its course. We have already seen that the industrial and commercial advance of the Fatherland was and still is more rapid than that of the United Kingdom, and in this blatantly commercial age, it is natural enough that the traditional friendship dating from the days of Frederick the Great should be weakened. But this alone would hardly have led to extreme tension: Anglo-American relations have steadily improved in spite of increasing commercial competition. Two quite different factors are responsible for the breach.

Bismarck disliked England and particularly "Professor" Gladstone, but he was willing to co-operate with it under ordinary circumstances. Since 1890, however, the Wilhelmstrasse has managed to cross the British government at every available opportunity. Whether it was the Armenian massacres and the Cretan question of the 'nineties, the interpretation of treaties in the Far East, the position of France in Morocco, or of Austria in the Balkans, Germany and England have taken opposing views. In many cases there was a real clash of interests, but the Kaiser's telegram to President Kruger after the Jameson raid and the fierce abuse of everything English during the Boer war has accentuated the psychological aspects of the quarrel. A few years ago war semed unavoidable, not because there was any issue to fight about, which fact was perhaps the root of the evil, but because the two nations had been lashed into a frenzy of mutal hatred which was deliberately abetted by the fishers in troubled waters. The Germans grew jealous of the imperial heritage of Britain, and the English resented that any one should dare to dispute the ascendancy they had exercised for almost two hundred years.

The real danger lay in the naval rivalry. The very life of England depends upon its navy. Drawing the food for its people and the raw materials for its factories from every corner of the globe, the island kingdom is bound to maintain a supreme navy. To lose command of the sea is to throw England open to invasion, starvation, and annihilation, and Germany has seen fit to challenge the mistress of the seas. Beginning in 1900 a series of naval laws has been passed which will provide the Empire in 1920 with sixty-one first-class battleships, ten armored cruisers, and an elaborate flotilla of torpedo and auxiliary craft. When completed, this fleet will be the most powerful aggregation of warships in the history of nations. In other words, the mightiest military state of our age is striking for nothing less than the control of the world. That Germany should succeed in this effort is unthinkable, and thanks to the inflexible determination of England, it will not. The reply of the British peoples has been magnificent. From every corner of the Empire have come presents of battleships and battle cruisers, and under the pressure of the German menace, the British Empire is fast becoming a reality.

> "The night is full of darkness and doubt,
> The stars are dim and the Hunters out;
> The waves begin to wrestle and moan;
> The Lion stands by his shore alone
> And sends, to the bounds of Earth and Sea,
> First low notes of the thunder to be.
> Then East and West, through the vastness grim,
> The whelps of the Lion answer him."

The Germans have been taught to believe that England is a land of fossilised inefficiency whose material resources are on the verge of exhaustion: yet British budgets have easily borne the tremendous new naval expenses, which have played such havoc with German finances. The British fleet will continue to be the surest guardian of the peace of Europe.

It is a bitter pill for the Emperor William II to swallow, for the fleet is emphatically his creation. Until he told the Germans on a famous occasion that their future lay on the water, they were content with the Bismarckian glories. But His Majesty, seeing how his splendid liners must pass beneath the guns of Dover Castle or around the rock of Gibraltar, imagined that to protect them, Germany, to quote the naval act of 1900, "must possess a fleet of such strength that even for the mightiest naval Power, a war with her would involve such risks as to jeopardise its own supremacy". Thus to the actual challenge was added a gratuitous insult, which served the purpose of arousing England to the real situation. The following figures of the distribution of British fleets will show how real is the fear of German designs.

In the Mediterranean		In the North Sea
1904	202,000 tons	Practically none
1907	135,000	166,000 tons
1909	123,000	427,000
1912	126,000	481,000
1913	50,000	500,000

It has been stated officially on innumerable occasions that Germany does not aim at a fleet superior to that of England, but in its actions it has strained every nerve to achieve this. Three times in the last seven years the British government has endeavored to effect a limitation of armaments, and Germany alone of all the powers of Europe, has refused its assent. As the creator of the German navy, William II is entitled to the enthusiastic devotion of his people, but in attempting to outdo Napoleon, he deserves the execration of the civilised world.

Of late the relations of England and Germany have improved, and really give little cause for concern. During the late Balkan wars they worked harmoniously and successfully to restrain their belligerent friends or allies. The Baghdad railway dispute is approaching a solution, and it is by no means impossible that another five years will witness a resumption of cordial relations.

Germany and Russia are often regarded as potential enemies, and their peoples do cordially hate one another. The imperial chancellor, Dr. von Bethmann Hollweg, demanded the recent increase of the army because of an inevitable struggle between *Deutschtum* and *Slaventum*. The assumption is not justified unless Germany intends to precipitate the conflict. Of all the governments in Europe that of Russia is the least belligerent, and now that Turkey has fallen a prey to the Balkan states, there is no reason why Germany and Russia should resort to the *ultima ratio*.

With the United States the German government has, since the gasconnades of Manila Bay, managed to preserve tolerably cordial relations, but public opinion, so far as it is reflected in the press and notably that of Berlin, is violently hostile. There is no institution or feature of our life, public or private, no policy of our government and no public officer from the President down that is not constantly ridiculed or abused by the young lions of Prussian journalism, whose prejudice, ignorance, and jealousy is equalled only by their almighty cocksureness and disgusting conceit. Not even the Panama Canal is exempt from the vitriol, though it means much to German trade. When I first began to read these diatribes, my blood boiled and my astonishment was immense; but I can now recommend them as an excellent sedative for tired nerves and an unfailing source of amusement.

Our account of German diplomacy would be incomplete without a brief reference to its vacillating character. It has been everything by shorts and nothing long, which is just what to expect from the restless energy of its dictator. To this day no one in France or England and probably very few persons in Germany know exactly what Germany wants in the world. Its public men give expression alternately to honeyed words of peaceful promise and the most truculent threats of impending war. Thus General von Bernhardi, in his book, *Germany and the Next War*, says frankly that Germany wants more territories for her people and new markets for her industry, and that it will take them by right of might. His only qualification is thus stated: "It must therefore be the duty of our diplomacy so to shuffle the cards as to compel France to attack us", and he concludes with the following words: "As long as we are afraid to be the aggressors, France and England can subject us to their will. Therefore if we wish to bring about an attack on the part of our enemies, we must initiate a political action which, without attacking France, yet will hurt her interests, and those of England, so severely that both states will be obliged to attack us. The possibilities for such a procedure present themselves as well in Africa as in Europe."

In the face of such language, which beyond a peradventure represents the mentality of the ruling classes, it is delightful to record the complete failure of William II and his five chancellors to secure the permanent safety of Germany. Fear of its incalculable intentions has sounded the knell of ancient animosities. France and Italy have composed their differences, England and Russia have seen through the German game, and France and England have developed such intimate relations that twice within ten years the British government has been ready to throw 150,000 redcoats, the finest soldiers in the world, upon the eastern frontier of France. German diplomacy stultified itself by allowing Italy to embark upon its Tripolitan adventure, by which it has given hostages to fortune. Let Italian troops march into France, as under the Triple Alliance they are bound to do, and the French or British fleet will promptly cut off communications with Tripoli. As for the other ally, Austria, it is face to face with a new Balkan problem which will paralyse its action in Europe for years to come. In other words, Germany is practically an isolated power, and the hatred with which it is regarded is aptly expressed in these words of a recent writer on Italy.

> "In these days when the second-rate efficiency of the Teuton threatens to engulf everything that is vital and characteristic in Europe, we should be eager to encourage and consider such little states as Andorra and San Marino. Not that they can in any way help stem the flood of mud that rolls over us all from the Germanies, but that in their happiness they serve as examples of all that we should lose by a Germanic domination, under which all that is most divine in us, most characteristic and genuine, will be smothered by the most accursed mediocrity that has ever appeared in Europe, and would be crushed out of existence by a system, a training and a tradition essentially barbarous atheistic, and hopeless."

Let us conclude by striking a balance. On the credit side may be recorded an enormous increase in population, a prodigious advance in every kind of industrial and commercial activity, the creation of the second most powerful fleet in the world, and some success with the new *Weltpolitik*. To offset this splendid showing, the extraordinary expenditure on armaments has thrown finances into disorder, and greatly increased the popular burden, more especially as the great prosperity of the earlier years has slackened perceptibly. Nearly one-third of the people regularly express, through the ballot, their dissatisfaction with existing conditions, so that a reactionary professor now proposes to destroy *Poebel*, *Presse*, and *Parlamentismus* as the three evils of the realm which must be extirpated. In foreign affairs Germany has aroused the enmity of England without securing the good-will of France, and has been fooled by its allies. From an American point of view, the balance is decidedly against Germany, nor is it countervailed by the personality of the Emperor. To William II the world will accord a due meed of praise for keeping the peace, but in other respects it will regret that a career of much promise has been marked by an excessive devotion to the ideals of the past and by a self-assertiveness not warranted by the test of proportionate achievement.

The War: Twenty Years After, 1914-1934

A lecture given at the University of Chicago on August 1, 1934, twenty years after the First World War began. It offers a view of the state of the discussion about the responsibility for the war and the question of American participation. Little is said about the peace treaties that came after the war or about the world created by them. The purpose of the lecture was expressed in the final sentence: "Let us be taught by the lessons of twenty years, recognize that, however much we may dislike the fact, we are inextricably involved in the affairs of Europe, and evolve a policy towards Europe which will strengthen the forces of peace and save our skins".

Rereading the lecture after 26 years, I find nothing to change. I note, however, that I do not discuss the possibility of a new war in Europe. Personally I was of the opinion, after Hitler had assumed power, that Germany would some day go to war again in order to tear up the treaty of Versailles, but in August 1934 it was not possible to guess how soon this would happen. Although the blood purge of June 1934 and the assassination of the Austrian chancellor Dollfuss in July were evil signs, in the summer of 1934 Germany did not possess the military power on land, at sea or in the air to challenge Britain and France. It was not until the following year, 1935, that Germany began to rebuild its army, air force, and navy. When Germany started rearming, both Britain and France, instead of following suit, embarked on a policy of "appeasement" and allowed Germany to get such an advantage that in 1939 Germany had become strong enough to precipitate war.

*   *   *

Twenty years ago to-day Germany declared war on Russia, and the Great War began. Some of you here present were perhaps not even born, and probably more of you were too young to realize what was happening. To such the years from 1914 to 1918 are no more than an historical episode analogous to the Civil War or the

American Revolution. But men and women who have passed forty will probably recall the mingled sensation of horror and incredulity with which they learned of the European tragedy. In 1914 few Americans knew anything or took any interest in the complicated politics of Europe, for the ordinary newspaper provided little information on foreign affairs, and the conviction was well-nigh universal that the affairs of Europe were no concern of ours.

To-day a large number of people are again proclaiming that the troubles of Europe are none of our business and are clamoring for a policy of isolation. But even the most determined 'die hards' must surely recognize that what happens in Europe does react upon us, whether we like it or not. Is German default of no interest to the thousands of Americans who bought German bonds? Is there no relation between the defaulting of the inter-allied war debts and the political and economic conditions of Europe? Paradoxically enough, those who insist most strongly on the payment of the war debts are also the bitterest advocates of isolation. Have twenty years of confusion verging upon chaos taught us nothing? And so, on this fateful anniversary, I propose to take a look backward at the war, to try to recapture its mood, and to discover, if I can, some of its lessons.

The most spectacular fact about the war was the suddenness with which it broke out. On July 23, 1914, when Austria hurled its ultimatum at Serbia, the only exciting circumstance in Europe was the possibility of civil war in Ireland over the question of Home Rule: two weeks later seven nations were at war. Even in Europe this abrupt transformation from peace to war caused a shock. It is true that for some years before 1914 certain men had been crying that a great European conflict was impending, but they were not heeded by the great masses. Four times in a decade—in 1905, 1908-9, 1911, 1912-13—Europe had been brought to the verge of war. But on each occasion the governments had drawn back, and in spite of ancient grudges and traditional rivalries, the idea had begun to spread that war was not only inhuman but also unprofitable. Statesmen and diplomatists in every country professed their devotion to peace and more or less sincerely believed their professions. Yet within a fortnight inhibitions and restraints were swept away as if they had never existed.

The moral of all this for us is clear enough, namely, that the peace of the world lies at the mercy of some untoward incident. The murder at Sarajevo of the heir to the Austro-Hungarian throne was not the cause of the Great War—it merely provided the occasion. So another assassination, or something else equally stupid, may again open the temple of Janus, just, for that matter, as the blowing-up of a bridge in Manchuria in September 1931 precipitated the Chino-Japanese conflict of recent years. Is there no way of escape from such operations of chance? Sir Edward, later Viscount, Grey, the British foreign secretary in July 1914, subsequently expressed the opinion that if the League of Nations had been in existence at that time war might have been avoided. In view of the League's failure to prevent what was actually, though not legally, war between China and Japan, one must be skeptical. But Grey's argument was sound in principle. What he meant to say, I think, was that when war threatens, the danger can best be exorcised by mobilizing the opinion of neutrals which shall demand that the disputants submit to some kind of mediation or conciliation. Events have shown that the present procedure of the League of Nations is ineffective, partly because of the terms of the Covenant, partly because certain Great Powers are not members of the League. But the principle is surely sound that because war anywhere affects the world at large, some machinery is required which will enable the nations not parties to a dispute to consult together on how to prevent the dispute from degenerating into war. This machinery needs to operate automatically and immediately, for time is the essence of success; in 1914 there was no such machinery and it could not be improvised in a few days. Also the consultation must be universal, or at least it must be participated in by all the Great Powers; in 1931 the action of the League was seriously handicapped by the absence of Russia and the uncertain attitude of the United States. To devise such a fool-proof machinery is the prime task of this generation. Perhaps it cannot be done. But we Americans should never forget that because an Austrian archduke was killed at Sarajevo more than fifty thousand Americans died in France and we are saddled with debts which will burden us for a generation.

Once the shock of war had been met, there began a fervid and passionate investigation of the causes of the tragedy. From a psychological point of view the very fact that the war had broken out suddenly—unlike previous great conflicts, which were long in coming to a head—made plausible the view that it had been deliberately plotted and then sprung at what seemed an auspicious moment. The conduct of German diplomacy in July 1914 seemed to bear out this theory, and ultimately there emerged a story, which first circulated in Germany itself, to the effect that early in July representatives of the Austrian and German governments had met secretly at Potsdam, under the presidency of the German Emperor, and there decided to bring on a European war. For some years this story was almost universally believed in the Allied countries and in the United States, not less so because there was seemingly good evidence to support it. The Germans were never able to fix so specific a plot on their enemies, but all during the years of the war they believed, and many of them still believe, that Russia, France and Great Britain had been sedulously preparing for a war to annihilate Germany and had therefore seized with alacrity the opportunity offered when Austria decided to punish Serbia for the murder at Sarajevo.

Recent historical research has disposed of many of these legends. The collapse of the empires of the Romanovs, Habsburg and Hohenzollerns has made possible the opening of secret achives in their respective countries, and this in turn forced the victorious powers, Great Britain and France, to publish their diplomatic correspondence. At present the number of documents dealing with international relations in the period from 1871 to 1914 which the historian can peruse is not far from 50,000 and may well reach twice that figure before all the material has been made available. Many private letters have also been published in the autobiographies or biographies of the principal personages involved. Anyone who reads this voluminous material will soon disabuse himself of the notion that the governments of pre-war Europe deliberately plotted a European war. That is not to say that individual statesmen did not, at given moments, toy with the idea of war or try to impress their adversaries by threats of war. Bismarck, whose policy after 1871 was generally pacific, did not hesitate on several occasions, to try to terrorize France and Russia, and his most famous successor, Bülow, boasted that during the first Moroccan crisis of 1905, he had let the situation develop almost to the point of war, confident that at the last minute he could wriggle out. The German Emperor also talked much of war and gave vent to many belligerent sentiments in the marginal notes which he scribbled on the margins of documents submitted to him. Such dangerous tactics contributed powerfully to the widespread distrust of Germany which prevailed for years before 1914, but they do not prove that the German government was pursuing a policy of deliberate war. Likewise French statesmen such as Delcassé, Clemenceau and Poincaré were at times ready to fight; so also the Russian Izvolsky and the Austrian Aehrenthal, and even a British Liberal like Sir Edward Grey and a British Radical like David Lloyd George could and did show their teeth. But it seems well established that responsible governments, however much they prepared for war by creating enormous armies and building huge navies, however much they might bluster and try to bluff, did not desire an armed conflict; one and all they preferred the maintenance of peace and not only were prepared to, but actually did, make concessions for its sake.

Of the military men one can speak with less confidence. Certainly General Conrad von Hötzendorf, the chief of the Austrian general staff, itched for war and from 1906 on did his utmost to bring it about. Germany also had its school which advocated 'preventive war,' notably Waldersee in the late 'eighties and early 'nineties; it would also seem that in 1914 the chief of the German general staff, the younger Moltke, welcomed war because he preferred to have it then rather than later. The Grand Duke Nicholas, who commanded the Russian armies in 1914, is thought by some to have been eager for war; so perhaps also certain French generals. The famous British admiral Sir John Fisher was keen to 'Copenhagen' the German fleet before it became too strong. But down to 1914 these generals and admirals were kept in hand by the civil authorities and had little influence on policy. What these men contributed was not so much a direct push towards war as the spread of suspicion and fear, for their never-ending demands for bigger and better armaments made for nervousness all around, and often embarrassed the diplomatists who strove for peace.

It cannot, then, be said that the war was the result of a fell conspiracy on the part of conscienceless and ambitious men; even those who in 1914 took the decisions and gave the orders that issued in war did so in the conviction that no other course lay open to them in the interests of their respective states. The one exception was Austria, which for several years had been desirous of a military reckoning with Serbia if a plausible excuse could be found—which was provided by the murder at Sarajevo.

Fundamentally the war of 1914 was caused by the fact that the frontiers of states did not correspond to the distribution of peoples. Germany and France were enemies because in 1871 Germany had taken Alsace-Lorraine against the wishes of the population who, whatever their racial origins and past connections, then considered themselves French. The Austro-Hungarian monarchy contained eleven different peoples, most of whom lived in subordination, both political and economic, to two or three privileged races and were vainly endeavoring to secure some measure of self-government. The Balkans were restless because the Christian populations desired to be emancipated from Turkish rule. Russia also had numerous non-Russian minorities who deeply resented Russian domination. Everywhere minorities were harshly treated by the governments under whom they were forced to live and gradually became more or less disloyal. Not only that, but many minorities had kinsmen across the frontier with whom they wished to be united. The Rumanians lived partly in Austria, partly in Hungary, partly in Rumania. The Yugoslavs were divided between Austria, Hungary, Serbia, Montenegro and, until 1812, Turkey. The Poles had long before been partitioned between Prussia, Russia and Austria. Bulgarians, Greeks and Italians also had failed to achieve national unity. The *Zeitgeist* made it inevitable that these several disunited peoples should strive for unity. They could achieve it only by the destruction of existing governments or existing constitutions and a wholesale remaking of the map of Europe. Since the existing governments were not in the least disposed to permit this, the only means to the end desired was war.

It was this irrepressible conflict which led the European governments to devote so much time, energy and treasure to the fashioning of armies. Germany was convinced that it could hold Alsace-Lorraine only by the sword and therefore maintained an army deemed sufficient for the purpose. Austria and Russia were in the same boat, for they could keep their subject races in submission only by force. France and Italy could hope to liberate their kinsmen under German and Austrian rule only by war. Thus the German system of universal military service had to be and was adopted by all the Continental powers, and once adopted, there was no escape from it. Every increase in strength, every technical improvement in *matériel*

made by one country had to be met all around, and after forty
years of competition, the relative strength of all was not greatly
altered. The principal result had been an increase of fear and suspicion.

A similar competition in naval armaments was engendered by
rivalries for colonies and concessions abroad. Unlike the conflicts
of nationality on the continent of Europe which often involved the
traditions of centuries, these overseas rivalries, which were of recent
origin, could be and were compromised. If we leave out of account
the Russo-Japanese war, the Great Powers of Europe managed to
divide Africa, parts of Asia and the islands of the Pacific without war.
Similarly, trade competition and commercial wars could be dealt
with by means of tariffs, either by raising or by reducing them,
and except in the case of Austria and Serbia, where the situation
was peculiar, trade rivalry had, in my judgment, comparatively
little to do with the war of 1914. But the steady building-up of vast
navies contributed powerfully to international ill-feeling, and the
primary issue between Great Britain and Germany was assuredly
their competition for the mastery of the seas.

Now the most fatal aspect of this enormous expenditure on
armies and navies was not the money involved or even the training
of millions of men in the ways of war, but the progressive insecurity
felt by every nation. Governments and generals invariably asserted
that armaments were necessary to secure peace, but actually the
greater armaments became, the less secure did any country feel,
because it was more and more alarmed by the armaments of its
neighbors. In 1912 the chief of the German general staff declared
that the position of Germany was more dangerous than at any
time since the establishment of the empire forty years before—yet
Germany, by general admission, possessed the finest military machine
in the world and the second strongest fleet. And Winston Churchill
talked in much the same strain, although the British navy was the
most formidable aggregation of fighting ships ever known. Thus
unstable political frontiers had created a feeling of insecurity, and so
recourse was had to armaments which might defend those frontiers.
Yet armaments seemed unequal to the task. What then?

Obviously, try to find friends who will help you, on condition
that you in turn will help them. Hence the system of alliances, which
began with the Austro-German alliance of 1879. When this alliance

was expanded in 1882 into a Triple Alliance by the inclusion of Italy, some counter-weight became necessary and was found by the conclusion of a Franco-Russian alliance between 1891 and 1894. Originally both alliances were defensive, being formed to preserve the *status quo,* and for some years they existed side by side, neither really threatening the other. But with the passage of time each alliance was modified, with a view to permitting changes in the *status quo.* In the end this new tendency was bound to become dangerous.

For many years the maintenance of equilibrium between the Triple and Dual Alliances was facilitated by the isolation of Great Britain, which co-operated now with one, now with the other group. But in the early years of this century Great Britain began to find its isolation costly and even dangerous, and it was forced to surrender its casting vote in favor of one group or the other. It tried to make a bargain with Germany—and failed. Thereupon it adhered to the other side, to France and Russia. Great Britain never joined the Dual Alliance, but it became a diplomatic partner, thereby creating the Triple Entente. Also it made certain military and naval arrangements with France which could be put into effect if Great Britain decided to join France in War. By July 1914 the schism of Europe was complete: Triple Alliance stood face to face with Triple Entente. Each side was determined to preserve, if possible, the balance of European power in its favor.

This explains what happened in July 1914. Theoretically the quarrel between Austria and Serbia which was brought to a head by the murder at Sarajevo concerned only those two countries. Actually Serbia occupied, at the moment, the key position in European politics. Were it brought under Austrian control, which would surely result if Serbia accepted the Austrian ultimatum, Austria and Germany would effectually dominate the Balkan peninsula and establish a close connection with Turkey where German influence was already predominant. The Central Powers would, in short, obtain the ascendency of Europe. Therefore Russia in the first line and France in the second resisted the pretensions of Austria, and if they could keep Serbia from the clutches of Austria, they might themselves secure the ascendency of Europe. And Great Britain was drawn into the conflict by the same consideration: it was unwilling to let Germany, with its threat to British naval supremacy, acquire a dominant position on the continent, because Germany would then be able to make good its challenge on the seas. Thus, in the end, the principle of the balance of power proved no more effective for the maintenance of peace than bloated armaments. Stripped of diplomatic verbiage, this was the issue which lay behind the thousands of telegrams exchanged between July 23 and August 4, 1914.

The Great War, then, was the consequence of the system of alliances and armaments which had grown up since 1871. But while all the Great Powers were involved in this system, it does not follow that all were equally responsible for the crash of 1914. The documents now available leave no doubt in my mind that the primary responsibility rests with the Central Powers, for it was they who put the system to the test. Austria-Hungary decided to seize the opportunity offered by the murder at Sarajevo for the long-desired reckoning with Serbia and formulated a plan of military invasion. The Austrian statesmen were well aware that this would probably provoke intervention by Russia and not unnaturally, before making their final decision, inquired what would be the attitude of Germany. There was the possibility that German support of Austria would deter Russia from action; if it did not, only German assistance would permit Austria to fight Russia as well as Serbia.

The German Emperor and the German government, having had the Austrian plan explained to them, accepted it with alacrity and urged its immediate execution. According to the existing evidence William II and Chancellor Bethmann Hollweg believed, or affected to believe, that Russia would not intervene; why they did so remains to this day a complete puzzle, for both had previously declared, on more than one occasion, that an Austrian invasion of Serbia would cause Russia to interfere. Nevertheless both recognized that Russia might come forward as the defender of Serbia. Therefore, when they sanctioned the Austrian policy, they knew that they were running the risk of a European war. Since they assumed that Great Britain would not take part in a European war arising out of a Balkan question, they may have argued to themselves that Russia, even with the support of France, would back down before the superior military power of Germany and Austria-Hungary. In either case, they put the system to the test. If Germany had said to its ally that Austria must be content with some punishment of Serbia less severe than military action, Austria would have had to submit to this advice, and in all probability war would not have broken out in July 1914. It may be noted that the German decision was taken by the political authorities, for the military chiefs were not consulted, only being informed of the decision when made. The soldiers were, however, nothing loath, and certainly did nothing to prevent the crisis from developing into war.

The crisis was created by the action of Austria, which refused to recede one jot or tittle from its demands that had been calculated to make war with Serbia unavoidable, and of Germany, who supported the Austrians to the limit. But the crisis was immediately regarded by Russia and France as a test of the balance of power. They would have preferred to fight later, and they offered their opponents numerous opportunities for negotiation and compromise. But because they thought themselves sufficiently well prepared to risk a war, they refused to accept the Austro-German programme *in toto.* The Russians did their best to make clear to the Central Powers that they would fight if necessary, but Germany either would not take the Russian warning seriously or did not care if war did come. In such circumstances peace had no chance.

But peace might have had a chance if the one country which, more than any other, namely Great Britain, sincerely desired peace, had pursued a different course. As already stated, the German government, when deciding to support Austria to the limit, did so in the expectation that Great Britain would remain neutral—although the German ambassador in London had for eighteen months consistently reported his conviction that Great Britain would assist France if it were attacked by Germany. When, as the crisis developed, it began to appear that Great Britain would probably not remain neutral if war came, the German Emperor and the German government became alarmed: to fight Russia and France was one thing, to add Great Britain to the list of enemies completely altered the situation. In consequence Berlin began, within certain limits, to urge Vienna to make concessions which might possibly prevent war. Unfortunately, these moves were made too late, because Austria had already declared war on Serbia and Russia had begun mobilization; also the German pressure was relaxed at the critical moment, and in the end Austria yielded nothing. But it can certainly be argued that if Great Britain had made clear, before Austria declared war on Serbia, that it would join in the fray, Germany would have prevented an Austrian declaration of war (which actually it had encouraged) and would have negotiated for a compromise. Both the Russians and the French believed this at the time, and probably they were right, and I suspect that Grey believed it too.

The irony, the tragedy, was that British public opinion would not permit Grey to make the one declaration which would have saved the situation. It is not, I hope, belittling representative government to say that in time of grave crisis it can effectively prevent those in authority from taking steps which they believe necessary. The British thought they were keeping their hands free to decide what to do when the moment came: actually they found that they were not free, that the decision had been made for them by events which they had refused to control. And in this year 1934 British opinion seems still unwilling to learn the lesson of 1914. It is still trying to avoid taking sides betwen France and Germany, though at the moment it seems to be leaning somewhat to France. But if, unhappily, a new war should break out between Germany and France, Great Britain will again find itself just where it was in 1914—and I doubt not that the result will also be the same.

So much for the origins of the war and its lessons. Obviously this is no place to attempt even a summary of the military operations from 1914 to 1918. But certain emotions of those years may be recalled and some observations offered. In the first place, very few persons had the slightest notion that the war would last so long— if they had, there surely would have been no war. The general staffs expected a short struggle—the Germans counted on smashing the French within six weeks, and nearly did so. The shortage of ammunition which soon manifested itself tells the same story. And the general public everywhere long cherished the illusion that victory lay just around the corner. Many of you can doubtless remember the eagerness with which you read of some small victory, in the expectation that this was the beginning of a 'push' which would be decisive. Anyone who in 1914 had dared to say that the belligerents could hold out for more than four years would have been dubbed an unreasoning pessimist or a traitor. The moral is that war is incalculable and that in the long run, it is much safer not to run the risks it entails.

A second conclusion is embodied in the remark ascribed to

Clemenceau that war is much too serious a business to be entrusted to soldiers. All things considered, the military mind did not distinguish itself. It is true that Kitchener predicted the war would last at least three years, but he often showed himself obtuse in his psychological handling of vital problems, notably the question of Irish recruiting. Nor was he able to break through the red tape which stood in the way of providing the British army with the munitions and supplies it needed. In vivid pages Mr. Lloyd George has described how he had to make guns and munitions in spite of the British war office, which resented having a civilian tell it what to do and how to do it. The classic example of military obtuseness is, of course, the tank. The British generals were long opposed to it; when finally they accepted it, they insisted on using it prematurely and thereby nearly ruined its chances. Fortunately for the Allies, the Germans also at first refused to take the tank seriously and neglected effective counter-measures until too late. Similarly the Germans began to use their submarines before they possessed nearly enough for really effective action and thus gave the Allies time to experiment with methods of defence.

Both Mr. Lloyd George and Mr. Winston Churchill have denounced in glowing terms the high strategy of the war, as imposed by the French and British general staffs, that is, the insistence on attacking the enemy at his strongest point instead of seeking the weak places in his armor. It was the civilian ministers who insisted on the expedition to Salonica that finally contributed so much to the ending of the war. The German general staff, in turn, has to be credited with the entry of America into the war, for they, and not the German government, were responsible for unrestricted submarine warfare.

Even on the strictly military side, the generals can hardly be said to have won great distinction. On the western front trench warfare continued for nearly four years, neither side being able, until 1918, to devise any method except that of frontal assault in which they persisted long after its failure had been demonstrated. But perhaps one should not condemn the generals too severely, for in fact the huge armies used in the war were a new phenomenon in military history and the art of handling such enormous bodies of men had to be improvised more or less by the method of trial and error. It is probably true to say that if the war had been fought by small professional armies, it would have come to an end much sooner, and the political consequences might well have been much the same as were achieved by mobilizing entire nations.

On the political side, the most important discovery was the possibilities and dangers of propaganda. In spite of forty years of universal military service in the continental nations, the belligerent peoples had to be kept up to the top pitch of enthusiasm by incessant governmental encouragement. 'War weariness' was a universal disease, inevitably so in the face of the tremendous losses and the incredible privations suffered by the civilian populations, and it was counteracted only by relentless propaganda. But if the governments were thereby enabled to fight the war to a finish, they became at the same time prisoners of public opinion. Having whipped up their peoples to believe that nothing less than a knock-out victory was tolerable, they dared not negotiate for a compromise peace, even though they were one and all aware of the dangers of economic exhaustion or social revolution that might result from prolonging the fighting. Lord Lansdowne's appeal for a negotiated peace got scant hearing in England; the Emperor Charles of Austria had to conduct his negotiations in complete secrecy; the German government was never able to issue a declaration for the restoration of Belgium. But in spite of this obvious lesson, it must be assumed, I fear, that in the event of another war, governments will once more mobilize public opinion and act precisely as they did in 1914-1918.

Possibly one hopeful sign can be detected in the circumstances in which the war was fought. Modern war is essentially a war of *matériel,* and it is permitted to doubt whether, in spite of all the present portents of war, Europe is in a position to fight again on the scale of 1914-1918. By common consent Germany is the nation most disposed and likely to risk another conflict. But the Germany of 1934 is not the mighty German Empire of 1914. Its resources in iron, without which guns and munitions cannot be made, are much smaller than they were twenty years ago. Unless it were able to capture the Briey basin in France and the iron fields of Polish Upper Silesia, it might have considerable difficulty in equipping its armies. The oil fields of Galicia, which were so important to Germany and Austria-Hungary in the late war, belong to Poland. And in its present economic condition, which may continue indefinitely, it will not be able to buy abroad beforehand large supplies of iron and oil and cotton.[1] Italy also is poor in coal and iron. France and Great Britain are undoubtedly better placed than they were in 1914, but they too would probably have to import many materials—and how would they find the price? In 1914-1917 both countries were able, up to a certain time, to finance their purchases in the United States by the sale of American securities, but to-day the amount of such securities held in France and Great Britain is relatively small. Failing such means, the only other course would be to raise loans or secure credits. In the present state of American opinion, surely neither could foreign loans be floated nor foreign credits raised. Economic considerations may not prevent a new war, but lack of resources may make it shorter and less exhaustive than the last one.

Such a statement of course presupposes that a new war will be fought by the old methods. But that is of course highly doubtful. Many military men now believe that airplanes and gases will be the deciding factors, not ships and shells. That, however, opens up vistas into which a layman cannot safely peer.[2]

Whatever the nature of the next war may be, American opinion is clearly determined that we shall not be drawn into it. But in August 1914 probably no American seriously believed that we would participate in the conflict then beginning. I cannot recall hearing anyone at that time express such an opinion, and certainly nothing was further from the mind of President Wilson. Yet in the end we did go in. Can we escape if a new war occurs? Before attempting to answer that question it is worth while trying to discover why we did, after long hesitations, throw in our lot with the Allies.

At the present time many people are persuaded that it was the devilishly clever propaganda of the Allies which did the trick, and since the Allies were no better than the Germans, as is proved by the famous secret treaties for dividing the spoils of victory, we were the simple victims of egregious misrepresentation. Personally, I believe this estimate incorrect. The German invasion of Belgium made an ineradicable impression on the American mind which was further deepened by the reports of Belgian atrocities. From the

[1] This was a bad guess. The German army that took the field in 1939 lacked nothing!

[2] General de Gaulle published his book on armored warfare in 1934, but I had not read it.

very beginning of the war American sentiment was preponderantly pro-Ally; this is not merely my own conviction, but the opinion of numerous historical writers and, it may be added, of Count Bernstorff, the German ambassador. That this sentiment was strengthened and stimulated by Allied propaganda, may be conceded, but the maladroit German activity helped not a little. If, however, American felling was strongly anti-German, it was not, except in certain circles along the Atlantic seaboard, in favor of intervention. The Middle West and West wished to keep out of the war, and for that reason reelected Woodrow Wilson in November 1916. Furthermore the peace efforts of the President in December enjoyed wide popular support. It is no doubt true that Allied propaganda encouraged us to regard the Germans as devils and the Allies as saints, but after all the German case was constantly presented in the American press by sympathetic correspondents, and it should not be forgotten that Russia was much disliked by many elements in the United States. My own guess is that propaganda had much less to do with the formulation of American opinion than is generally supposed.

Equally wide of the mark, in my judgment, is the view that business interests drove the United States into the war in order to save investments in the Allied countries. As a matter of fact, most of the purchases made by the Allies were paid for in cash or by the sale of American securities. The credits established by the Allied governments, while considerable, were not worth the gigantic cost of our participating in the war. Again, Wilson was the last man to yield to the pressure of business, and there is no evidence that such sordid reasons influenced him or any important section of opinion. Undoubtedly many people cherished the belief that Great Britain and France ought to be saved from the clutches of Germany, but it remains to be proved that any large number wished to see this done by the arms of the United States.

Until convincing evidence to the contrary is produced, the verdict must be that until Germany embarked upon unrestricted submarine warfare in February 1917, American opinion was overwhelmingly against intervention. Even so, President Wilson was by no means resolved on war when he sent Ambassador Bernstorff home. He continued to hope that this action would bring the German government to reason, and he waited for what he called "actual overt acts" before he took the plunge. As late as the morning of April 2, he was still uncertain in his own mind.

The policy of the President which had brought him and the country to this pass has been criticized from many points of view. From 1914 to 1917 he was assailed because he did not act with sufficient vigor. Pro-Germans wished him to stop the British interference with American trade with Germany, while some pro-Ally partisans urged a rupture with Germany over the *Lusitania* or the *Sussex*. Both complained that while the president wrote magnificent notes of protest they failed to secure results. Instead of confining himself to words, he should, they said, have "acted," and the movement for preparedness was intended to provide him with the means of action. Colonel House, the confidential adviser to Wilson, consistently argued that if the United States greatly increased its army and navy the European belligerents would listen to our protests, and it is at least significant that the British feared we might adopt the plan of convoying our merchantmen. Wilson did ultimately come out for preparedness, but by that time the situation had become hopeless.

The Wilsonian policy was also criticized on the ground that it was not a policy of genuine neutrality, but of partiality for the Allies. This was, in fact, the truth of the matter. Because of the British blockade, the Allies could import whatever they needed from the United States, whereas the Central Powers could not. Legally, of course, the position of the United States was unassailable, even in the matter of munitions, and the German government admitted it. To have changed the existing law would have been an unneutral act. Moreover, the immediate interests of the United States were served by the trade in munitions and war materials. In 1914 business was seriously depressed in the United States and the international trade balance was against us. By 1916 we were enjoying great prosperity. To have tried, in the name of neutrality, to shut off the export of war materials to the Allies would have revived economic distress and have alienated both manufacturers and workmen who were profiting by the war trade. In a presidential year, such a course was politically impossible and would, moreover, have been condemned by the great body of Americans who desired the defeat of Germany. But when all is said, the fact remains that it was precisely the continued flow of American goods to the Allies which drove Germany to the desperate course of unrestricted submarine warfare.

To what extent Wilson appreciated this is not clear. In any case the president undoubtedly applied one standard of conduct to the Allies and another to the Central Powers. From a legal point of view there was no difference between the British forcing neutral ships into British harbors for examination of cargoes and the Germans sinking ships because they could not take the ships into port, no difference, that is, in the sense that both acts were violations of international law. But Mr. Wilson very early established a distinction. Interference with the course of American trade could at any rate be compensated for, but the loss of American lives through the action of German submarines was irremediable. This distinction was legally and technically sound, for under international law, a man-of-war was bound to rescue the crew and passengers of a captured ship if it were sunk—and this, of course, the submarine could not do. The Germans contended that they were not adapting existing international law to a new situation any more than the British were in their extension of the rules of blockade. But American opinion heartily supported the president, and thus the German contentions got little hearing.

It must not, however, be supposed that Mr. Wilson, though he talked less sternly to the Allies than to the Central Powers, was indifferent to the conduct of the Allies. Indeed he grew more and more indignant as the months and years passed and finally secured power from Congress to institute reprisals. Most unfortunately, whenever the president was getting into a frame of mind to deal severely with the Allies, the Germans would perpetrate some new submarine atrocity or deport Belgian workmen and thus redirect attention to themselves. They committed their crowning stupidity in January 1917, and since one aspect of this is not generally known, a brief statement will not be without interest.

By the end of 1915, President Wilson had realized that waging neutrality had become increasingly difficult and was likely to become impossible. The only avenue of escape, if America was to keep out of the war, was to bring the war to a close. In the spring of 1916 he made a proposal to the Allies according to which the United States would intervene if Germany refused to discuss reasonable terms of peace. He was greatly annoyed when the Allies practically ignored this offer, and his irritation steadily increased on account of the blockade. By the end of the year 1916, Mr. Wilson was actually more disgusted with the Allies than he was with the Germans, who had kept their pledge about submarines since the sinking of the *Sussex*. Then in December he made his overture for peace to both groups of belligerents. The Allies replied with a refusal, together with a statement of terms which Wilson and Lansing, the secretary of state, thought ridiculous. The Germans refused to communicate their terms, and instead took their fatal decision for unrestricted submarine warfare. This much is common knowledge. What is not generally known is that, if we may believe Count Bernstorff, the German ambassador, who claimed to have had it from Colonel House, Mr. Wilson intended, if the German terms proved at all reasonable, to use the power of reprisal vested in him by Congress, to compel the Allies to enter upon peace negotiations with the Central Powers. Bernstorff was enthusiastic and finally secured a statement of the German terms which he transmitted to Wilson. But it was too late, for at the same time he had to hand over the note announcing unrestricted submarine warfare. Thus the Germans lost the supreme opportunity to bring the war to an end, and precisely because they had spoiled his plans, President Wilson turned upon them with all possible bitterness.

Could we have stayed out of the war, should we have stayed out? The answer to both questions is in the negative. Once we had begun to sell war supplies to the Allies on a large scale, our economic prosperity was bound up with this trade, which was approved by a majority of the people. Inevitably that brought us face to face with the submarine issue. That issue we might have avoided by forbidding Americans to travel in the war zone, except at their own risk. But Wilson refused, and was supported on the whole by public opinion, to admit any such derogation of Americans' legal rights, on the ground that it would not be becoming to the dignity of the United States, and he finally made the issue one of humanity as well as of legality. International law being what it was, no other policy seemed practicable or worth considering.

If we had not entered the war, it is very unlikely, nay almost certain, that the Allies could not have won, especially after the collapse of Russia. The terms of peace might have been a compromise which, in the minds of many, would have been better than the treaties imposed on the Central Powers in 1919. But it is more likely, in view of the actual military situation, that the Germans would have been able to dictate a peace comparable to the peace of Brest-Litovsk which they forced on Russia in 1918. At the best the German military party would have remained masters of the situation—and such was their hatred of the United States for having supplied munitions to the Allies, such would have been their power even in the event of a compromise peace, that in the end we should probably have had to reckon with them. So, in spite of all the disillusionments of the past fifteen years, I remain convinced that both the honor and the interests of the United States required us to intervene. And I am equally persuaded that if a new war breaks out in Europe, we shall be drawn in again—unless we modify our policy of neutrality. Mr. Wilson's experience convinced him that neutrality would be impossible in the future, and it was precisely for that reason that he wished to create some kind of world organization which would make wars impossible.

In a striking article in *Foreign Affairs* last April, Mr. Charles Warren, who was the solicitor general of the State Department during the years of our neutrality, has examined what he calls "troubles of a neutral," and I commend it to you. In essence, he believes that if we attempt to insist on our theoretical 'rights,' we cannot escape war. Therefore, has not the time come for us to reshape our traditional attitude and give up 'rights' which we can enforce only by means of war? But any change must be made *before* a new war begins, in order to escape the reproach of unneutral conduct. And be it remembered that all the contested points about blockade and submarine remain, in 1934, exactly where they were in 1914, so that the same issues would arise again to plague us. For detailed suggestions, I refer you to Mr. Warren's article, but no thoughtful person can fail to see that the problem is one of the most momentous confronting the country.

Much of our confusion in the matter of foreign policy arises out of disgust with the spectacle of post-war Europe. Certainly the Europe of to-day is far removed from that Europe safe for democracy which, in 1917-18, we expected to create, and it is perhaps natural that we should distrust and criticize the European states which seem to have learned so little from the late war and to be headed for another one. Nevertheless, if we are fair, we shall have to admit that the United States bears a large measure of responsibility for the present state of things. It is fashionable to denounce the peace treaties of Paris as the *fons et origo malorum*. Undoubtedly the treaties have played their part in the unsettlement of Europe. But may I remind you that in 1918, when the treaties were being formulated, American opinion desired a 'strong' peace? That the Central Powers, and particularly Germany, should be let off easily, was not a popular notion, and the criticisms offered in the liberal and radical weeklies found very little echo in the daily press. In the next place, those who denounce the frontiers established by the treaties should remember that the United States had much to do with determining these frontiers. Americans sat on all the boundary commissions at Paris and often served as mediators between rival claimants. The frontiers finally drawn were not perfect, but in most cases they were better than the old lines, and good or bad, the United States was just as much responsible for them as Great Britain or France. By refusing later to ratify the treaties, the United States escaped any legal obligation, but that does not discharge our moral responsibility. Thirdly, the whole peace settlement was based on the hypothesis that the United States would join the League of Nations. Whether our failure to join the League is to be explained by the animosity of Senator Lodge, the stubbornness of President Wilson, or some other cause, our absence from Geneva completely upset all calculations and has had incalculable consequences. The irony of it all is that, after first ignoring and later discounting the League, we finally came to find it a useful and even necessary body and within certain limits are actually co-operating with it. I can only express my opinion that if the United States had been in the League from the beginning, the French invasion of the Ruhr in 1923— which was the first step in Germany's road to economic ruin— would not have occurred, that the limitation of armaments would long ago have been settled, and that the Manchurian crisis of 1931 would never have arisen.

In the minds of many, our refusal to ratify the Covenant of the League and the peace treaties was justified because the treaties did not conform to Wilson's Fourteen Points. In some respects the treaties did not conform to the president's program: futile to deny it. Yet without Wilson's work, the treaties would have been more severe than they actually were. Suffice it to say that the treaties were probably as good as could be secured at the moment, and that if the

United States had ratified them, the modification of their evil features would have been much easier. Looking back over the events of the last fifteen years, one cannot avoid the melancholy conclusion that the present situation, which causes us so much indignation and so much worry, is partly of our own making.

Is there anything that we can do about it? Our primary interest is not to be drawn into another war, and therefore we must be profoundly concerned with trying to prevent war. Many still believe that we should join the League. But President Roosevelt has said, No, and public opinion is still either hostile or indifferent. Yet because Mr. Roosevelt has formally recognized the usefulness of the League, we certainly should define our relationship to it as precisely as possible. My own solution is that the United States should negotiate with the League *now*, before a new situation arises, an agreement whereby, without becoming a member, we should promise to consult with the League, that is, through the Council, in the event of war breaking out or threatening to do so. This can be done by an appeal to the Pact of Paris, which practically all nations have signed. For the purpose of such consultation, we should accept *ad hoc* membership in the Council. This would not commit us to any action without our consent, but it would enable the United States to define its position and to ascertain the attitudes of other powers. A repetition of the uncertainties which prevented effective action in the Manchurian crisis would thus be avoided, and the chances of keeping the peace would be greatly increased. If peace could not be preserved, our freedom of action would remain unfettered. I see nothing to lose and much to gain from such a procedure.

When all is said, Americans have two things to remember. (1) War broke out in 1914 so suddenly that a method for preventing it could not be improvised quickly enough. Today, to be sure, a procedure exists through the action of the League. But that procedure will inevitably be gravely handicapped without the participation of the United States, which, in spite of the depression, remains the most powerful nation in the world. (2) A new war in Europe will have disastrous consequences for us. Either it will involve us or, if to avoid being involved, we modify our traditional policy of neutrality, we shall suffer huge losses. In either case the result will be disastrous. Wherefore, my final word is this: let us be taught by the lessons of twenty years, recognize that, however much we may dislike the fact, we are inextricably involved in the affairs of Europe, and evolve a policy towards Europe which will strengthen the forces of peace and save our own skins.

After Munich

In February 1939 I gave four lectures at the University of Chicago on "Twenty-Five Years". The first, "August 4, 1914", dealt with the origins of the war. The second, "April 6, 1917", discussed the entry of the United States into the war. The third, "June 28, 1919" was an analysis of the peace treaties, beginning with that of Versailles which was signed on the date given. The fourth was entitled "February 23, 1919?" and is here reproduced. It reflects the uncertainty that was widespread as to what lay ahead, and in the lecture I tried to point out how uncertain Britain, France and the United States were as to the best course to pursue. In my own mind, there was no doubt that we were drifting towards war. In a convocation address delivered to the University of Chicago on December 20, 1938, I warned the graduating class that their life would be "neither easy nor simple" and that they would probably "be called upon to fight for the honor and interests of the United States". The only course I could suggest was an increase in armaments, which I admitted was a "confession of bankruptcy".

In 1960 the menace of Soviet Russia and Communist China is greater than was the threat from Nazi Germany and Fascist Italy in 1939. The west is certainly better prepared, from a military point of view, to meet a Russian attack than Britain and France were to resist Hitler and Mussolini. But on the larger issues of general policy, there seems to be considerable lack of agreement between the United States, Britain, France and Germany—as much uncertainty as existed in 1939, an uncertainty perhaps best reflected by negotiations for an Anglo-French-Soviet alliance against Germany which began auspiciously in March 1939, only to peter out miserably in August.

*   *   *

After the lecture last week, a criticism was made that I seemed to rely too much upon the recent book of Lloyd George about the peace treaties. As it happens, I made no statement last week concerning the literature of the peace conference. Most of our information about the Paris peace conference derives from American sources. Books have been written about or by each of the five American commissioners—Woodrow Wilson, Robert Lansing, Colonel House, Henry White, and General Bliss. We have also the extensive *Dairy* of David Hunter Miller, the most elaborate documentation dealing with the treaty. There are also numerous German accounts, several by Frenchmen, and one, at least, by an Italian. Hitherto, there has been no authoritative account of the peace conference from the British point of view. For that reason I deemed it wise to emphasize Lloyd George's contributions to the debate, but I was careful to say that I did not necessarily agree with all his contentions, because his books, like his life, are always controversial. In that connection, I may remark that the State Department, according to recent information, has at last received permission from the governments associated with the United States in the war to publish the American and other documents in the possession of the State Department relating to the peace conference, and will do so as soon as it can.[1]

For the years since the war, we do not possess the information which is available for the pre-war and war years. Very few documents, except those of the most routine kind, have been published since the war. The European governments occasionally issue documents for the information of their respective legislatures, but there is nothing comparable to the great collections of pre-war documents, and even *Foreign Relations of the United States* comes down only to 1923 at the present time. In other words, the student of post-war Europe, or as the late Frank H. Simonds used to say, what we must now call pre-war Europe, has to depend in large measure upon newspapers. My own impression is that the newspapers find out a good deal more about what is going on than they did before 1914, but from the few, very few, glimpses which I have had of politics behind the scenes in the last twenty years, I am well aware that the newspapers do not begin to tell us the whole story, and that is, I am sure, very much the case with respect to the crisis which culminated in Munich last September.[2]

My lecture today I find somewhat embarrassing, firstly, for the reason that I do believe that it is possible to say anything new about

---

[1] Publication did not begin until 1942 and was not completed until 1947 (13 volumes).

[2] Even in 1960 much remains unknown.

Munich. That episode has been so thoroughly discussed from every conceivable point of view in the last few months that there is nothing new to say, because we have no additional information. People are for or against Munich. The second difficulty I face is that I have written a little pamphlet, which I know some of you have read, called *From Versailles to Munich*, and I am somewhat in the position of having either to repeat myself today or say nothing at all. I have, however, tried to approach the matter from a somewhat different angle from that which I have presented in my pamphlet.

Let me begin by asking why the treaties of 1919-1920 failed, as obviously they have failed, to bring peace to a war-weary world. Why are we once more living under the shadow of war? Perhaps it is not generally realized in this country, where until quite recently we felt very safe from the machinations and dangers of Europe, that in the last twenty years the world has been going through a series of revolutions or attempted revolutions, or revolutions which failed to come off.

In the first place, we have become gradually aware of what is commonly called the technological revolution, a modernization and speeding up of the processes of industry, so that industry is carried on in 1939 by machinery which represents a vast improvement over that of 1919. While I do not profess to know, any more than the economists do, whether in the long run technological improvements make for unemployment, it would seem obvious that many improvements have thrown a lot of people at least temporarily out of work, and thereby contributed to human misery. That explains in part, though not altogether, the second revolution of which I wish to speak, the one of which we are becoming increasingly conscious—what I should call the revolt of the masses against the classes. That has been induced in large measure by the misery created by and since the war. I had occasion in an earlier lecture to point out that the battle losses of the United States were insignificant in comparison with the losses of the European states. Similarly, our privations were not really privations at all, and when the war was over we were able to resume life on the standard and scale to which we had been accustomed.

That was not true in Europe. The destruction of property and the disarray into which the European economic system was thrown by the war made it impossible for Europeans since the war to maintain the standard of living to which they had grown accustomed before 1914. Sometimes their difficulties were the consequences of the peace treaties, notably in Germany, where the occupation of the Ruhr by France and Belgium led to inflation on a tremendous scale, in a large measure destroyed the middle class, and in my judgment paved the way for Hitler. Then, as I pointed out last week, high tariffs and the interruption of old trade routes prevented the old economic machine from functioning properly. The result has been, therefore, a diminution of the standard of living in Europe since the war, and it is that which explains this revolt of the masses against the classes.

That occurred earliest and has proceeded furthest in Russia, where a nominally Communist, though more accurately a State-Capitalist state has existed for more than twenty years. The Fascist revolution in Italy, the Nazi revolution in Germany, was each, I think, a revolt of the lower middle classes, who had been driven desperate by economic conditions, against property. Curiously enough, both revolutions were in the first instance fostered by the propertied classes in the hope that Communism would thereby be staved off, but it is notorious that in both Italy and Germany the revolution is tending more and more toward the left.

Far behind these three most conspicuous revolutions, I would place the revolution in Spain, which overturned the monarchy in 1930; the rise of the Popular Front in France three years ago; and, though some may be horrified to hear me say it, others may be pleased, the New Deal in our own country. There is a great difference, obviously, between the regime established in Russia and the aims of the New Deal in this country, but both have this in common, I think—they represent the revolt of the masses against the classes. That has been going on, in greater or less degree, for twenty years, and no one will dare say what the end may be.

Secondly, there has been a revolt against the peace treaties, which goes back at least to 1931, when the Japanese marched into Manchuria. Technically, Manchuria was not involved in the peace treaties, but it should be remembered that the peace treaties did give Japan the German rights, titles, and privileges in the Chinese province of Shantung; that the pressure of Great Britain, France, and the United States at the Washington Conference of 1921 forced Japan to give up in Shantung what the treaty of Versailles had awarded it, and the Japanese seizure of Manchuria in 1931 may be regarded, I think, as a retort for the loss of Shantung. This was the first stage in the program for recasting the world as settled at Paris in 1919-1920. It has been followed by the Italian conquest of Ethiopia, and the German conquest of Austria and part of Czechoslovakia.[3] The revolt against the peace treaties, then, is in full swing, and again, no one can say where it is going to end.

Fourthly, there was an attempted revolution in international life. I refer, of course, to the establishment of the League of Nations, and the attempt to bring about a reduction and limitation of armaments. The idea of an association of nations and the idea of reducing armaments are both quite old; but not until the treaties of 1919 was an association of nations actually set up, or did the governments of the great powers pledge themselves to a reduction and limitation of armaments. If those high hopes had been realized, a revolution would have occurred in the conduct of international relations, and probably a good deal of the misery of the world at the present time would have been avoided. Unfortunately, that revolution failed to take permanent root in the case of the League, because it never had full membership. The United States never joined; Russia did not join until after Germany and Japan had left; and obviously a League of Nations, an association of nations, whatever you choose to call it, can be effective only if all the great powers of the world belong to it. Subsequent efforts of the United States to cooperate politically with Geneva have failed. The fault has not been entirely with the European members of the League. There are many inherent difficulties which it is impossible to discuss here. Suffice it to say that the attempt of the United States in 1931 and again in 1935 to cooperate with Geneva came to naught.

In the second place, disarmament proved impossible of realization. When the United States failed to ratify the Franco-American treaty of alliance which was regarded by the French as an integral part of the peace settlement, and when the British took advantage of our refusal to refuse to ratify the corresponding Anglo-French treaty, the French became "jittery." They refused to rely upon the Covenant of the League, they refused to disarm. They built up a system of alliances in eastern Europe to replace the Anglo-French and Franco-

[3] Germany seized the rest of Czechoslovakia in March 1939.

American alliances, and they felt that with 65,000,000 Germans on their frontier they dared not disarm.

True, in December 1932, six weeks before the advent of Hitler to power, Great Britain, France, Italy, and the United States signed a declaration at Geneva recognizing, in principle, the right of Germany to an equality in armaments, but before that could be translated into reality, Hitler arrived in power, and subsequently, in 1933, the Allied governments refused to implement their declaration of 1932, and the last chances of disarmament disappeared.

The revolution, then, that was hoped for in the conduct of international relations has not materialized, but the revolt against the peace treaties is still in progress, and the revolt of the masses against the classes is still in progress. We are, therefore, in a period of revolution of which we, in the United States, are far less conscious than the inhabitants of Europe. Against that general background, let me attempt a brief and necessarily inadequate chronological summary of the last twenty years.

The first period extends from 1919, the signature of the treaties, to the year 1924, the period in which an attempt was made to apply and enforce the peace treaties. During these years the ex-enemy states were still too exhausted from the war to do anything more than submit to the orders of the Allied powers. The territorial settlements were imposed. The new governments were established, and the principal concern of the time was to get the economic machine started so that Europe might recover from the ravages of the war.

But that problem was greatly complicated by reparations, on the one hand, and by the Allied war debts to the United States, on the other; the effect of those two problems was to prevent the establishment of normal economic relations between the European states. Germany had suffered very little physical disruption during the war, whereas a considerable section of France and Belgium had been devastated. It was perfectly natural, perfectly human, for the French and the Belgians and in lesser degree Italians and Serbs and Poles to demand that Germany make good the damage done during the war. The trouble was to find some way in which the Germans could make good the damage in a practical fashion, and so the problem of transfer, the problem of transferring reparations from Germany to the Allied countries very soon became a burning question, and Great Britain and France quickly fell out.

Lloyd George, still prime minister, took the view that the figures of the Reparations Commission were excessive, that the Allied countries could not afford to take German goods beyond a certain amount. He had seen to it that the principal British losses, namely ships on the high seas which had been sunk by German submarines, had been made good ton for ton, but when the French in turn asked that the factories in northern France be made good machine by machine and destroyed houses be replaced by new houses, Lloyd George objected. So France and England fell out on the issue of reparations.

In the end, the French decided that the only way to make the Germans pay was to invade the Ruhr, and that invasion unquestionably had the effect of creating in Germany more of a will to pay than had existed before. On the other hand, the invasion of the Ruhr was the beginning of Germany's economic distress. It led to boundless inflation, from which Germany never really recovered, and it was during the days of the Ruhr that Adolf Hitler first began to organize his party and to write *Mein Kampf*. The Ruhr occupation was in no small degree responsible for the misery of the classes who subsequently flocked to the support of Hitler.

During that same period, Germany and Russia, strange as it may sound today, were not only on speaking terms, but were actually concluding a treaty between themselves (1922), because they were both outcasts—the Russians because they were Reds; the Germans because they would not pay reparations.

The second period begins in 1924, and extends to 1929. Those five years represent the best years of Europe since the war. The occupation of the Ruhr had brought all concerned to a realization of the difficulties involved in reparations. The Germans were made to see that they had to pay something, and the French had found out by experience that it profited them very little to occupy German soil. In the end, it was the United States, through the so-called Dawes Committee, which was largely responsible for a compromise on the question of reparations. The Dawes plan was accepted by the European states, went into effect in 1924, and functioned until 1929. During those years, Germany paid reparations, and France was satisfied, relatively. During those same years, a beginning was made towards an adjustment of the war debts of the Allies to the United States. So from the economic point of view, Europe, as the phrase ran in those days, had "turned the corner," and much encouragement was derived from the fact that the German foreign minister of those days, Gustav Stresemann, believed that the best way for Germany to recover its position in Europe and the world was to pursue a "policy of fulfillment," and seemingly he had converted the majority of his countrymen to that view.

Hence it was possible to negotiate the treaties of Locarno between Germany, France, Britain, Italy, Belgium, Czechoslovakia, and Poland, which created a greater degree of political stability in Europe than had existed at any time since the war. By the Locarno treaties, the western frontier between Germany and France was guaranteed by Britain and Italy, and the eastern frontier of Germany between Poland and Czechoslovakia was likewise declared inviolable, and those three states agreed to settle any disputes which might arise among them by methods of conciliation.

Looking back, those years from 1924 to 1939 do seem like a golden age. What we are apt to forget is that the German reparations were paid in large measure by American loans. We loaned money to Germany, and Germany used the loan to pay England and France, and they in turn used that money to pay the interest on their war debt to the United States. So a considerable part of the money never left the United States at all, thus involving no question of transfer, and as a friend of mine rather amusingly remarked about 1927, all that had happened was that there was a little bookkeeping in the office of J. P. Morgan and Company. We did not then realize that Germany could continue to pay reparations on the scale of the Dawes plan only if we lent it the money to do so.

Nor were the political issues clearly faced in those years. There was no adjustment of territorial disputes; no concession to the ex-enemy states in the matter of minorities; no serious attempt in the direction of a limitation of armaments. What the Germans attached great importance to, though an exaggerated importance I think, was Article 231 of the treaty of Versailles which, as the Germans interpreted it, assessed them with the responsibility for the war.

The year 1929 marks the beginning of the third period, which extends to 1933. The period begins with the crash in Wall Street in October 1929 and ends with the advent of Herr Hitler in Berlin and of Mr. Roosevelt in Washington in 1933. The crash of 1929 was in its earlier manifestations little more than a stock market crash.

It took two years for the ramifications of the Wall Street disaster to make themselves felt. But by 1931 serious financial difficulties arose in Austria, then in Germany, next in Great Britain, and lastly in the United States. The crash in May 1931 of the famous Viennese bank, the Credit-Anstalt, put the German banks in great financial difficulties, and since they in turn were in debt to London, English banks suffered severely, and the result was that by September 1931 England had to go off the gold standard, and from that day to this the financial difficulties of all governments have been acute.

By 1932, with the cessation of American loans and the increasing difficulties in Germany, reparations were brought to an end. The Allied governments recognized that, whatever their legal or moral rights might be, it was impossible to get any more money out of Germany, so reparations were written off, for all practical purposes, by the Lausanne agreement of 1932. But that helped a sinking world comparatively little, because in September 1931 the Japanese, sensing the troubles of Europe and America, invaded Manchuria, and that I regard as the beginning of our present woes. Because of the Japanese invasion of Manchuria, the disarmament conference which met at Geneva in February 1932 was not able to accomplish anything. I happened to be in Geneva during the conference and was keenly aware that the whole proceedings were profoundly affected by what the Japanese were doing in Manchuria.

Meanwhile, economic distress in Germany, after the cessation of American loans, was mounting so rapidly that Chancellor Brüning, who enjoyed the respect of French and British statesmen as had none of his predecessors, was forced to govern in most dictatorial fashion, and thereby made the way easy for the establishment of a formal dictatorship when Hitler arrived in power.

The fourth period begins with the advent of Hitler in January, 1933, and ends with the agreement of Munich in September, 1938. During those five years there was considerable economic recovery throughout the world, but it is becoming evident that in large measure that recovery was due to the process of rearmament which Hitler inaugurated shortly after he attained power. In fact, the outstanding feature of the five years from 1933 to 1938 is the rise of Germany to power. In 1932, Germany was still disarmed and practically helpless. In five years, Hitler had raised it to the first military power in Europe. During those five years, both Great

Britain and France, as it seems to me, refused to face the issue presented by the recovery of Germany. On the one hand, they refused practically all concessions to Germany, and they made very little concession to Italy. That was an intelligible attitude, if at the same time they provided themselves with the power necessary to confront German and Italian demands, but on the other hand in neither Britain nor France did the process of building up military power keep pace with the political attitude of refusing to make concessions to Germany and Italy.

In Great Britain, there was indeed considerable sympathy with Germany, a feeling that many of Germany's demands were justified. So, when Hitler took the crucial step of re-occupying the Rhineland, the British government accepted it without protest and refused to support France in a policy of forcing the Germans out.

In France, ever since 1934, the cleavage between Right and Left has become more and more marked. From 1936 to 1938 the Popular Front was in power, but whereas in an earlier period the Left parties in France were in favor of concessions to Germany, the government of Leon Blum and his successors was not willing to make concessions to Germany because they disliked the dictatorial regime which prevailed in Germany. Unfortunately also, Britain and France could not agree upon the proper method of dealing with Italy over the Ethiopian crisis. France would have liked to buy off Mussolini, but Britain was unwilling to do that, and the result was that Italy was neither bought off nor brought to terms through the operation of sanctions. Likewise, Britain and France showed considerable reluctance, after what may be called the return of Russia to Europe in 1934—that is to say, when Russia joined the League of Nations—to cooperate with Russia in building a common front against Germany and Italy.

The result was that when the crisis of 1938 arose, Great Britain and France were not able to oppose to the totalitarian states either military force sufficient to overawe them, or a diplomatic combination powerful enough to restrain them. On the other hand, the totalitarian states, both Germany and Italy, have known exactly what they wanted to do, and long ago came to the conclusion that the only way they would be able to revise the treaties would be by force or the threat of force, and they provided themselves with the force. Mussolini used it in Ethiopia, and Hitler used it in the

Rhineland and used it in Austria and threatened to use it in Czechoslovakia.

The United States sat back and looked helplessly on, partly because of disgust with the quarrels of Europe, partly because our hands were tied by neutrality legislation. So we reach the crisis of last September.

The only point I wish to make about Munich is that I do not believe there was a Chamberlain-Hitler plot to "put something over." A former distinguished member of this University[4] has declared that Chamberlain and Daladier were in "cahoots" with Hitler and Mussolini to stage a fake crisis, knowing all along that war would not result, but planning to terrorize the British and French peoples by the threat of war so that they would consent to the dismemberment of Czechoslovakia. Now, my personal opinion is that Great Britain and France had got themselves into a desperate situation, diplomatically and militarily, by September 1938. They both were reaping the fruits of mistakes during the past five, ten, twenty years. But I am not convinced on the basis of the evidence now available that Mr. Chamberlain and Monsieur Daladier deliberately staged a fake crisis in order to bamboozle their own people. Those who were in England and France last September do not believe that the crisis was faked.

I was told about a month ago by a distinguished British statesman who was in Chicago, who though not a member of the British government has access to excellent sources of information,[5] that in his judgment not only was Hitler not bluffing, but that he actually regards Munich as a diplomatic defeat. That may sound like an extraordinary statement. What he means is that Hitler was all set to march the German armies into Czechoslovakia. He wished to do that in order to demonstrate to the world the might and power of the German armies. After all, that was the same attitude that William II took on several occasions before the late war. According to this theory, then, Hitler was determined to march his armies into Czechoslovakia, and therefore, when, under the pressure of Chamberlain and Daladier and Mussolini, he had to content himself with a peaceful handing over of the areas which he demanded, he felt that he had been diplomatically

---

[4] Professor F. L. Schuman, of Williams College.
[5] The late Lord Lothian, who became British ambassador to Washington in August 1939. His view is now known to have been correct.

defeated, and there is certainly a good deal in the events of the last six months to bear out that interpretation of the situation.

As for Mr. Chamberlain—does he really believe in the policy of "appeasement," or was he seeking to gain time? Frankly, I do not know. The best judges appear to think that from a military point of view, Britain and France were not in a position to face Germany and Italy in September 1938; that the German-Italian air force was far superior to that of Britain and France; and that therefore the motive behind the Anglo-French surrender was to gain time. That is a question which we are not likely to be able to answer in any authoritative fashion in the lifetime of those who took the decisions. We shall have to wait for the opening of archives and the publication of private documents before we can answer such questions with any degree of certainty. So that brings me now, at last, to the subject of my lecture, the prospects on February 23, 1939.

To me it seems clear—I express all these opinions very tentatively—that appeasement has for the moment failed; that neither Hitler nor Mussolini is satisfied; and that the chances are unfortunately only too good that both Hitler and Mussolini will presently put forward new demands which will precipitate a new crisis. As to which way they will move or when they will move, I do not pretend to guess. There are those who also expect Japan to move against the Soviet Union.

That raises the double question: *Should* the dictator states be stopped? *Can* they be stopped? Some persons argue that it is folly to try to stop the "dynamic" states. There are 43,000,000 Italians, 40,000,000 Frenchmen. There are 80,000,000 Germans, 45,000,000 Britons. What chance, it is argued, have Britain and France of permanently stopping Germany and Italy, especially as the British and French peoples show considerable reluctance to disciplining and organizing themselves in such fashion as will enable them to build up the kind of war machine which Germany and Italy possess at the present time?

From that it can be argued that the world had better be re-divided. Let Germany dominate eastern Europe and the Balkans. Let Italy have a free hand in the Mediterranean, and let Japan take China, if it can. The Soviet Union will still be a world by itself; the British Empire is a commonwealth spread all over the world, more economically self-sufficient than any other single power; the French empire is not far behind. Why should the European states fight each other to the death when they can divide the world between them at the expense of China and small nations in eastern Europe? The logical conclusion of that theory would be that the new world, the western hemisphere, would remain the preserve of the United States, which would assume a kind of guardianship, wanted or not, over the states lying to the South of us.

Well, it may be that such a reorganization of the world is on the cards, and if one could be assured that such a re-division would mean permanent peace, I am sure a large number of people all over the world would be in favor of it. For us Americans, of course, the question at once arises, will the dynamic states allow us to dominate Latin America? Will they not insist upon carrying on there propaganda against us, impeding the progress of American trade, American institutions, and putting as many spokes as possible in our wheel?

The other question is a more difficult one. Can the dynamic states be stopped by the democratic, peace-loving states of the world? I saw the other day a review of a book by the former correspondent in Geneva of the *New York Times*, Mr. Clarence Streit. I have not read the book, so I know only what I read in the review. According to the review, Mr. Streit points out that the democratic, peace-loving nations of the world far exceed the dynamic states in number, in population, in resources; that it is up to them to decide whether they wish to stop the dynamic states. His argument apparently is that if the United States, Great Britain, and France, and the other democratic states of Europe, are willing to pool their resources, and if necessary to shut off or reduce their dealings with the totalitarian states to a minimum, that they are in a position to stop the totalitarian states. But obviously that is the greatest question facing us at the present day. I do not propose to answer that question here, because I know that I, like yourselves, can not answer it.

Of one or two things I am, however, certain. One is that if we decide that the dynamic powers must be stopped, we cannot do it by wishful thinking. We have to address ourselves to the problem with the same deadly earnestness that we manifested in 1917-18. Talking will not stop Hitler or Mussolini or the Mikado. If we are to stop them, we have to organize ourselves in some fashion so that the dynamic states will realize that the United States cannot be trifled with.

Here I come back for a moment to the experiences of 1914-1917. In October 1914 Colonel House urged upon President Wilson that the

United States should add greatly to its army and navy, pointing out that unless we did so, we should be treated with scant respect by both belligerents in the European war. Events proved Colonel House right. The British turned the screws of the blockade as tight as they felt they could. The Germans defied us on the submarine issue because they thought we would not or could not fight. I am convinced that if, when Congress met in December 1914 President Wilson had said to Congress, "We are facing an unparalleled situation; we are being affected in one way or another by both groups of warring powers; it is necessary to add in large measure to the army and navy of the United States and do so as quickly as possible"—if he had taken that attitude and could have persuaded Congress to accept it, I doubt very much if the British would have turned the screws of the blockade so hard, or if the Germans would have applied submarine warfare so recklessly.

I admit that to advocate armament is a counsel of despair, a confession that statesmanship is bankrupt. But I, for one, see no possible alternative but for the United States to proceed as rapidly and as thoroughly as possible to the accumulation of armaments to such a strength that if, unhappily, war does break out in Europe, all belligerents will feel that they must proceed to deal very cautiously with the United States, and that the knowledge that the United States will be strong enough to defend its interests may—I will not put it more strongly—may have some effect in preventing the outbreak of war.

I say that because nothing is more encouraging to me than the cries of rage now emerging from Germany and Italy over the armament program of the United States. They know, both Germany and Italy, that if it does come to a test of endurance, however reluctant we may be to do so, the United States can outbuild Germany and Italy in ships and planes. We have more resources than both of them put together. They are furious with our proposed program precisely because they know that if we cast our weight into the balance, their game will be definitely lost.

Therefore, whatever the cost to us, it seems to be an elementary precaution for us to gird our loins and make it clear to the world in unmistakable fashion that we can and will fight, if necessary.

The United States on the Verge of World War II

As soon as the Second World War broke out in September 1939, I was called upon to explain the causes of the catastrophe, and in the course of the next few months, I delivered three speeches on this subject in Chicago.

I put the blame squarely on Adolf Hitler, who for years had announced his intention of tearing up the Treaty of Versailles imposed on Germany in 1919; I admitted that Germany had some just grievances under the treaty and that the Allies—Britain and France—had been to slow in making concessions which might have staved off the Nazi regime; I also recognized that Britain and France had allowed Germany to get ahead of them militarily and that by 1938-1939 they were so weak that Hitler was convinced he could defeat them and was thus encouraged to precipitate war. Finally, I contended that the United States, by not joining the League of Nations and by withdrawing from European politics, bore some measure of responsibility for the second German war.

After the fall of France in June 1940, I soon became convinced that Britain, standing alone, was not likely to defeat Germany and Italy, especially as Russia was supplying Germany with raw materials. So I supported the Committee to Aid the Allies organized by William Allen White, and then Lend Lease. In this cause I made speeches in Chicago and at Kenyon College, Gambier, Ohio. The address here reproduced was given before the international section of the southwestern meeting of the American Association for the Advancement of Science held at Lubbock, Texas, on April 29, 1941, that is, nearly two months before the German attack on Russia and more than seven months before Pearl Harbor. In the summer of 1941 I joined with 130 other members of the faculty of the University of Chicago in urging President Roosevelt to take whatever action was necessary to keep the sea lanes open from the United States to Britain, even at the risk of war.

In 1960 the American people are more aware of the danger to which they are exposed by the policies and ambitions of the Soviet Union than they were in 1941 conscious of the situation created by Hitler,

*and there is a great deal of uneasiness about our future. But whereas
in 1941 the administration of President Roosevelt was moving, step
by step, in a policy designed to defend the interests of the United
States, neither the Republican administration of 1960 nor the Democratic Congress seems to have a clear idea of what they want to do or
what should be done. In an election year, both seem reluctant to impose the taxes which the exigencies of the situation may demand.
Having lived through the crises of 1915-1917 and 1940-1941, I am
more conscious of drift than in either of the earlier periods. By the
time this paper appears in print, the presidential election will have
been held, and one can only hope that the new president will be able
to formulate a convincing policy around which the people of the
country can rally.*

*   *   *   *

We are facing the greatest crisis in the history of our country since
we obtained our independence, and are facing it without clear convictions. During the Civil War of 1861-65, each side fought with a
passionate belief in the justice of its cause. In 1917 we went to war as
a united people, with the sincere intention of making the world safe
for democracy. Today we feel so overwhelmed by the events of the
last few years that we do not know what we think. A recent Gallup
poll put the question, Are you in favor of going into the war or of
staying out? and eighty-three percent declared for staying out. Another
Gallup poll revealed that nearly as large a majority—seventy-two percent, if I remember rightly, as opposed to eighty-three—supported the
Lease-Lend Bill, that is, accepted the plan of aid to Britain even at
the risk of war. That two such contradictory attitudes could be assumed almost simultaneously is surely proof of the confusion in which
the American people find themselves. For this desperate situation, we
are in no small degree ourselves responsible, because for twenty years
the American people, in my opinion, followed false gods.

In 1919-1920 the United States threw away the fruits of victory
which it had won in the First World War. Because the peace treaties
did not in every detail measure up to the Fourteen Points of President
Wilson and the ideals for which we had fought, it was possible for a
small group of irrepressibly partisan politicians so to confuse the issue
that the Senate of the United States rejected the treaties. The verdict

was seemingly confirmed by the election of 1920. Not only did we thus reject the principle of international cooperation, but by refusing to join the League of Nations we destroyed the fundamental basis of the peace treaties and encouraged those who did not like the treaties to try to tear them up.

The treaties were not perfect, but they were far better than partisan criticism admitted, and they contained the means for improvement and change. By rejecting the treaties because they were not perfect, the United States restored a kind of international anarchy to a world which had at least caught a vision of something better. Competent observers of the years from 1919 to 1939, who approach the question as historians and not as vote-seeking politicians, are now pretty generally agreed that our share of responsibility for the chaos of the world is a large one. When all is said, the United States did help to formulate the treaties; and although by failing to ratify them, it escaped any legal commitment, its moral obligation was immense.

What might have happened if we had joined the League of Nations and played our proper part in the politics of the world is, of course, an academic question. But one guess may be ventured. Had we ratified the treaties, we should have sat on the Reparations Commission, and the probability is that we should have voted against declaring Germany in default on the payment of reparation at the end of 1922; in other words, we should have prevented the invasion of the Ruhr by France. It was that invasion which destroyed the German economy and paved the way for Adolf Hitler, who wrote *Mein Kampf* during the last period of the invasion.

It would, of course, be absurd to contend that all the problems of a world recovering from the most devastating war in history could have been automatically solved by the adherence of the United States to the League of Nations, for on many issues the policy and interests of the United States are not the same as those of European and Asiatic countries. Nevertheless, our absence from Geneva injured the League both positively and negatively: positively, because we contributed nothing to such constructive steps as it tried to take; negatively, because its policies were often timid so long as the attitude of the richest and most powerful nation in the world remained obscure. The more the League failed to deal successfully with problems thrust upon it — Manchuria, Ethiopia, Spain — the more dangerous and desperate the situation became; but American opinion did little more than denounce the League for lack of courage and prevented the government of the United States from offering effective help.

In the ten years from 1919 to 1929, the United States extended its economic empire to the most distant areas of the globe. In some mysterious fashion a majority of the American people persuaded themselves that they could protect these vast interests without taking part in the politics of the world, while a minority, belonging chiefly to the Left, thought the interests not worth protecting. After 1931 the Japanese conquest of Manchuria and the subsequent invasion of China caused enormous losses to American enterprise in the Far East. After 1933 the crooked finance of Nazi Germany cost American investors in German bonds millions of dollars. Yet few Americans were apparently willing to recognize that our peace and prosperity depended on stability elsewhere.

Since we were foolish enough—as I think—to reject the League and withdraw into our shell, we should have drawn the logical conclusion of isolation, that is, we should have built up a military, naval, and air force so powerful that we could defend our interests against all comers. Instead of doing that, we disarmed; at least we went much further in disarmament than any European or Asiatic power, and assumed that treaties were more effective than guns. Would to God we had today the battleships, cruisers, and aircraft carriers that we scrapped in 1922! For the next ten years we cherished the cheap and comforting theory that public opinion in Europe and Asia, still remembering the horrors of 1914-1918, would be both anxious and able to prevent another war. Those who preached international cooperation were denounced as the tools of British and French propaganda (whereas the most energetic propaganda came in fact from Germany), and those who advocated a large navy were alleged to be subsidized by munitions makers. Since America seemed fully protected by the two oceans, what happened on the other side of those oceans was none of our business. The most we would offer to the cause of world peace was the Briand-Kellogg pact, which did not provide for any implementation or even for consultation among its signatories—and which broke down as early as 1929 when Secretary of State Stimson unsuccessfully tried to apply it on the occasion of a dispute in Manchuria between China and Russia.

Not content with assuming an unrealistic attitude of political virtue, we embarked upon an economic policy which was fatuous in the extreme and which was repeatedly denounced by the most competent economists in the United States. On the one hand, we urged our European associates in the war to reduce the amount of reparations which they wished to collect from Germany, and at the same time we tried to collect from them the debts which they had contracted with us in order to win the war and to start their reconstruction after the war. Oblivious to this inconsistency, we also raised our tariffs to such a point that our debtors found it very difficult to pay us what we demanded in the only way open to them, namely, goods. Not even the collapse of the fragile structure in 1929 disabused American opinion of its folly, for in 1930 the tariff was again raised. It will also be remembered that we loaned large sums of money to Germany. In so far as these loans could be floated because many Americans believed that Germany had been unjustly treated, that it needed help, and that the payment of German reparations would facilitate the recovery and stability of Europe, they did credit to American generosity and sentimentality; but these enormous investments also helped finance the building of factories which would sooner or later compete with our own industries.

From 1933 to 1939 the Democratic administration tried to offset the consequences of these mistakes. President Roosevelt attempted to restore some measure of international cooperation by overtures to Geneva. Secretary of State Hull aimed to restore international trade to its normal channels through the Reciprocal Trade act. A historian has to recognize, however, that what they tried to do met with much resistance from the American people. Mr. Hull's trade policy aroused no great enthusiasm, and effective co-operation by the United States against Italian aggression in Ethiopia and Japanese aggression in China was blocked by the indifference of the public and the hostility of Congress.

These aggressions, followed by the German seizure of Austria and the partition of Czechoslovakia, did strip us of illusions to some extent. At least they made clear that force, naked military force, was still the determining factor in international relations, and consequently President Roosevelt's plans for increasing the American navy were accepted. But if old illusions were partly dissipated, new delusions appeared in their stead. A group of politicians was pleased to investigate the circumstances in which the United States went to war in 1917 and announced the conclusion, preposterous and unproved, that bankers and munitions makers had maneuvered the American people into war for their own profit. At the same time another group wrote books alleging that British propaganda, rather than German misdeeds, had been the cause of our entering the war; that the German misdeeds had been intelligible and excusable, and no worse than British misdeeds; that in short, we had been bamboozled or betrayed into war. Such conclusions can be reached only by a distorted reading of the evidence. But the American people, worn down by years of depression and disgusted by the troubles of Europe and Asia, were in a defeatist mood and disposed once more not to face realities. This, I submit, is the only plausible explanation of that last word in fatuity, the Neutrality Act, which was deliberately intended to hamstring us as a great power in the affairs of the world.

This neutrality legislation probably had much to do with the outbreak of war in Europe in 1939. In my opinion it convinced Adolf Hitler that the American people had become so soft, so sunk in sloth and materialism, that they would and could not rise again to the heights of 1917 and that Germany, with her highly perfected war machine, could conquer Europe in short order. And have we not become soft? A considerable number of young men are opposed to any policy which may necessitate their fighting, and a great many parents are equally determined that their boys shall not be exposed to such risks. There was no such holding back in 1861, North or South. In 1917 the men of my generation did not hesitate. In each case the American spirit asserted and vindicated itself. The present inclination to place personal safety ahead of national interest is, I respectfully submit, the last word in that muddled thinking which has brought us to our present desperate pass.

When war broke out in 1914, the instinctive American reaction was to keep out of it, for we knew very little about Europe and what we knew was none too good. In 1939, we knew a great deal about Europe and what we knew was all too bad. More than ever before we wished to keep out, and for the first nine months, down to the fall of France, it was easy to believe that we could stay out. But my own belief, as you may already suspect, is that the foreign policy of the United States cannot be constructed on any abstruse hypothesis that we must stay out of war, that is, stay out at all costs. Any nation can stay out of war, theoretically, if it is cowardly enough to submit to any terms which a would-be conquerer may try to impose on it. That might bring peace, peace of a kind, but not peace with honor or security. In my opinion, we must pursue a foreign policy which will protect the interests of the United States—by peace, if we can, but if necessary, by war.

Lest you think me a warmonger, let me say now that I served in the army of the United States in the last war. I was above the draft age, but I enlisted when I could pass the physical examination. If I am today not a peace-at-any-pricer, I am not assuming a position other than that which I was willing to defend twenty-four years ago when I was of military age.

A recent visitor to the United States, the Archduke Otto of Habsburg, the pretender to the throne of Hungary, was much impressed by the freedom of speech, meeting, and religion which we enjoy— and by the fact that we took it for granted. Why can we take this freedom for granted? Not because it is innate in human experience! We enjoy those blessings in the United States today because some three hundred years ago Englishmen fought a civil war, deposed King Charles I and cut off his head, and later deposed King James II and sent him into exile. Did they accomplish these things by act of parliament? No, they accomplished those things by appeal to the sword. In 1783 we achieved our independence from Great Britain. Did Great Britain willingly grant that independence? No, it was compelled to grant it because it was faced by the superior military force of France and the United States. In 1865 union triumphed over secession. Did the South willingly submit to that? No, it submitted because of the superior force of the Northern army. In 1918 William II fled to Holland and the German Empire collapsed. Did he do this of his own volition, because Woodrow Wilson had hinted at it? No, he did so because of the superior force of the Allied and Associated armies.

So it has been from the beginning of time, and so it is in our own time. We shall not be able to preserve our American way of life in the world of today by wishful thinking, but only if we are willing to fight for it. We must become as hardboiled as our ancestors were in 1776 and 1861 and 1917.

What are the legitimate interests which we must be prepared to defend, if necessary, by force? First of all, the territorial integrity of the United States which, I may remind you, includes, until July 4, 1946, the Philippine Islands. Whether the Japanese have designs on those islands may not be conclusively proved, but there is ample ground for suspicion, and until the islands become independent, we are in honor bound to defend them. This will not be an easy job, but we have to face it.

Secondly, we intend to maintain our political independence, by which I mean the right to determine our own government and institutions free from external pressure and without the interference of fifth columnists of any stripe. In view of what happened last year in Norway and elsewhere, it is obvious that this is not an imaginary danger.

Thirdly, we have learned in the last twelve years that economic security is a complicated and delicate business. Though we are more happily situated than any other nation, we do not provide within our borders all the raw materials needed in our industry, and we do not consume all the products of our machines and fields. In other words, access to natural resources and the continuance of international trade are of vital concern to us.

Lastly, we have vast cultural and non-material interests throughout the world of which we are very proud, notably in China.

To me it seems obvious—only too obvious—that an Axis victory would greatly jeopardize these vital interests of the United States. The most immediate consequence will be to place us in a position of naval inferiority. With the British fleet out of the picture, the Axis will have more of every kind of fighting ship than ourselves—battleships, cruisers, aircraft carriers, destroyers, submarines. According to a statement in the *New York Times* for Sunday, April 20, 1941, we have 322 ships with a tonnage of 1,250,000, as against 658 ships with a tonnage of 1,835,000 for the Axis. No doubt our present feverish construction will reduce the Axis lead, but if Germany succeeds in dominating Europe, it will have at its disposal the ship-building facilities of the continent—which are many times larger than our own. Even if we exert ourselves to the uttermost, the chances are that Europe can build more ships than we can.

Now it pleases some people to argue that although our position at sea would remain one of permanent inferiority, we shall not be in danger for the following reasons: (a) Germany will be so weary of war and so exhausted that it will not dream of attacking the United States; (b) it will not have enough ships to convey a force sufficiently large to attack us; (c) according to Colonel Lindbergh, an attack by air is out of the question; (d) in any case, the United States is so large and so rich that in the long run it cannot be defeated.

The first argument strikes me as complete nonsense. If the Germans win this war, after having lost their other war in 1918, they will feel that their system of government and economics has been justified by events, as indeed it will have, and so far from being war-weary, they will look around for something more to conquer. It is inconceivable that they should feel satiated. Throughout history, military conquerors have never been able to stop, and for at least fifty years Germans have been telling each other that they are a super-race whose mission it is to rule the world.

It is also dangerous to assume that the Germans could not send troops across the Atlantic. We sent 2,000,000 troops to France in 1917-18, when the British dominated the sea. If the Germans get control of the Atlantic, why can they not reverse the traffic? Colonel Lindbergh may be justified in saying that in 1941 an invasion by air is out of the question. But 1946? 1951? One thing is certain: the general staff of the army and the general board of the navy think that we are in grave danger, and I prefer to trust them. I may also be told that if Hitler cannot invade England he cannot invade the United States. As a matter of fact, Hitler has not yet attempted to invade England; if and when he does, no one knows what the result may be. We cannot afford to take any chances.

We have also to remember that if Britain collapses, we shall have to face the prospect of Germany's trying to assert itself in South America politically as well as economically. Without going into the ramifications of that possibility, I think it safe to assume that the establishment of German political control anywhere south of the Rio Grande would give Hitler an excellent base for attacking us by air.

Quite apart from the contempt which a Nazi Germany feels for the democratic United States, there are two special reasons why a victorious Germany will be anxious to have a go at us. Firstly, because the assistance which we have already given to Great Britain has greatly prolonged the war, and the Germans would be no more than human if they wished to punish us for this. Secondly, Germany has never forgotten that without American help, Britain and France would probably have been defeated in 1917-18. In my visits to Germany between the two wars, I was more than once made to realize that Germany had not forgiven us for our intervention. The late ambassador Dodd, in his recently published *Diary*, reveals that he had similar experiences. The people of the United States may count upon Germany's trying to revenge itself in the most uncompromising fashion and, if we remember the repeated assurances of Hitler to Poland, Czechoslovakia, the Low Countries, and France, we may be sure that his constant asseverations that he has no quarrel with the United States afford the best possible proof to the contrary.

The most immediate consequence of a British defeat will be that in the Far East, we shall be left to face Japan single-handed. Singapore will not be available to our fleet, and the defense of the Philippines will become extremely difficult. Given time, we can no doubt construct the necessary naval and air bases, but probably the Japanese will not leave us time, especially now that they have concluded a five-year agreement with Russia which relieves them of worry from that quarter. And the Japan which we should have to face would be greatly strengthened by whatever British and Dutch possessions it chooses to pick up. Furthermore, if Britain falls, China will probably fall also, for the Burma Road will be cut, and we shall not benefit from whatever resistance China has thus far been able to make against Japan. And just as Germany has never forgiven us for our intervention in 1917, so Japan has not forgotten the Immigration Act of 1924 which permanently excludes Japanese from the United States. The proud islanders think that they possess a real grievance in that matter. Our isolationists and hyper-patriots may honestly believe that we can defend ourselves against a German or a Japanese attack; but they do not appear to have sensed that probably we shall have to face both Germany and Japan at the same time.

But, I may be told, we can save ourselves by building a navy and an air force so powerful that we can withstand simultaneous attacks from the east and west. Whether that is technically possible I do not know, but I do know that the cost would be terrific, and I very much fear that a totalitarian victory will make it impossible.

Throughout our history foreign trade has been a vital factor in our national economy. Freedom to buy and sell anywhere in the world, without either restraint or preferential treatment, has been our insistent claim, and our prosperity has depended in considerable degree (though not exclusively) upon the maintenance of a large import and export trade, as the years of depression have brought home to us only too vividly. Since the advent of the Nazi regime, however, Germany has pursued the opposite course of rigidly controlling its foreign trade. For freedom of exchange on the basis of cash, it has substituted barter and resorted to many devious and dishonest tricks, from which we have suffered not a little. If Germany wins the war, there is no reason to suppose that it will not continue its crooked methods. Its leaders boast that in Europe the non-German peoples will be reduced to a kind of serfdom, and there is no reason to doubt this. We, with our high standards of living for the working people, shall not be able to compete with German products, and we can be very sure that the Germans will do their utmost to deprive us of access to raw materials, such, for example, as tin in Bolivia and rubber in the Dutch Indies. Our free economy will be gone, probably our vast accumulation of gold will be rendered useless, and we shall face utter disaster. In such circumstances, we shall not be able to build sufficient defenses to resist the final German attack.

In the meantime, while our economic position has been deteriorating, we shall have been tinkering with our political institutions. Nothing succeeds like success. In 1918 the victory of the democratic states over the autocratic powers was followed by the springing up of democratic governments all over Europe. If, however, Germany wins this present war, Europe will go Nazi, and it will be difficult for us not to do likewise, if for no other reason than that increasing economic distress will demand more and more governmental control. This will please a few reactionaries, who think that Fascism will enable them to deal severely with labor and perhaps also a few labor leaders who expect to feather their own nests at the expense of capital. But the experience of both Italy and Germany shows us only too clearly what Fascism means in every-day life—regimentation of body and soul, lowered standard of living, permanent organization for war. The American people will not relish all this, but it is likely to be our lot if Germany wins this war. Personally, I believe that the majority of the American people, who detest the Nazi system and all its works, are at last beginning to see clearly what lies ahead of us, and that the few who assert that Naziism cannot be beaten and that therefore we should compromise with it are becoming less numerous each day.

Politics and economics aside, our non-material losses will be stupendous if the Axis wins. Will America be strong enough to remain a country of refuge for the oppressed of all lands? If we have to become Fascist ourselves, we shall not want them! Will not true religion be suppressed in Nazi or Bolshevik fashion? The United States would then be as bound spiritually as it was sick economically. Will not our literature and our art succumb as have those of Germany, Italy, and Russia, and become dull and lifeless? Will not the efforts we have made in China to point a new course to that heroic nation be undone by the Japanese? I for one do not believe that we are so craven as to submit to such a fate.

But if we are to avoid this fate, we must act and act quickly. By means of the Lease-Lend Bill, the President, Congress, and the country have committed themselves to the defeat of Hitler, not because we love the British Empire, but in the interests of the United States. We plan to spend seven billions of dollars to that end. But of what earthly use will planes and tanks and guns be unless they reach England and are put to use? To load these precious weapons on to ships only to have the ships sunk by German submarines and planes is fantastic and will not long be tolerated.

The answer? A first answer is, clearly, convoys; that is, the use of American naval vessels to protect merchant ships against German submarines and airplanes. For the moment American opinion seems confused on this point, as on many others. According to last week's Gallup poll, only 41% of the people favor using the American navy *now* for convoys, but 71% believe that we should thus use the navy if there is danger of Britain being defeated. These contradictory reports suggest that we do not know what we want, or perhaps it would be more correct to say that we are still trying both to eat our cake and have it. By which, I mean that we are, at heart, still hoping that Britain will win the war for us, that her people will do the fighting while we share the benefit. This is not a very honorable attitude, and public opinion is in fact coming to be ashamed of it: witness the Fight for Freedom Committee recently formed in protest, with the program of fighting our own battles. But I do not wish to dwell on this inconsistency, for the events of the last two week in the Balkans and North Africa seem finally to be removing the last blinders from American eyes and it is increasingly evident that the decision about convoys cannot be long postponed. If we wait until Britain is at its last gasp, it will be too late. Now or never!

The President is reported as saying recently that "convoys mean shooting and shooting means war": wherefore he hesitates because, while he is believed personally to favor convoys, he fears that the public will not support him if he uses his undoubted constitutional authority and orders the navy to convoy merchant ships. Now Mr. Roosevelt is universally recognized as the shrewdest judge of political forces that this country has produced in a long time, and certainly his technique of waiting has thus far been highly successful. He induced Congress to modify the Neutrality Act so as to permit the sale of munitions; he carried through the exchange of destroyers for naval bases; and he secured the enactment of the Lease-Lend Bill. Each of these measures aroused much opposition when first proposed, but the President, instead of forcing the issue, allowed the slow democratic process of debate to function and in each case carried the day. So it may be in the matter of convoys. The upsurge of sentiment in favor of convoys in the last weeks has been unmistakable; and while I personally wish that Mr. Roosevelt would assert his leadership and tell the country flatly that convoys are necessary, in which case he will, I believe, receive the backing of most citizens, still I had rather wait a little longer and let the demand for convoys be so outspoken that no possible doubt will remain that the country approves. It is much better in the long run for the President to follow public opinion than for him to exercise his legal power before the public is convinced that such exercise is necessary and thereby expose himself to the charge of dictatorship. If this is a correct diagnosis of the situation, then all persons who believe in the use of convoys should write the President and urge him to go ahead.

Will convoys lead to formal war? I assume that the United States will not declare war on Germany, for that would enable Germany to claim the assistance of Japan under the Axis treaty and the Japanese government has declared that it would recognize the obligation to attack us. Our naval vessels will shoot at German vessels and planes and they will shoot back: acts of war will be committed. Will Japan then move? I do not know, for however much Mr. Matsuoka[1] may talk, Japan clearly does not wish war with the United states, treaty promises to the Axis notwithstanding. Here I may remark parenthetically that Mr. Roosevelt may be playing for time. In a few months our newest battleships will be in service and the naval situation will be enormously improved to our advantage; if the use of convoys can, without disaster, be put off until the *North Carolina* and the *Washington* are ready, we can certainly act more effectively. This is all specula-

[1] Yosuke Matsuoka, Japanese minister of foreign affairs.

tion, but I mention it to show that there is more than one angle to the problem of convoys.

It seems to me unlikely that Germany will declare war if we use convoys. In spite of the fact that the Nazis hold us up to ridicule and declare that it is too late for us to save Britain, the German people have not forgotten that our intervention in 1917 turned the tide against them and their morale would certainly get a terrific shock from learning that their Führer had declared war on the United States. Still, Hitler has a genius for doing the unexpected, and he might surprise us. If he should declare war we shall have to face it and we shall face it. The Lease-Lend Bill was passed on the clear understanding that it involved the risk of war, and the people will not flinch.

The president of the University of Chicago argued in a recent speech that the United States is not morally or intellectually prepared to face the issue of war, and that if we should go to war, we should have to become a totalitarian state in order to wage war effectively. As for his first point, there is no doubt that the American people have been confused by the false teachings of the last twenty years; but inasmuch as Mr. Willkie apparently agrees with Mr. Roosevelt on the tremendous issue before us, namely, that the United States cannot afford to let Britain fall, I refuse to believe that the American people will not respond if the call comes.

As for the second point, Britain has not become a totalitarian state, and there is no sign that it intends to do so. Yet it is "producing the goods" in the matter of war materials, and the morale of its people is the wonder of the world. In our own case, President Wilson was given vast powers in 1917-1918, but the controls then set up were promptly relaxed after the end of the war. In short, the assumption that a democracy, in order to fight totalitarianism, must itself go totalitarian is not warranted by either logic or history.

No one can say today whether we shall go to war, but I for one believe that we should and will go to war rather than allow Hitler to win. While we are waiting on events, we can not only send material aid to Britain, but we can and should exert economic pressure against the totalitarian states. In particular, I think that we should stop the export of gasoline to Japan and of other commodities to the Soviet Union. Experience seems to show that the "tougher" we are towards Japan, the less likely we are to have trouble with her; and as for Russia, its recent treaty with Japan affords new proof that we gain nothing by being nice to the Soviets. The question of sending food to France and the other conquered lands is tremendously difficult. My own belief is that there is sufficient food on the continent to keep life going and that the Germans will dole out just enough to prevent starvation; and in spite of Mr. Hoover's arguments, I very much fear that the Germans will profit by the sending of American food more than will the occupied lands. Incidentally, the governments in exile have not, so far as I know, asked for this help, and apparently the conquered peoples prefer short rations to letting the Germans get any food from the United States.

Thus far I have discussed, so to speak, the past and the present of the war. Now it is time to look towards the future. The view has been presented that the vital interests of the United States require a British victory and that we should take whatever steps may be necessary in order to insure that victory. In that event, we shall, it may be assumed, participate in the making of peace. What considerations should guide us in so complex an undertaking?

First of all, we must take to heart the lesson of 1918. You will remember that just as the fighting was coming to an end, political partisanship, which had been fairly quiescent during the war, reasserted itself. In the election of November 1918 the Democratic party was defeated and the Republicans won control of both houses of Congress. Thus President Wilson became, as it were, a minority president, and his position at Paris in the negotiations for peace, was greatly weakened. It is, therefore, of the utmost importance that if and when the United States takes part in another peace conference, the President shall be able to speak for a united nation. This will be possible only if the American people have been made familiar with the issues at stake and have been able to express their opinions frankly. Until such a clarification of ideas has taken place, until the American people know what it wants, it would be unwise, in my opinion, for the government of the United States to commit itself to any specific program, for otherwise the tragic experience of 1919-20 may be repeated. The time has accordingly come for men of good will to take up the problems of peace and try to reach such a measure of agreement that our government can, at the proper moment, speak with full authority.

In 1918 two main conceptions had been presented to the American people as the bases of peace: the self-determination of peoples, and the establishment of a League of Nations. The peace treaties of 1919-1920 followed these precepts. A League of Nations was set up, and the frontiers of Europe were so drawn as to give every racial or ethnic group unity and self-government. At the time the treaties were drafted, there was not much comprehension of two problems which in the long run undermined the treaties and helped precipitate the present war. Those were the question of minorities and the question of tariffs.

Because racial lines are not clearly marked in eastern and southeastern Europe, minorities were unavoidable, no matter how the frontiers were drawn, and the peacemakers very properly tried to guarantee these minorities against oppression by special treaties imposed on the new states. Generally speaking, these treaties failed to work and in fact caused more harm than good. The problem remains, however, and will have to be dealt with at the end of this war.

Political self-determination logically involved complete economic independence, but it appears not to have been foreseen that the desire of every state to be economically self-sufficient would lead to much duplication of industry and to disastrously high tariff walls. Consequently the new states never achieved economic stability or real prosperity, and the way was opened for Fascist and Nazi intrigues.

Since the treaties of 1919 failed to bring permanent peace, self-determination has been under a cloud. Yet the Czechs, Poles, Romanians, and other peoples continue to exist, and some way will have to be found for them to live in peace with each other and with their more powerful neighbors.

At the moment, the formula which wins most favor is "federation," and the exiled governments of Poland and Czechoslovakia have agreed to a federation of their states when they are restored. But federation may prove as much of a delusion as self-determination unless—and this is what I have been leading up to ever since I mentioned self-determination—the problem is thoroughly thought out. Is federation synonomous with customs union, or does it connote political union as well? Is a European federation to include Great Britain or is it to be confined to the continent? If the latter, is Russia to be a member? Certainly the idea of a European federation is intriguing, but before adopting it as a specific war aim, we should try to make a blue-print for it.

The central problem of peace is, of course, Germany. The Germans are the most numerous people in western Europe and the most highly organized, but they are also the most dangerous. Twice, in 1914 and in 1939, they supported their government in precipitating war and have fought these wars with more cruelty and terror than any other people in modern history. The fundamental task of the future is to prevent Germany from running amuck a third time.

There seem to be three possible solutions. The first is a negotiated peace. This has a few advocates, some of whom believe that Germany cannot be beaten and argue that compromise is better than ruin. Others contend that the best treaties in the past have been those which do not humiliate either side and therefore have some chance of lasting. The prospects of a negotiated peace, however, seem remote unless the war develops into a military stalemate.

A second course is to impose on Germany terms so severe that it will be crushed for an indefinite period, terms which will make the Treaty of Versailles look like the Sermon on the Mount. By this is meant the partition of the country, permanent disarmament, and the destruction of German industry on a large scale. This policy of a "strong" peace has many supporters, if I may judge from the remarks of friends and acquaintances.

The third possibility is to accomplish the military defeat of Germany, but to leave it to the German people to deal with their Nazi tyrants. Germany would be given reasonable terms, in the hope that, having lost two wars, it would settle down to a life of peace which would bring prosperity and content.

Thus we can choose between a peace of compromise, a peace of punishment, and a peace of moderation. Which is most in line with American opinion? Frankly, I do not know, and I wish that Dr. Gallup would give us a poll on the matter. But it seems to me very important that we should make up our minds and give the President a lead.

At bottom the war is a struggle between the "Haves" and the "Have Nots," a struggle precipitated by the latter and precipitated, we believe, quite unnecessarily. Because of this we intend to defeat them. But those who favor a peace of moderation will contend that when we have beaten the Have Nots, we should make concessions which will reconcile them to defeat. If that is to be our policy, then we should begin to think of what those concessions might be. Loans? Lower tariffs? Guaranteed access to raw materials? Revision of immigration quotas? I put the question, but do not answer it. What again I am concerned with is that when peace negotiations begin, American opinion shall not be taken by surprise.

In the opinion of practically all students of international problems, it is hopeless to expect that any peace settlement will be permanent unless it is based on some kind of international organization and that such an organization can succeed only if the United States is a member of it. Is American opinion ready to accept this premise? To any one living in Chicago, this may well seem doubtful; but in other sections of the country, sentiment is certainly more favorable. Whatever the present temper of the people, the question should be tackled soon. At the end of the war, the President must know whether he can declare that the United States will participate in a world organization of some kind or whether he cannot. President Wilson pledged the United States to membership in the League of Nations and was subsequently repudiated. President Roosevelt must not make the same mistake. Because we place our faith in the democratic process, this issue should be debated now and decided, and not left to the decision of chance and circumstance.

I have done. My proposition has been three-fold: (1) From 1919 to 1939, the American people were hypnotized by the unrealistic notion that they could live alone in the world, that what happened beyond their frontiers was of no concern to them; the war has, however, demonstrated the complete folly of this notion.

(2) The habit of muddled thinking in which we have indulged for twenty years made it difficult for us to realize that the war is our war; but the Lease-Lend Bill, passed after exhaustive debate, puts us on record as determined to support Britain and its allies to the limit, even at the risk of war, for we have no alternative if we are to retain our independence and our honor.

(3) In expectation of victory, we must now think out the main outlines of the peace which will prevent a repetition of the catastrophe, and then at the future peace conference give united and unlimited support to the President. This is surely democracy at its best, and if we really believe in democracy, we can do no other.

The United States, Germany and Europe

An address delivered, at the invitation of the Canadian Institute of International Affairs, to its branches at Winnipeg, Saskatoon, Regina, Calgary, Edmonton, Vancouver and Victoria in March 1949. Although I was at the time a member of the Historical Division of the Department of State, the address was not an official pronouncement of the Department. I wrote it in my private capacity as a historian, not as an officer of the Department; it was submitted to the Department, in order to make sure that I did not say anything which might embarass the Department, and it was approved without change, except for one small question of fact on which I was misinformed.

I concluded on a despairing note, for I did not see how the western powers and the Soviet Union could agree on the future of Germany. The same note has to be sounded in 1960. The western powers— Britain, France and the United States—are committed, in principle, to the reunification of Germany, that is, the union of the Federal Republic of Germany and the German Democratic Republic in a single German state. As this is not in the interest of the Soviet Union —unless the unified state be established as a Communist state, which the western powers will not accept—the prospect of German unification is nil. Equally uncertain is the fate of Berlin, but, so far as one can see, the Soviets cannot change its status without using force. Will they risk an atomic war to accomplish this? I certainly do not know.

*   *   *

In August 1914 Germany, the most military state of the time, precipitated a European war for the purposes—so its enemies believed—of becoming master of Europe. The democratic states headed by Great Britain and France would probably have been defeated had not the United States in 1917 intervened on their side. In November 1917 the Bolshevist Revolution in Russia introduced Communism as a third factor in European affairs. From that time to the present the history of Europe is fundamentally that of the conflict between Western democracy, German militarism, and Soviet communism.

In the years immediately following the First World War, the defeated Germans and Russians combined to a certain extent against the victorious allies. Then for some years the Soviets pretty much withdrew from European affairs—only in 1934, that is, after the advent of Hitler, to join the League of Nations and draw closer to France, Great Britain, and even the United States. But a firm Anglo-French-Soviet alliance failed to develop, and in August 1939 the Soviet Union concluded an agreement with Germany which made it possible for Hitler to start his war against Poland. In little less than two years, Hitler attacked Russia, and the Anglo-Soviet coalition was formed, to which the United States adhered after it became involved in the war. This mighty coalition succeeded in defeating Germany, and until the end of 1947 it maintained some of the outward symbols of unity. However, the failure of the Council of Foreign Ministers in December 1947 to reach agreement concerning Germany led the Western powers to lay increasing emphasis on the building up of a (Western) Germany that would be economically sound and democratically oriented, because such a Germany would contribute materially to European recovery and at the same time offer a formidable obstacle to the threat of Communism. This policy was adopted in spite of certain misgivings as to the possible resurgence of German nationalism and militarism.

From this very brief historical summary, it is clear that in the course of thirty-odd years various combinations have been restored to by the three rival forces represented by Western democracy, German militarism, and Soviet communism. How permanent the 1949 "line-up" may be will depend upon circumstances and factors which it will be the purpose of this paper to indicate and evaluate.

At the end of hostilities in May 1945 the present situation would have been regarded in the United States, by both government and people, as inconceivable. During the war, the White House, the Department of State, and the public generally hoped that, by manifesting a generous attitude toward Soviet requests and war aims, the United States would be able to convince the Soviet government that we cherished no hostile intent toward the Soviet Union and that in return the latter would admit the possibility that Communistic and non-Communistic regimes could exist side by side in a world longing for peace. Although certain actions of the Soviet government in 1944 and 1945, that is, after ultimate military victory seemed assured, were somewhat disturbing, nevertheless the Soviets, at the time the Potsdam

Conference opened in July 1945, possessed an enormous reservoir of American good will, and even the stiff line they took in the negotiations, while annoying, did not destroy the confidence of the United States that the Soviet Union was anxious to cooperate with its wartime allies for bringing about the recovery of Europe and laying the foundations of a joint and lasting peace. The fact that the Soviet government had made numerous concessions in the United Nations Conference at San Francisco in order to facilitate the drafting of the Charter of the United Nations was held to be a truer sign of Soviet intent than the hard bargaining pursued at Potsdam.

The Potsdam agreements may be very briefly summarized.

1. In order to prevent Germany from embarking on a third war, the country was to be demilitarized and the population denazified. In addition, the educational system was to be reorganized in order to "make possible the successful development of democratic ideas," the judiciary was to be organized in accordance with the principles of justice under law and of equal rights for all citizens. Likewise freedom of speech and freedom of the press were proclaimed. All these reforms were regarded as essential for the establishment of democratic political parties.

2. Because the problem of reparation payments under the Treaty of Versailles had proved to be probably the greatest obstacle to the restoration of normal economic conditions in Europe in the 1920's, it was agreed that reparations should be made not from current production but by the removal of capital goods from German assets abroad; it was further agreed that the Soviet Union should receive 25% of the removals from the zones occupied by the Western powers, with 15% compensated for by certain products, especially food, from the Soviet zone.

3. Germany was to be treated as a single economic unit, and steps were to be taken to ensure the equitable distribution of essential commodities between the four zones of occupation. Common policies were to be adopted with regard to imports and exports; in particular, it was agreed that the first charge on German exports should be to pay for the imports necessary to get the German economy into operation. Common policies were also to be worked out for currency and banking. On the other hand, Germany's economic life was to be decentralized in order to get rid of the "excessive concentration of economic power" represented by cartels, syndicates, trusts, and other monopolis-

tic arrangements. It was also agreed that German economy should be reorganized by the development of agriculture and peaceful domestic industries.

4. On the political side, the goals set were the decentralization of the central government and the development of local responsibility. But no central government was to be established for the present. Instead, central administrative departments were to be established to deal with finances, transportation, communications, foreign trade, and industry. The supreme authority was exercised, according to the quadripartite agreement of June 5, 1945, by the Allied Control Council, which was established to coordinate policy in the four zones of occupation and to decide matters affecting Germany as a whole.

5. The Allies agreed to the Polish occupation for administrative purposes of German territory lying east of the Oder and Neisse rivers.

This is not the place to recite the dreary history of the meetings of the Council of Foreign Ministers in March-April and November-December 1947. Suffice it to say that on each of the main issues concerning Germany, deadlock was reached between the Western powers and the Soviet Union.

1. Since the Soviets professed to regard renewed German aggression as possible, the United States in 1946 proposed a treaty of disarmament and demilitarization between the Four Powers for a period of twenty-five years (or even longer). But although Generalissimo Stalin had been originally receptive, the Soviet government rejected the offer —yet continued to denounce the Western powers for not suppressing the remnants of Naziism with sufficient energy.

2. In spite of the Potsdam undertaking that the new government of Germany, when constituted, should be constructed on the principles of decentralization and the recognition of local responsibilities, the Soviet government advocated a centralized regime for Germany and made its acceptance a condition for the discussion of other issues with the Western powers. Furthermore, the Communist-dominated Socialist Unity party was the only effective political group in the Soviet zone of occupation, the other parties being discriminated against in one way or another. The Western powers, on the other hand, advocated a federal system for the future Germany, and allowed free rein to all political parties subscribing to prescribed democratic requirements, the Communists included.

3. Thanks to Soviet tactics, the economic unity of Germany stip-

ulated for in the Potsdam Agreement was never realized. The Soviet authorities treated the Soviet zone as their private preserve and exploited and bled it in a variety of ways, at the same time refusing to provide information about their operations. At every turn the Soviet member of the Allied Control Council blocked action desired by the other powers. Particularly grievous was the Soviet refusal to let food from Eastern Germany flow freely to the Western zones, which did not produce enough for their own consumption; with the result that the Western powers had to import and pay for food to feed the population of their zones. In such circumstances, economic unity was non-existent, and economic recovery was seriously retarded, even though the British and United States zones were united, economically, in January 1947. By way of retaliation for the Soviet tactics, the United States had stopped the transfer of capital goods from its zone to the Soviets as reparations, but this did not make the latter any more conciliatory.

4. Matters were made worse by the fact that, not withstanding the clear language of the Potsdam Agreement to the contrary, the Soviet government insisted that the administrative frontier between Germany and Poland was permanent and the Polish government was accordingly allowed by the Soviets to expel the Germans living east of the line. These Germans, as far as possible, made for the Western zones, thereby increasing the already surplus population. On the other hand, the Soviet declined to accept the incorporation of the Saar in the French economic system or to agree to the establishment of commissions to study frontier questions.

5. Possibly these issues could have been settled if agreement had been reached on the question of reparations. Although the Potsdam Agreement laid down the principle that reparations were to be paid by removals of plant and not from current production, the Soviet government in July 1946 demanded payments from current production. Furthermore, it insisted—in defiance of the evidence—that at Yalta President Roosevelt and Prime Minister Churchill had agreed to the Soviet Union's demand for ten billion dollars of reparation. Not only did the Western powers decline to admit the Soviet interpretation of Yalta; they insisted that Yalta had been replaced by Potsdam, which mentioned no figure. Acceptance of the Soviet demand would effectively prevent the recovery of Germany, all the more so since the Russians in December 1947 asked for the calculation of reparations at 1938 prices, which would have increased the amount de-

manded from ten to fifteen billion dollars. In reply to the Soviet demand, the Western powers refused point-blank to allow reparations to be paid from current production, because they themselves would have to make up the deficit in the German economy which would result from such payments to the Soviet Union. Since the Soviet government would not negotiate on other matters until its reparation demand was accepted, the deadlock was complete.

Thus at the end of 1947 it seemed clear that the Soviet government, so far from desiring German economic recovery, desired the continuance of German misery, hoping thereby—so the Western powers were bound to believe—to promote the growth of Communism and make easier the bringing of all Germany under Soviet control. After two and a half years of concessions by the Western powers, they could only conclude that further negotiations with the Soviets were futile, at least until the Soviet position on basic issues was modified. They also deeply resented Soviet charges that they were exploiting German production to their own advantage or buying their way into German industry. Exasperating also was the circumstance that by advocating a centralized government for Germany, the Soviets were able to pose as the champion of German unity, whereas of course it was the Soviet policy of keeping Germany disunited economically which was responsible for the *de facto* partion of the country. But to meet this propaganda and to prevent the Soviets from getting control of Germany, more than indignation was necessary. Positive action was required.

Meanwhile, the United States had come forward with the Marshall Plan for promoting the recovery of Europe as a whole. The Plan involved help for Germany to get that country on its feet, and help by Germany to make the Plan work, since Germany, for all the damage suffered in the war, was still the king-pin of European economy. In keeping with this analysis, the United States in July 1947 had revised the original directive of 1945, which, formulated during the war, had aimed at keeping Germany at a subsistence level, by a new directive which recognized that Germany could recover its economic health only if its industry were allowed to attain a much higher level of production. The level of 1936 was accordingly set as a goal.

These decisions to rebuild the German economy in defiance of Soviet opposition, which were dictated partly by the necessity of encouraging German resistance to Communist propaganda, partly by

the understandable desire to reduce the burden of the American tax-
payer, who resented having in large part to foot the bill for feeding
Germany, were not taken lightly. The United States is aware that
the German people are not very penitent about the Nazi regime and
that the democratization of political life is only skin-deep. We have
certainly not forgiven Germany for starting the Second World War
and for its atrocious conduct of the war. Those of you who may be
familiar with my writings will not suspect me of tenderness toward
the Germans, and I personally should have preferred it if a decision
to build up Germany could have been avoided; but the situation
created by Soviet intransigence leaves us no real choice, and for
reasons to be set forth in a few moments, the decision may work a
turning point in European history.

The decision immediately raised two delicate but fundamental
problems. Any rebuilding of German industry on a large scale, and
particularly of the Ruhr, the century old arsenal of German aggression, instantly aroused the deep-seated apprehension of practically
all Frenchmen, who could not forget and could not be expected to
forget the thre invasions of France in seventy years. Much as France
needed German coal, it would require a good deal of reassurance
before it sanctioned a policy which might, some day, make it possible
for Germany to rearm; in particular, as regards the Ruhr, France
was prepared to be stubborn. Secondly, the possible revival of German industry, involving an increase of German exports to pay for
imports of food, aroused some apprehension in Great Britain, which
was also struggling desperately to increase its own exports. Fortunately, the United States government was aware of these attitudes in
both France and Britain. It believed that the fears were exaggerated
and was confident that Germany could be kept under control; but it
realized that the issues had to be met and the fears alleviated.

The task of the United States was made easier by the growth of
the idea of a Western European Union. In order to implement the
Marshall Plan, the countries of Western Europe were feeling their
way to a degree of economic cooperation which had never before
seemed possible. A further step was taken when in January 1948 the
British government announced a policy of extending the Franco-
British Treaty of Dunkirk of March 4, 1947, which provided for
mutual military defense and economic cooperation, to include first
the Benelux countries and later the nations of Western Europe. On

March 17, a fifty-year treaty of military and economic alliance was signed in Brussels by the British, French, and Benelux foreign ministers. Although the treaty is not directed specifically against the Soviet Union, there can be no doubt that it was inspired by fear of Communist aggression, and the Soviets, whose propaganda never ceases prating about hostile *blocs,* have only themselves to blame if a solid *bloc* has been formed in Western Europe. Just as Hitler's seizure of Czechoslovakia in March 1939 was followed by an Anglo-Polish alliance, so the Communist coup in Czechoslovakia in February 1948 was followed by the alliance of the Western democracies.

After economic cooperation and military alliance the next logical step is some form of political union, and, no doubt you recall, a Conference on Western Union was held at The Hague in the spring of 1948. While no positive achievements can be recorded, both France and Britain have made definite suggestions which are being explored. For centuries men of good will have dreamed of some kind of European union, but never before has it appeared to be practical. It will certainly not be realized over night, but it is definitely "in the air". For this good omen, we can thank the Soviet Union, for it is the understanding of the fate that will overtake Western Europe if its does not stand united against Soviet aggression which has brought Western Union into the realm of practical politics.

Now we Americans have long reproached Europe for its continuing national rivalries, and therefore the present trend towards Western Union is welcomed by the people and government of the United States. As my personal opinion, I venture the guess that the more effective Western Union becomes, the more readily will the Congress of the United States appropriate funds for the continuation of ERP (European Recovery Program). Be that as it may, the idea of Western Union has an important bearing on the United States policy towards Germany.

When I interviewed the late German Emperor, William II, in 1928, he contended that the Germans were an Eastern people, not a Western, his argument being that like Orientals they could not govern themselves but required to be governed. Certainly the Germans have not displayed great skill in governing themselves, but it is silly to deny that for a thousand years, Germany has been part of Western Europe, and it is hard to imagine any future for Germany except as a member of Western Union. Today, the Germans, apart from the fanatical Communists who constitute only a small portion of the people, apparently both loathe and fear the Russians.

For the United States, this circumstance is of the utmost importance. General European recovery is largely dependent on German recovery, but to make German recovery safe for Britain, France and the other countries injured by Nazi aggression, it is necessary to bring Germany into the Union of Western Europe. This will not come about tomorrow, in fact no one can predict when a German government will be established which can be admitted to whatever organization may evolve in Western Europe; but in our opinion, it is sound policy to work toward that end. Our task, therefore, is to create in Germany a sound economy and a political regime which will be acceptable in Western Europe and to persuade the Germans that their only hope lies in accepting such an orientation of future German policy. To accomplish this will not be easy. It will require patience, imagination, and will power, but we are in the game to stay.

It is against this background that I now invite you to consider the events of 1948-1949.

As a result of informal discussions held in London between February and June 1948 by representatives of the United States, Britain, France and the three Benelux countries, far-reaching measures were announced.

I. It was agreed that the Benelux countries should be associated with the three occupying powers in matters of policy regarding the Western zones of Germany—this being in substance a renewed rejection of the Soviet contention that the terms of the treaty for Germany should be worked out by the Council of Foreign Ministers without participation of the smaller powers.

II. Three related decisions concerned the role of German economy in the European economy:

a. It was agreed that "for the political and economic well-being of the countries of Western Europe and of a democratic Germany, there must be close association of their economic life", which was ensured by the inclusion in the Organization for European Economic Cooperation (under the Marshall Plan) of both the Anglo-American combined zone and the French zone.

b. It was agreed to recommend the establishment of and international authority for the control of the Ruhr, in which the

Western powers, the Benelux countries, and Germany would participate.

c. The principle of non-discrimination against foreign interests in Germany was reaffirmed.

As a practical step to end the economic stagnation and promote recovery, the Western powers announced and put into immediate operation a new currency, the German mark, which was intended to get rid of inflation and the black market.

III. On the political side, it was recognized that it was "necessary to give the German people the opportunity to achieve on the basis of a free and democratic form of government the eventual re-establishment of German unity at present disrupted", and plans were announced for the meeting of a Constituent Assembly to lay the bases for a federal form of government which would be submitted for ratification by the people of the several German states in the three Western zones. The government thus established would be provisional, but would permit the Germans to deal with their own affairs. At the same time, an occupation statute would be framed by the military governors in consultation with German representatives which would delimit the powers reserved to the occupation authorities.

IV. Proposals would be submitted for certain minor territorial adjustments of the Western frontiers of Germany.

V. The Western powers declared that "there could not be any general withdrawal of their power from Germany until the peace of Europe is secured and without prior consultation". They proposed to establish a Military Security Board to ensure the maintenance of disarmament and demilitarization in Western Germany, and they foreshadowed a continued system of inspection and control for as long as necessary after the end of the occupation.

Great Britain and the United States justified this program by the argument that it had been forced upon them by the violations of the Potsdam Agreement on the part of the Soviet Union. They and France, however, stated that their proposals in no way precluded eventual four-power agreement on the problems of Germany and should even facilitate agreement. Actually, they had no expectation that the Soviet government would modify its attitude of hostility and obstruction, and indeed they were prepared to face Soviet counter-action.

This brings us to the blockade of Berlin.

II

On the night of January 24, 1948, the night train from Berlin to Bielefeld carrying British officials and 120 Germans was detained for 11 hours in the Soviet zone. This was the first step in a long series of measures extending over six months by which the Soviet authorities shut off access to Berlin by land and water and compelled the Western powers to supply their sections of the city by an air lift. Inasmuch as this action was taken before the conference of the Western powers in London, it was obviously not taken as a rejoinder to the decisions announced in London in March, even if the restrictions were intensified after that date. Furthermore, the Soviet authorities for weeks alleged that their restrictive measures were necessitated by "technical difficulties". It was not until July that the Soviet government formally charged the Western powers with violating the Potsdam Agreement and the Four-Power agreements for joint control of Germany and tried to justify its conduct as a defense against the alleged illegal action of the United States, Britain, and France. On March 20, 1948 the Soviet delegation walked out of the meeting of the Allied Control Council, and on June 16 they left the Allied Kommandatura of Berlin—steps which put an end even to the pretense of four-power cooperation.

If the Western powers had been badly fooled in their assumption that the Soviet government was ready to carry out the Potsdam agreement and promote the recovery of Germany and of Europe, the Soviet leaders had also guessed badly. The elections in Germany had shown that Communism possessed little appeal for the average German; only in the Soviet zone had the Socialist Unity (Communits) party been able to win, and then only because the Soviet authorities had discriminated in its favor; in Berlin they had been routed. On the economic side, things were beginning to improve in the Western zone, whereas in the Soviet zone, they were beginning to deteriorate, thanks to Soviet looting and to the practical cessation of trade with the Western zones. So, in spite of Soviet championship of German political unity, Soviet prestige was slipping.

While one is never sure of the motives behind Soviet action, the Western powers assumed that the purpose of the blockade was to compel them to abandon Berlin and thus leave the Russians in complete possession of the German capital. The Soviets would then be in a position to set up a puppet government in Berlin and appeal to all Germans to rally around it. Presumably the Soviets, who usually plan their moves carefully, believed that the Western powers were so craven that they would submit to such pressure; that is, when the blockade became intolerable, they would yield rather than fight.

To the Western powers the Russian pretention was indeed intolerable, for it was a clear violation of the agreements of 1945 between the Four Powers concerning the administration of Berlin. The Western powers asserted that they were in Berlin by right of defeating Germany, and that they had withdrawn their troops from Saxony and Thuringia only on condition that they could share in the occupation of Berlin. To make clear that they intended to stay in Berlin, they began to supply the city by air lift—and have continued to do so to this day. It is believed that the Soviets had not calculated upon the ability of the Western powers to carry out this program—although if they had possessed a sound interpretation of American psychology, they would have sensed that their action offered a challenge to American technical capacity which would be accepted with alacrity.

I remarked some minutes ago that the Western powers had introduced a new currency for their zones. Although they took this step only after the Soviet had not only refused to sanction a reform for the whole of Germany, but also introduced a new currency in their own zone and into all Berlin, the Soviet military governor declared it a violation of the Potsdam agreement and represented it as justifying the blockade of Berlin. On June 23 the Western powers announced that they would introduce their new currency specially stamped "B" in their sector of Berlin. When it became evident that the Soviet authorities in Berlin had no intention of raising the blockade in spite of the protest of the Western powers, the latter decided to approach the Soviet government directly.

So we come to the negotiations between the Four Powers, beginning with identical notes from the United States, British and French governments to the Soviet government on July 6 and ending with their notes of September 27 announcing that they would refer the dispute to the United Nations. The British and United States governments have published extensive accounts of these negotiations which you may have read or can read, so I will content myself with a summary. The initial positions of the two sides were far apart. The Western powers insisted that Berlin was not part of the Soviet zone, and that they would not negotiate with the Soviet government until the blockade of Berlin was lifted. The Soviets contended that Berlin was part of the zone; they would not negotiate solely about the situation in Berlin as proposed by the Western powers; they could not accept the German B mark in Berlin. The real issue, however, according to Generalissimo Stalin, was the plan of the Western powers to establish a German government in the Western zone.

The representatives of the Western powers in Moscow held two conferences with Generalissimo Stalin and four meetings with Mr. Molotov, the Soviet foreign minister. Although the Soviet government expressed an urgent desire that the Western powers should not proceed to the formation of a German government before the Four Powers had discussed the whole problem, it did not make this a condition of negotiations concerning the lifting of the blockade. The Western powers, while declining to commit themselves, pointed out that no date had been set for the formation of a German government and that it would first be necessary for the Germans to frame and adopt a constitution; they also affirmed their desire for a Four-Power agreement whereby a government for the whole of Germany would be established. With this understood, an agreement was reached on August 30 for the following steps to be taken simultaneously:

A. The Soviet blockade of Berlin and the restrictions laid down by the Western powers on intercourse with the Soviet zone would be lifted.

B. The German B mark would be withdrawn from circulation in Berlin and replaced by the Eastern mark of the Soviet zone. The Western powers agreed to this on the understanding that the use of the Eastern mark in Berlin would be subject to regulation by the Four Powers operating through the Berlin Kommandatura, and a directive to the four military commanders was formulated enumerating certain stipulations concerning the use of the Eastern mark. It was certainly the intent of the Western powers that the legitimate interests of the Soviets should be protected as well as their own. In short, a compromise, seemingly acceptable to both sides—an essential of good diplomacy—had apparently been reached.

But when the four military commanders discussed the technicalities of the introduction of the Eastern mark into Berlin, the Soviet commander, Marshal Sokolovsky, put forward new demands:

1. While willing in large measure to life the blockade, he pro-

posed to introduce restrictions on air transport—an entirely new idea.

2. He would not admit that the emission of the Eastern mark should be controlled by a Four-Power financial commission.

3. He insisted that the Soviet military authorities should be exclusively responsible for approving agreements for trade between Berlin and the Western zones of Germany and for issuing import and export licenses.

In the view of the Western powers, these demands "constituted a departure from what was agreed in Moscow and struck at the very foundation upon which these discussions were taken". But the Soviets would not admit this, and after each side had addressed a second note to the other, the Western powers referred this dispute with the Soviet Union to the Security Council of the United Nations as a threat to peace. In their view, the issue was no longer one of technical difficulties of comunication or of currency, for Berlin. The issue was that the Soviet government had clearly shown by its actions that it was attempting by illegal and coercive measures in disregard of its obligations to secure political objectives to which it was not entitled — that is, the withdrawal of the Western powers from Berlin—and which it could not achieve by peaceful means.

The proposals of the Security Council called for simultaneous lifting of all restrictions on trade and communication by both sides, settling of the currency question by the four military governors, and, within ten days, a meeting of the Council of Foreign Ministers for a discussion of "all outstanding questions concerning Germany as a whole". They were accepted by the Western powers, but rejected by the Soviet Union, whose representative on the Security Council declared that the blockade would be continued until the Eastern mark was established as the sole currency of Berlin on the Soviet terms.

There the matter rests. The President of the Security Council has appointed a committee of technicians to try to work out a solution of the Berlin currency question, after consultation with the technicians of the Occupying Powers, but that committee has not yet produced a report.

This episode in the long struggle between the Soviets and the Western powers is more important than the specific issues, serious as they are. London, Paris and Washington had long before reached the conclusion that it was futile to negotiate with Moscow; but because (1) the Soviet blockade of Berlin and the counteracting air lift had created an obviously dangerous situation, where some incident might precipitate a clash of arms and because (2) Communists everywhere were charging the Western governments with deliberately provoking the Soviet Union, the three Western powers decided to try negotiation once more. They thought they had secured Premier Stalin's personal and formal acceptance of the proposed compromise —only to find that like other Soviet agreements it was worthless.

Whether this repudiation was a deep-laid Russian scheme from the beginning or whether the Generalissimo was overruled by the Politburo, is immaterial. The agreement saved the Soviets' face on the question of the blockade, secured their mark for Berlin, left open the question of a German government. Yet is was rejected by the Soviet government. Why? The only possible conclusion — what many observers have contended for a long time — that the Soviet Union did not desire even a short-term understanding with the Western powers. Western opinion was profoundly disillusioned — and hardened accordingly. Personally, I think the Soviet leaders committed a grave error of judgment, for they destroyed the fond hopes which the peace-loving Western peoples had raised on the basis of Mr. Stalin's seeming conciliation. Henceforth, the West is likely to be "tougher" than ever.

It is probably too much to expect that the Soviet leaders will be able to form correct opinions about the Western powers, for they have little contact with the peoples of the West and apparently dislike what little they do have. Thus they guessed wrong about the elections in Germany in 1946, and for several years they have been banking on a depression in the United States—which hasn't come yet.

Apparently the Soviets do not desire and do not expect an accommodation with the West, and on that point, the evidence is, I submit, increasingly convincing. First, there is the remarkable article by "Historicus" in the January *Foreign Affairs* which many of you may have read. After reading all of the books written by or for Marshal Stalin and considering his various speeches, statements, and interviews over the past twenty years, Historicus quotes chapter and verse again and again to show that the Soviet leader has always proclaimed that a conflict between Soviet communism and Western capitalism is, sooner or later, unavoidable. Because the Soviet state, ever since its inception, has been weaker than its capitalist or Fascist enemies, it has tried by various devices to postpone the show-down. Among those devices is the issuing of a statement from time to time by Stalin himself that Communism and Capitalism can live side by side or that the disputes between them can be adjusted by compromise. These statements are designed to impress peace-loving and gullible people all over the world, and to a certain extent have succeeded in doing so. But whenever negotiations are begun for compromise, one of two things is apparent: (a) The Soviet idea of a compromise is to maintain the Soviet position intact and demand that the other party, in the interest of unity, accept it; or (b) if absolutely necessary to achieve the appearance of agreement, it makes concessions, but repudiates or ignores them afterwards. On this latter point, I should like to refer you to the paper presented by the Department of State to the Committee on Foreign Relations of the United States Senate on June 2, 1948, listing 52 violations of agreements by the Soviet Government. Wherever Soviet policy has operated—Germany, Austria, Eastern and Southeastern Europe, Korea, Manchuria—the Soviet Government has consistently evaded the clear meaning of the engagements it has made. Not even the Nazis established a more consistent record—such tactics make sense, I submit, only on the assumption that the Soviet government regards conflict with the Western powers as unavoidable and even desirable.

This is not to say that such conflict is imminent. It is generally conceded that the Soviet armies could now overrun Western Europe in short order. There is, however, no evidence that they are planning to do so at this time. But apart from the superiority of its ground forces, the Soviet Union is weaker militarily and economically than the United States and is likely to remain so for some indeterminate period. Admitting that opinions are divided, I for one do not believe that war is around the corner.

It is possible that agreements may be reached on specific issues between the West and the Soviet Union, agreements which the Soviets will actually execute. The United States has repeatedly declared its readiness to negotiate, along with its Allies, on questions relating to Germany. Nevertheless, any reconciliation between our aims and the efforts of the Soviets to spread communism throughout the world appears at the present time to be unlikely. In these circumstances, two tasks confront the United States.

1. To try to remain stronger than the Soviet Union, especially as, with the passage of time, the present "spread" of power in our favor

may decrease. Even if war does not seem likely now or in the immediate future, there is always the danger that the Soviets, misjudging badly the situation at a given moment, may commit some rash act—like their attempted *coup d'état* in Berlin last September, only on a much larger scale. We must be so strong that the Soviets will hesitate to attack us, directly or indirectly. This will be extremely expensive, and we may be sure that the Soviet government will denounce us for planning a preventive war. As you know, the United States is already well launched on its program of rearmament, a program, be it remembered, accepted by a Republican Congress from a Democratic President and therefore not likely to be abandoned now that both executive and legislature are held by the Democratic party. As a historian, I have to admit that in the past competition in armaments has not succeeded in keeping the peace; at the same time, it should be noted that prior to 1914 and again in 1939 the superiority in armaments was possessed by a war-minded power, namely Germany. Now it is a peace-loving country, the United States, which proposes to achieve superiority. Both as an officer of the Department of State and as an American citizen, I do not believe that the United States will provoke war against the Soviet Union.

2. The second task of the United States is to help organize the peace-loving nations to defend themselves. Close military cooperation between Canada and the United States, begun during the war and continued since the close of hostilities, is the first step. The Treaty of Brussels between Britain, France, and the Benelux countries is the second. Now the culminating step is in process of accomplishment, namely, the conclusion of the North Atlantic Pact between the nations of Western Europe, and Canada, and the United States. This is so much the most momentous event since the close of hostilities that comment seems superfluous. Nevertheless two remarks may be in order:

In the first place, it is the Soviet Union which will have brought the Pact into being. Fear of a revived Germany would never have accomplished it.

Secondly, as a corollary of the Pact, the United States will provide arms for the European members of the alliance. When that has been accomplished, the military preponderance of the North Atlantic nations should be so overwhelming that, whatever may be the desires of the Soviet rulers, they will not risk an appeal to the sword.

I know that millions of persons in Canada, the United States and elsewhere will deeply deplore the colossal expenditure which this military-political program will entail. But what is the alternative? If our conflict with the Soviet Union were a mere matter of territory, the British Commonwealth and the United States might make an old-fashioned deal with the Soviet Union by agreeing to divide the world between the three powers. But we do not want territory and the Soviets want more than territory, for they demand control of our minds as well as of our bodies. In other words, the conflict in which we are engaged is a war far more of ideas and ideals than it is a struggle for mere material possessions. Unhappily the Bolshevists are not content to leave the result to the competition of ideas. They were aware that their ideas were not popular in Russia, so they imposed their will on Russia by force and have ever since gloried in having done it. So I ask anyone who is skeptical about our armaments program whether he is willing to take a chance that the Soviets will let us alone if we don't rearm and to accept the consequences if they don't.

It may be replied that instead of relying on military force to keep out Communism, we should create a society based on justice and freedom from want which will be immune to Communist propaganda. Americans generally subscribe to the doctrine that we must continue to seek social justice—but we insist on deciding for ourselves just how this is to be done—whereas the Soviets wish to impose their own brand and make us like it.

So, referring back to the question raised at the beginning of my remarks as to how long the present "line-up" against the Soviet Union might last, I answer it by saying that it will last as long as the Soviet challenge continues to threaten our way of life—provided, of course, we are determined to maintain and defend our way of life.

I had reached this point in the preparation of my paper when Generalissimo Stalin answered the questions put to him by the representative of the International News Service. Viewed in terms of the blockade of Berlin, which is the incident that is responsible for the present high tension, his feeler does not indicate any tendency to be conciliatory. At first the Russians explained the blockade by "technical difficulties". Later they justified it as a means of protecting themselves against the introduction of the German mark into Berlin.

Now they make the lifting of the blockade dependent on our giving up our plans for the creation of a German government in the Western zones. In other words, the Soviet terms, in spite of a seeming conciliation, are now stiffer than they were six months ago. Since we continue to insist that we will not discuss the German problem as a whole until the blockade is lifted,[1] there seems to be no escape from the circle.

Meanwhile the success of the air lift, which keeps the Berliners encouraged and at the same time disconcerts the Russians and reduces their prestige, leaves the Western powers in an advantageous position. They can wait for Marshal Stalin to show his hand—which is exactly what President Truman and Secretary Acheson did.

III

It is now time to get back to a consideration of the German problem.

Since the collapse of the negotiations over Berlin the most important event has been the meeting, at Bonn, of the minister—presidents of 11 German states for the drafting of a provisional constitution for Germany. Subject to the requirements laid down in the London decisions of June 1948, that the constitution must be democratic and federal, provide a guarantee of civil liberties, and be ratified by two-thirds of the states, its acceptance by the Western powers seems assured. In order to give the new German government as much responsibility as possible, an occupation statute is being drafted by the Allied governments which will reduce to a minimum—subject always to the requirements of military security—the right of the occupation authorities to interfere with the action of the new German government. In other words, the Western powers propose that the new German government shall not be a mere puppet regime, but one that will command the respect and loyalty of Germans. Provision is also made for the subsequent adherence of other German states, i.e. those of the Soviet zone.

How awkward this prospect is for the Russians may be grasped from the Soviet action in forming a People's Council, which included

---

[1] The blockade was at last lifted on May 12, 1949, as the result of a Four-Power agreement.

unofficial representatives from the Western zones and to which a full-blown constitution for a united Germany was presented. But if the population of the Soviet zone is allowed a free vote, it will most probably plump heavily for the regime being organized in the Western zones rather than for the constitution *octroyé* by the Soviets. No wonder that Generalissimo Stalin is trying to make postponement of the Western government the price of lifting the blockade!

The Soviets are also losing out on the question of the Ruhr. In the Potsdam negotiations of 1945 they claimed a voice in the management of the Ruhr, but since they have blocked the economic unification of Germany, they have not been admitted to the recent negotiations. The Ruhr question presents extraordinary difficulties, but we may be certain that those difficulties would be infinitely greater if the Russians had been allowed any voice in the matter.

The question was brought to a head by the announcement on November 10 by the British and United States military governors of law no. 75 dealing with the international trusteeship of the heavy industries of the Ruhr. While it declared certain enterprises to be excessive concentrations of economic power or otherwise objectionable, it provided that the operation of the coal mines and steel plants of the region should be transferred to German hands operating under Allied Control boards and that the question of the ultimate ownership of these industries (that is, whether they should be socialized) should be decided by a representative freely-elected government either for Germany as a whole or for Western Germany alone. In the Anglo-American view, this concession to the Germans was necessary in order to obtain greater production and thus insure that Germany played its proper role in the recovery of Europe, and they declared that the German industrialists who had cooperated with the Nazis would not be allowed to recover control of the Ruhr industries. But the French were of course greatly upset, and in order to keep the present middle-of-the-road group in control—the alternatives being either a DeGaulle or a Communist government—concessions had to be made.

On December 28, 1948, Britain, France, the United States, and the Benelux countries announced the signing of an agreement for the establishment of an international authority for the Ruhr, the purpose of which was declared to be to insure that "the resources of the Ruhr shall not in the future be used for the purpose of aggression but shall be used in the interests of peace" and to "provide the means by which a peaceful democratic Germany can be brought into the European community to play its part as a fully responsible and independent member".

The Authority is to make a division of coal, coke, and steel from the Ruhr as between German consumption and export, and it can require the German authorities to modify or terminate their measures. The Authority will consist of a council of representatives of the six signatory governments and of Germany, with Britain, France, the United States and Germany possessing three votes each, the Benelux countries one vote each. The German votes will be cast as a unit by the joint representatives of the occupation authorities until such time as the occupying powers decide that Germany shall cast them. However, as a result of the fusion agreement under which the United States bears the chief financial responsibility for supporting the German economy, the three German votes will be virtually cast by the United States military governor. In other words, the United States and the United Kingdom will be able to outvote France and the Benelux countries. They may well hesitate, however, to impose a decision to which France and the Benelux countries should be strongly opposed. It is also to be noted that no date has been set for the termination of the occupation. The agreement further provides that the continuance of direct controls over the Ruhr industries after the termination of the occupation shall be assumed by the Ruhr Authority, the Military Security Board, or some other body created by international agreement. In return for these concessions, France agreed to exclude from the Six-Power agreement establishing the Ruhr Authority the question of the ultimate ownership of the Ruhr industries.

While the French have not obtained that separation of the Ruhr from Germany which they desired, they seem reasonably well satisfied with the compromise and anxious to assure the Germans that they— the French—will be reasonable. Naturally, the Germans do not like the Agreement because it establishes permanent international control of the Ruhr, unless and until revised by the peace settlement, and the Russians are even more indignant because they are excluded.

No one can say how this experiment in international control will work, for there are no precedents which might furnish a clue.

At the moment, in connection with the report of the Humphrey Committee of the ECA, a difference of opinion has arisen between

France and Britain on the one hand and the United States on the other as to the dismantling and removal of certain Ruhr plants, the United States being anxious, in the interest of increased production, to retain more than seemed desirable to the British and French, who are fearful of the possibility of too great German competition with their own industries and are interested in maximum reparations deliveries. No doubt some kind of compromise will be worked out. As the United States sees it, the plan is a sincere effort to get the Ruhr plants into operation as soon as possible and thereby provide German and European recovery; to insure that the Ruhr is not allowed to pass under Nazi control; and to take account of the legitimate fears of France. Undoubtedly the policy involves certain risks, but a successful solution of the highly difficult problem will certainly not be obtained by either timidity or inaction.

Meanwhile the Military Security Board has been set up and public announcement of this has been made.

The United States would also like to see the present moratorium on private investment in Germany lifted, with the object of producing a speedier recovery of German economy and its integration in the European Recovery Program.

It is clear that only large-scale aid from Britain and the United States has prevented German collapse. The United States is contributing at the rate of $1,100,000,000 a year. At long last, thanks to the currency reform, Germany is showing marked signs of recovery, the most important perhaps being that the people are now working. It is also evident that while the Germans have no love for the Western powers — there is no reason why they should — they have come to love the Russians even less, apart, of course, from the Communists and Nazis accepted by the Soviets. There is now little chance of a collapse which will make Communism appeal to the Germans. From day to day the Western position becomes stronger. On the other hand, the Germans have certainly not abandoned hope of playing off the Western powers against the Soviets.

Sooner or later there are bound to be renewed discussions between the Four Powers about Germany. The Soviets make no effort to conceal their desire for such discussions because the tide is running against them and they hesitate to use force to drive the Western powers out of Berlin. The latter have repeatedly declared that they are ready for discussions—when the Russians lift the blockade of

Berlin. Meanwhile, the partition of Germany is a fact, and will become even more so if and when a provisional German government is established in the Western zones.[2]

Obviously, until the Council of Foreign Ministers meets and the two sides state their respective positions, no positive analysis of the situation can be made. However, since the Western powers do not intend to give up their plan for a democratic, federalized Germany, in which there would be economic unity, and the Soviets, so far as is known, have not abandoned their demand for a highly centralized Germany, the prospect of agreement seems remote. The Western powers have announced that their occupation of Germany will continue until peace is secure, whereas the Russians have certainly been toying with the idea of proposing the withdrawal of all occupying forces. While such a proposal would please the Germans and put the Western governments on the spot, they could hardly accept it lest (a) the German Communists, with the backing of the police force of the Soviet zone or even of Soviet troops in Poland, attempt a *coup* similar to that in Prague and/or (b) the German nationalists get out of hand. We cannot forget that Nazi and Communists more than once in the past joined forces, so we are not likely to make it easy for them to do so again.

Personally, I do not see any present basis for agreement on Germany between the West and the Soviets, that is, agreement determining the future of Germany to the satisfaction of both sides. On the contrary, the present tension is likely to continue, and we must simply get used to it. Germany will remain divided, and the Soviets may very well set up a Communist government in their zone to match the provisional government in the Western zones.[3] What the next developments may be is anybody's guess.

2 This was done in September 1949.
3 Which they did in October 1949.

DESIGNED AND MANUFACTURED UNDER THE
TYPOGRAPHICAL DIRECTION OF D. REX EATON
COMPOSITION, PRINTING AND BINDING BY
JACKSON TYPESETTING COMPANY OF JACKSON, MICHIGAN
AND HOLLERITH-EATON, INC., OF JACKSON
THE TEXT IS SET IN 10 POINT BASKERVILLE
AND THE HEADINGS IN 18 POINT GARAMOND

DATE DUE

FEB 16 '82

FEB 19 1982

MR 31 '91

GAYLORD   PRINTED IN U.S.A.